Island of Terns

Island of Terns

Warden of Scolt Head

·

Bob Chestney

Quiller Press
London

First published 1993 by
Quiller Press Limited,
46 Lillie Road,
London SW6 1TN

ISBN 1 870948 86 6

Produced by Book Production Consultants Plc,
Cambridge.

Typeset by Cambridge Photosetting Services.

Printed by St Edmundsbury Press,
Bury St Edmunds, Suffolk.

Jacket photographs: Front – Phyllis Chestney
Back (both terns and Bob) – Denis Vincent MA, ARTS

Contents

Foreword

It gives me very great pleasure to write a foreword to this book. I have known Bob Chestney for most of his life. My family has been coming to North Norfolk since the late 1920s, and we have seen many changes. We were in fact staying on the island a few days before the second world war was declared on September 3, 1939. We have stayed on the island frequently since then. It is a unique and unforgettable experience. At high tide you know that you are alone on the island with a wonderful view of the salt marshes to the south and the North Sea on the other side of the sand dunes, with an uninterrupted passage to the North Pole. It can be quite a challenge to be dropped off at the top of Hut Creek and to carry all your supplies up the steep path to the Hut. Woe betide if you have left anything important behind.

We knew and admired Bob's father, Charles, and were all delighted when Bob succeeded him. He has carried on and improved many of the ideas started by his father. He says quite a lot about his early life and experiences, and even more about the extraordinary island of Scolt Head and its fauna and flora. He has written it in the delightful way in which he talks, explaining so many things about birds – especially terns – and other natural phenomena. Much of the bird behaviour which he describes has been deduced purely by painstaking and intelligent observation. He has frequently been ridiculed by scientists for his ideas, but very often it has been found that he has had the correct solution. Generations of scientists, students and schoolchildren have benefited from the 'Chestney Knowledge'. I can well remember finding my sons enthralled by Bob's explanations, illustrated by drawings in the sand, exactly the way that I had sat at his father's feet forty years before.

It is hoped that people like Bob will still be here in the future. Without them much of our unique natural history will disappear forever under a tide of twentieth-century predation and pollution.

William Shakespeare
March 1992

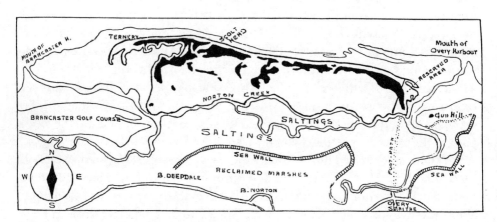

Scolt Head Island: Scale, 1 inch to 1 mile (approx.) The black areas represent sand dunes. The Southern Boundary of the island is Northern Creek, which connects Brancaster Harbour with Overy Harbour. The "Reserved Area" is the only part of the island not conveyed to the National Trust.

Introduction

I was born on January 19 1926 at Abington Cottage in Brancaster Staithe, one of many small villages of chalk and flint dwellings along the North Norfolk coast between Hunstanton and Wells-next-the-Sea.

The previous October my father, Charles Chestney, had been appointed warden of Scolt Head nature reserve. This event would prove scarcely less important to my future life than my birth itself.

I cannot remember exactly when I first visited Scolt. I had badgered Father many times, and cried as many times when he said 'no'. I do know that it was one fine evening after school, in May. The terns had just started nesting. Father said, 'I have to go back to the ternery this evening, I don't suppose you want to come with me, do you? We will have our tea when we come back.'

I dashed out of the house and down the Hard to the sailing boat, which was not quite afloat. Father arrived and we pushed the boat down the mud into the channel. The tide was just making (flooding). We hoisted the sail. With the light wind we just stemmed the flood tide, and sailed down the harbour, passing the whelk boats returning with their catch after a day at sea. Each time a boat passed it rocked our smaller vessel, causing the sail to flop from side to side.

A host of birds was diving into the water as we reached the Hole (a stretch of the main channel where the water remains deep even when the tide is out, trapping shoals of small fish and shrimps).

'What are those seagulls doing?' I asked.

'Seagulls! Don't you call them seagulls, they are terns, and if they hear you calling them gulls they will more than likely come and peck you on the head!'

That was my introduction to terns. On our landing at the ternery, hundreds of them took to the air, screaming and wheeling overhead. As we walked into the colony one swooped down several times, finally striking me on the head with surprising force from its sharp pointed bill. Blood spurted and ran down my forehead into my eyes. (Unknown to me the bird had pierced a small blood vessel.) Wiping the blood from my eyes with my hand, I screamed my head off. I was convinced that there was a large hole in the top of my head!

Father took me to the nearest pool of seawater, scooped some in his cupped hands and poured it over my sore head. As the blood and water spread over the pool I thought I was bleeding to death, and screamed even louder!

The blood soon stopped. Father said, 'You aren't going to die yet, making all that fuss!'

As we continued a bird dived at us again, and he added, 'I bet that be the same bird that pecked you on the head.'

When I thought he wasn't looking I picked up a stone and hurled it as hard as I could at the bird in question. My head was still very sore.

Unfortunately Father saw me. Instead of punishing me, he said, 'Don't let me ever see you do that again. All that bird was doing was trying to protect its nest. They don't like humans. We are their natural enemy, and this is their only defence against anyone or anything which might take their eggs or young.

While we were returning to the boat Father noticed footmarks in the damp sand, which the tide had covered earlier that morning. He asked me which animal I thought had made these tracks. I had no idea.

'That's a stoat's footmarks, and we don't want stoats in the ternery at this time of year. You stay here while I fetch some traps.'

On returning he searched the area. Finding four rabbit holes he set a trap in each of them; but I never found out if he caught the stoat.

The tide was ebbing fast, and it was time to go home. The boat was now high and dry, so we slowly edged it into Cockle Bight channel to refloat it. Father said, 'If I didn't have you to help with the boat pushing I would have to stay here until the next tide.'

Hoisting the sail we slowly made our way into the main channel, which separates Scolt from the mainland and Brancaster. Because of the light wind I rowed with one oar most of the way home, while Father steered close to the shore out of the main flow of the tide. When we were almost home I was allowed to steer until we ran aground.

After mooring the boat we walked up to the house. Mother had been watching our progress from the kitchen window. Tea was waiting for us on the table. I had never felt so hungry in all my life! Afterwards, I lay on the couch; but when I woke up in the morning I was in my own bed.

CHAPTER ONE

The Father Figure

Jacquetta Hawkes, authoress wife of J. B. Priestley and one of Scolt's many distinguished visitors, left this description of my father in her book *A Land*:

Chestney, a Brancaster man, had a large quiet body and a magnificent head, set with a formal pattern of curls, now white. He, more than any other man I have known, seems to draw strength and repose from his countryside, that coast of tidal creeks, wide saltmarshes and dunes. His life is adapted to the rhythm of the birds, their coming, mating, nesting and departure. When he dies, I should like to see a miracle. An artist, a true primitive, should paint a picture showing his body turned to a monolith and set up forever on the marshes, while his soul, a structure fine and clear as glass, is carried up to the blue Norfolk heavens by a flock of his terns, their exquisite white angled wings playing like lightning about it.

My father was certainly a man of strong character. Everyone respected him, including my mates. If they were getting up to mischief, he would go straight up to them and tell them off. He wouldn't say, 'I'll tell your father,' he dealt with the situation there and then.

He never changed his dress for anyone. Whether he be in his work clothes or his best suit the rich and famous, as well as ordinary folk, had to take him as they found him. He insisted on a clean shirt every day and, even at work on a warm day, wore a collar and tie, the latter fastened through the collar with a pin.

He was born at Burnham Overy Staithe, on the coast between Brancaster and

Wells, and was one of seventeen – the eighth in line. Like his brothers he experienced what growing up in the conditions of the day involved. He recalled in later years that his father repaired all the family's boots and shoes, and that his mother made all their clothes, which were handed down from one child to the next.

In those days, as it cost a penny per week to go to school, the boys obtained food for the family in any way they could. Poaching was the main source of meat. The boys started work at thirteen. At that age, Father was doing a man's work on the farm for three shillings and sixpence (17.5 pence) a week. With such a background it was little wonder that he was something of a 'rough diamond' as a young man.

In 1912, aged 26, he emigrated with some of his mates to Canada, in the hope of making his fortune. There he worked on what was by Canadian standards a 'small' spread – some 150,000 acres – near Winnepeg. He had charge of forty horses and as many farmhands. I've heard him say the winters were so cold that when they slaughtered the cattle they could hang the carcases outside to freeze. They would remain frozen until the spring.

At the outbreak of war, instead of enlisting in the Canadian forces, a sense of patriotism urged him to return to England. He volunteered for the Royal Navy and served on minesweepers, becoming a leading seaman. Four of these ships were on duty in the English Channel, each named with the prefix Liberty (Father was serving on the *Liberty Bell*). Being paddle steamers of shallow draught, when sweeping they could go over the top of a mine without being blown up by it.

On leave he visited the Army Pay Office in London, to draw money due to him, and while there got chatting to the chief cashier, a woman, Ethel Seaman. They found a common bond in their Norfolk roots she had been born only a few miles away from him, at South Creake.

They got to know one another and ended up getting married, in London. After the war, my father, a true countryman at heart, longed to return to Norfolk; but Mother's job was well paid for the time and she was unwilling to give it up. Besides which, life in the capital suited her and she didn't want to leave it behind. So instead she found him a job in London – as a store detective at Harrods. Physically, Father was probably well suited to this work; but it evidently didn't suit him. So Mother found him employment in the Fire Service as a fireman, which he found very boring. He complained that half the time he wasn't doing anything.

The lure of the coast was proving too much for him – he had to return home. He gave Mother an ultimatum – she could come with him or stay behind. This was in 1919 and she, under the circumstances, had little choice in the matter – she was pregnant.

Back in Norfolk they chose to settle in Brancaster Staithe and moved into Abington Cottage. My eldest sister, Eileen, was born on January 16, 1920.

From pre-Roman times the North Norfolk coast had supported a thriving fishing industry, and when my parents moved back there whelking was still a good commercial proposition. Mother invested £300 of her own savings in a boat and gear so that Father could get started. The harbour at Brancaster Staithe (Staithe meaning a discharging and loading point) was a flourishing little port. Coal from the North of England, bricks, pottery and general cargo from the Continent were landed, while sheep, cattle, barley, smoked and salted herrings were exported. With the arrival of the railways and then motorised transport, however, it ceased to flourish.

People were either fishermen, smallholders (such as my mother's family) or agricultural workers. The horse and two-wheeled cart or tumbrel had a dual role. Not only was it used on smallholdings to cart swedes, turnips or muck, but it also served for the collection of cockles and mussels that grew in abundance in the harbour. The latter supplemented the meagre income of the smallholders. Shellfish were carted to the railway stations at Burnham Market, Docking, Hunstanton or Wells, the latter two stations involving round trips of sixteen miles.

By the mid 'thirties smallholdings ceased to be viable. The horse and cart slowly became redundant until, by the end of the decade, motorised transport was being used.

Unfortunately the price of whelks dropped from ten shillings (50 pence) to two shillings (10 pence) a bag. My father, like many others, was out of business. He and his good friend Henry (Harry) Southerland found work on a ship which used to collect the whelks from Brancaster and deliver them to Lowestoft – a sea journey of some seventy miles in each direction. He took on other jobs, too, to support his growing family (another girl, Daisy, was born in 1923).

One of them was to take out gentlemen wildfowling and shooting. Although it might seem strange to those with 'modern' conceptions about nature conservation, as well as being keen sportsmen some of these were also good ornithologists and conservationists, and were connected with the Norfolk and Norwich Naturalists' Society. My father also met similar people ('the gentry', as he called them) at Brancaster's Royal West Norfolk golf course, where local men (not women, in those days!) had the privilege of playing on Sundays. Prior to the course being laid out, in 1891, the area had been grazing land, to which local people had had common rights. The arrangement was to compensate them for the loss of such rights. They could also compete for certain trophies, including the Sutherland Cup, which my father won in 1923. (I still have the silver replica of this which he was permitted to retain.)

Scolt Head Island was purchased by the Norfolk and Norwich Naturalists' Society from Lord Leicester's Holkham Estate, with money raised from an appeal to which principally Norfolk people contributed. It was handed over to the National Trust, at a special presentation on the island, on June 11, 1923.

The Society's chairman, Russell Colman, arranged for six rowing boats and a motorboat to ferry visitors from Burnham Overy Staithe to Scolt Head. Their journey from Norwich to the coast could be made, according to the public notice of the event issued by the Society, "by pneumatic-tyred Char-a-banc (14 seats) or open Motor-car". Tickets cost seven shillings and sixpence (37½ pence) each for the charabanc, or fifteen shillings (75 pence) each for parties of five travelling by car. The excursion was advertised as entailing a walk of from five to eight miles. Each visitor had to take his or her own lunch, etc., "as even water is not obtainable on the Island". A tea (for which tickets also had to be obtained in advance) was, however, arranged for the hardy trippers upon their return to the mainland!

For the first two years the reserve was wardened voluntarily by Miss Emma Turner, a distinguished naturalist and pioneer bird photographer. She monitored nesting and migratory species, as well as the human one. Her report at the end of the two years strongly urged the employment of a full-time warden, if Scolt Head was going to be successfully run as a nature reserve.

The post was advertised locally. There were only four applicants, including my father. Harry Loose, a local fisherman who had supplied Miss Turner with stores and fresh water during her sojourns on the island, had been offered the job prior to its advertisement, but had refused it.

Father's interview was only a formality. Dr Sydney Long who, in addition to being the Norfolk county medical officer was also honorary secretary and treasurer of the Scolt Head committee, wrote to Russell Colman:

Loose has turned down the warden's post, for reasons of his own. I have spoken with Chestney, and he is agreeable to taking on the watcher job, commencing in October. The job must be advertised to show that justice is being done.

During a conversation soon after Father's death I asked Harry why he had turned down the warden's job. He laughed and said simply, 'I was earning more money in one day than the job paid in a month.'

4

CHAPTER TWO

Island of Terns

S colt Head is a National Nature Reserve of some 1850 acres, and lies north and east of Brancaster Staithe and the Royal West Norfolk golf course. A long thin wisp of an island, thrown up by the North Sea storms and capped by wind-blown sand, Scolt dates back at least eight hundred years. It is believed to originally have been an offshore shingle bar or ridge, which was subsequently pushed landwards by onshore northerly winds assisted by east-west longshore drift. During a severe storm the ridge finally arrived in shallow water, and when the storm abated a section remained exposed above the normal high tides.

This allowed seeds, transported by wind and tide, time to germinate, soon establishing an embryo dune system which in turn stabilised the wind-blown sand, increasing the dunes to a height above even the highest tides created by the severest weather conditions. As more sand and shingle were carried landward, the establishment of dunes the length and breadth of the island inceased. Northerly winds curled the most westerly tip towards the south, creating a lateral ridge. As the island continued to extend westwards, this lateral remained, a procedure which has been repeated several times.

Between the laterals are bays, or 'bights', where the base consists of sand. Mud sediment builds up, creating mudflats over the sand. As the height of the deposits increases, these areas eventually reach a level where saltmarsh plants slowly take over. Thus develops the first stage of saltmarsh, crisscrossed with innumerable drainage ditches meandering to the main channel. There are thousands of these little gullies and creeks. From the air they resemble a huge jigsaw puzzle.

Often, when standing among these creeks or channels at dusk, waiting for duck to flight in to feed, I have heard what sounds like thousands of little sea animals talking to one another. In actual fact the noise is the top and bottom

5

shells of cockle-like creatures scraping together as they open or close. (It is safe for them to open under cover of darkness, as wading birds cannot feed while it is dark.)

In late October or early November, one of the widespread saltmarsh plants, an edible glasswort known locally as 'samphire' or 'sandfire' (some call it also the 'poor man's asparagus') takes on autumn tints, turning from deep green to a deep reddish brown. In the light of the setting sun the whole marsh appears to be aglow, as though on fire.

Today Scolt is appproximately four miles long and three-quarters of a mile wide. It comprises one-third shingle ridges and foreshore, one-third mudflats and saltmarshes and the remaining third sand dunes. That of Scolt Head itself attains a height of seventy feet, and is the highest sand dune in Norfolk. To the south stretches a low marshland coast. In the lee of the island, these marshes, mudflats and estuary provide shelter in winter for wintering brent and grey geese, diving and surface-feeding ducks and a variety of wading birds.

By contrast, during the summer months (April to September) the shingle banks and embryo dunes of the island's long backbone (especially those at the west and youngest end) become important. They are ideal habitat for tern species to nest. Many hundreds of pairs arrive from their wintering quarters (principally on the African coasts) during April and May. The rising sea temperatures, especially in the shallower water inshore, support large fish shoals on which the adult terns and their chicks totally depend. Round fish, sandeels, whitebait and shrimp are their main food supply.

It was this essential yet fragile ecological system which had attracted the attention of the Norfolk and Norwich Naturalists' Society. Although much has been learned about the island's origins and ecology, particularly during comparatively recent times, it still manages to retain mysteries. Even its name is not certain – it is spelt several ways on old maps, including Scalt, Scott and Scolt. The Head is the big sand dune where the Hut now stands. This is thought by some authorites to have been the site of the original shingle bank from which the island developed, although others claim this to have been where the present House Hills stand, farther to the east.

Areas of the island are pinpointed by highly individual place names. Smugglers Gap, to the east of the Head and Hut Hills, was where smugglers used to land. From here a track once led across the marshes, to join the Cart Road on the southern side of Scolt. (This was before the present sea wall was built.) And if someone says, 'I'll meet you at the entrance to Hut Drain,' it is like saying to someone in London, 'See you at Hyde Park Corner'!

In the original appeal for funds it had been recognised that a residence would

The HUT at SCOLT HEAD.

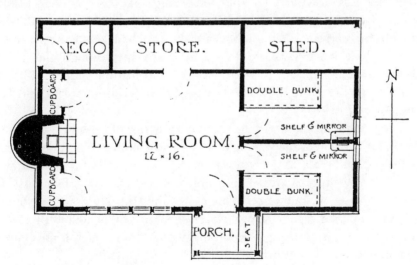

Edw. Boardman & Son.
Architects Norwich.

have to be erected for the watcher, and for those undertaking future scientific investigations on the island. £100 in excess of what was required for the island's purchase was therefore raised. An additional £200 was also subscribed, principally by Norfolk people, towards the building. An associate of Dr Long and the Colmans, a distinguised Norwich architect, Stuart Boardman, designed what was to be known as the Hut.

Alfred Cushion, of Norwich, undertook the building of this shelter, providing seasoned Norfolk-grown oak for its exterior and for the oak roofing shingles. The material was carted down by boat on the high spring tides. This made it possible for the flats, even fully loaded, to go across the even terrain of the marsh, where at high tide the water was about two feet six inches deep. The wood was thrown out onto the ground under the foot of the hill, and the boatmen had just enough time to get back into the main channel once again before the tide went out. (These big tides rise and fall very quickly.)

The workmen could not stay on the island. They had to come and go daily. When tidal conditions permitted, they could be transported by boat both ways, but more often they would walk one way and go by boat the other. Sometimes they had to walk both ways.

As I mentioned previously, the resulting bungalow was called the Hut. This might seem strange, considering it appears to be an almost palatial residence for five persons.

The explanation is that there was already a 'house' on Scolt Head. In actual fact this was a warrener's hut, measuring some eight by ten feet (but brick-built!). It was located about halfway along the island on a sand dune, and was used by the warrener killing rabbits for the Holkham Estate during the winter. (It has long since vanished from the landscape, though the site is still distinguishable.) As this was the 'House', and its dune House Hill, the new building and its more imposing vantage point became the Hut and Hut Hill respectively.

The first attempt to overcome the total absence of fresh water on the island was made early on by the sinking of a well, at the bottom of the west-facing steps below the Hut. Unfortunately, however, this was unsuccessful, becoming rapidly permeated with salt water. The problem was then solved by constructing a catchment area for rainwater, to the east of the Hut. This was done by erecting a frame, which originally carried eleven sheets of corrugated iron, down which the rainwater ran into a galvanised metal tank, from which it was bucketed as required by the Hut occupants.

Dr Long, the chief initiator of Scolt's purchase, had been born at Wells-next-the-Sea, and in his youth had got to know the North Norfolk coast well. He was aware of the hostility from the 'locals' to Scolt becoming a nature reserve. They strongly resisted change. Being from the area himself, Father also understood their resentment and, on his own initiative, turned a blind eye to their minor infringements, confident that in a few years time their hostility would run its course.

When he caught someone overstepping the mark, their argument was usually that they had been 'doing it for years and had not been stopped'. They also added that he had been one of them. In his own quiet way he would point out that it was his duty to implement the bye laws and that he had every intention of doing so. One case he told me about was confirmed by the person involved some years afterwards, when I met him in The Hero public house at Burnham Overy Staithe.

'I was eighteen at the time,' he told me. 'With two of my mates, I decided to ignore the ban on shooting on the dunes. If accosted by the warden, we would sort him out. We had several shots and then we saw your father coming straight towards us. Having no intention of running away, we joined up and waited for him.

On reaching us he was not even out of breath! While he was presenting the facts about shooting on the reserve (this was allowed only on the saltmarsh and shoreline) one of my mates, not having a gun but a cudgel, slunk to one side. Thinking your father hadn't seen him he raised the cudgel to strike him on the head. But Charlie had seen what was happening and moved to one side. The blow struck him on the left shoulder, knocking him to his knees. Without hesitation he straightened up and, with one blow to the chin, he knocked my mate out cold. Then he swung round and did the same to me.

The next thing I remember he was standing over me saying, 'Have you had enough?' In a dazed state I slowly got to my feet. My mate who had hit your father still lay on the ground, holding his jaw and moaning. I asked where our other mate was, and was told he had run away. 'And a good job he did,' Charlie added.

'My mate finally managed to get to his feet, holding his jaw, which he now discovered was broken. Your father had a broken collar bone, and was supporting it in his buttoned up jacket. After a lecture we were given our guns, with the cartridges removed, and made a hasty retreat. On the way home we realised the possible consequences of what we had done. Luckily for us your father took it no further. If we had known at the time,' he concluded, 'that from a teenager Charlie had been a 'handful', and had been Southern Region boxing champion in the Navy, we should have had second thoughts about intimidating him! Strange to relate, though, after this little episode we became good friends!'

Reminiscing about those early wardening days, Father wondered what the outcome would have been if an outsider, unaware of or not understanding the bitter resentment of the locals against the National Trust, had been appointed warden. For example, how could he justify to himself prosecuting a local man for taking the odd rabbit or two, when at that time the countryside was in the grip of what was known as the Great Depression, and people were very hard up and, in many cases, literally starving?

When I was three years old we moved to Dial House, Brancaster Staithe. For some time the Scolt Head Committee had been looking for a suitable warden's residence. After several setbacks this property came on the market. Dr Long attended the sale at the Ship Inn, Brancaster. He described the property as 'the most picturesque house in the village'.

Formerly the Victory Inn, Dial House was about 200 years old, "built of thin red bricks and flint with pantile roof, with a most picturesque porch surmounted by an old sundial". It comprised "two sitting-rooms, kitchen and office on ground floor, five bedrooms, two staircases. In front (to the south) is a large, open green, and to the north the property extends to the harbour." (In fact the kitchen overlooked most of the harbour.)

The entire property was purchased for £540. 'Compare this with trying to build a suitable house for anything like the money,' Dr Long enthused. 'We have already got possession, and minor repairs (painting, etc) are now being effected, so that Chestney will move on April 6th' (1929). He continued, 'We shall retain and furnish two of the rooms, which will be let to visitors, and the Brewhouse and barn can be used as parking places for cars.' In addition to the brewhouse, the extensive outbuildings included a grain store. Beer had been brewed not only for the Victory but many other local pubs. These buildings were, in time, converted to a laboratory for the use of Cambridge students visiting the island.

I remember that, after our cottage, it seemed such a barn of a place to me. How cold it was – terribly cold. I remember too the impressions of the wildness and openness of it and its gloomy oak beams. But it was also terribly exciting, with all those outbuildings to explore. I daresay it never was as bad as my childish imagination made out. My father guided and advised visitors to the reserve. Mother fed and looked after the students, and answered the many enquiries about tides, boats and what was happening 'birdwise' on Scolt.

A tall woman (five feet ten inches) she always seemed 'unflappable'. No matter what I had done, when I came home the first thing she wanted to know was 'what the damage was'. She worked hard, although she was never keen on housework – much of any remaining time she spent reading her weekly magazines. No matter what else was happening she would tidy the house last thing at night, irrespective of its state during the day!

Her talent for music showed itself in an ability to play a somewhat unusual combination of instruments – the violin, harmonium and mouth organ. Sometimes she would go away for a weekend or week with a lady friend to Ostend or France – that was her way of relaxing. Father would never do anything like that – he didn't enjoy travelling. The Committee's annual general meeting was always held at Dial House, starting at eleven o'clock and finishing precisely at twelve thirty. 'Chestney' was asked to sit in on this meeting. The day was organised to coincide with a flood tide after lunch, thus giving the members maximum time on the reserve. Some of them swam off the north beach. (Dr Long would swim on nearly every visit, even when staying on the island in December!)

Mother served the customary seafood lunch of cockles, oysters, samphire and sea trout, all acquired locally by my father. The trout, caught off Scolt's north beach, would weigh approximately ten pounds and be eaten slightly warm. She baked, on demand, apple and treacle tarts, insisting on no toppings, as they would spoil the flavour. All was washed down with a glass or two of wine. Eileen and Daisy (known as Dee) helped with the cooking.

Evelyn (three years my junior) and I kept well out of the way until the committee left for the island, when we 'appeared' for our sixpence, along with the others. One year I spent mine on an enormous sixpenny block of ice cream – and made myself sick!

Committee day was important to the family; but there were sighs of relief when it was over for another year! They were always a worry to my father, although Mother seemed to take them in her stride. My father spoke of them as being the reason why Scolt was always financially sound. Funds from voluntary subscribers in some years did not pay all the bills. Dr Long was a genius for obtaining money, especially for Scolt. Each reserve was expected to be self-supporting. When donations were insufficient to cover costs, he would say to the committee, 'Gentlemen, we have a small deficiency of 'x' pounds for the year. Would you be prepared to pledge 'y' pounds so that we can start the new year solvent? All agreed?'

This kind of sentiment was at that time typical not only of Scolt Head but of the village itself. I still meet people who remember those days, when they were children, and they talk about the magic and the everlasting impressions that have never been forgotten or equalled.

Virtually the same committee continued until the outbreak of war in 1939. Its founder members were: Russell Colman Esq, chairman; Lord William Percy

DSO; B. Riviere FRCS, FZS, MBOU; Robert Gurney MA, DSC, FLS; Major Anthony Buxton DSO, MBOU; G.E. Gurney Esq; R. M. Jarret Esq; Dr S. H. Long MD, FZS, MBOU honorary secretary and treasurer. Miss C. E. Gay was assistant secretary for many years.

My father's approach to life was to be generous, fair-minded and humorous. He could always find time to listen to our problems and troubles. Most days, before leaving for Scolt Head, he would ask me what I was going to do that day. When something new or with an element of danger was planned he would offer advice or show me the rights and wrongs of doing it. If I did anything mischievous I could guarantee he would hear of it. 'I understand you have done so and so,' he'd say. 'Why?'

Usually I had no reason or satisfactory explanation. He would then explain how stupid and irresponsible I had been, and tell me to have more sense in future. Rarely did he dole out physical punishment. Instead I would have to forego the Saturday treat (a visit to the 'pictures') and tidy around Dial House, or chop kindling sticks for the fire. He disliked dishonest people, and set great store by truthfulness. He always maintained that 'honesty was the best policy'.

Every night – rain, snow, hail or blow – precisely at a quarter to eight, he would walk the half mile to the White Horse for his pint and game of solo whist. The card school consisted of four. They had played together for years and would always wait for each other.

Despite the seriousness of his nature on the one hand, he also had a somewhat strange sense of humour. I remember when we were still very small we were blowing up balloons for Christmas. 'I'll blow them up,' Father insisted. They were huge balloons. He started to blow up his third one. He kept on blowing…

'No, Dad, don't blow it up any more,' we pleaded.

Obviously he was blowing it up to burst. It burst – he threw himself onto the carpet in our front room, kicking and choking. He terrified us children – Mother too, I think. Eventually he got up, laughing. It was only a joke. That was his sense of humour.

There were few girls of Evelyn's age in the village, so she would attach herself to us boys. We would try and avoid her, of course. Being the only boy, and small for my age ('puny', I believe they used to say) I must admit that I was thoroughly 'spoiled'. 'You spoiled little brat!' my older sisters used to yell when I got my own way, or had the cream off the top of the milk. I must have been a horrible little beggar! Many a time Eileen (who was as big at fourteen as she was at twenty) would have to help me out of a 'scrape'. She would sort out anyone who came after me!

It was, however, my father who retained the strongest influence over me. He was all the time teaching me to appreciate simple everyday things, to be aware that there were more satisfactory and rewarding things in life than those measured in purely monetary terms. When I grasped the situation, of course, I thought it was of my own doing! One of many examples was the pebble work in front of the Hut.

Both during construction of the Hut and subsequently, with the feet of many visitors to-ing and fro-ing, the surrounding vegetation was destroyed. This resulted in the wind creating a blowout, deep enough to be dangerous. To prevent further erosion, Father filled in the hole and the surrounding area with flattish pebbles carried from the beach in a skip on his back. (A skip is a Scandinavian word for a grain basket made of wickerwork.)

Although the pebbles were effective in stopping erosion, many visitors found them dangerous. When trodden on they moved one on top of the other, causing people to lose their footing. Some actually sustained sprained ankles. My father decided that something less dangerous was necessary, and presented the Committee with the idea of pebbles mounted in cement to stop them moving. The design was to be in keeping with the existing pebble-faced chimney, and

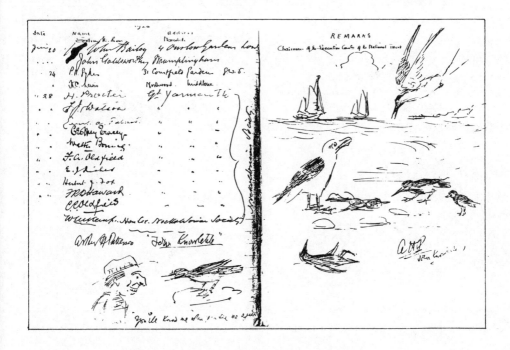

Extract from visitors' book, line drawing by John Knowlittle, naturalist and author, 1928.

13

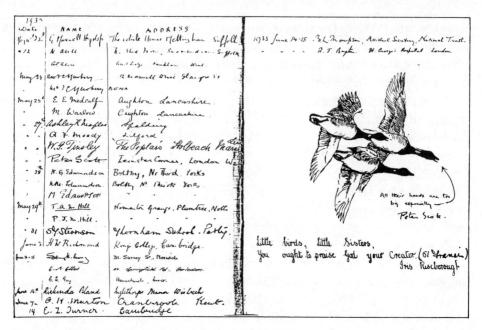

Extract from visitors' book, Brent geese by Peter Scott, 1933.

Extract from visitors' book, line drawings by Roland Green, Norfolk naturalist and bird artist, 1929.

consisted of a round centre piece, four feet across, with a needle in pebbles that pointed true north. This would be central to the door of the Hut. Either side of the circle would be ten foot squares. Both these and the circle were to be surrounded in Norfolk red brick, hand made at Holkham.

Before work started us boys – Ernie Loose (Harry's nephew) Derek Billing, Henry Helsdon and myself – went with him to the Hut at weekends. Each day we were given a pebble of a particular size and colour, plus a sack, and told to collect as many similar specimens as possible. Payment was to be a penny for each fifty delivered to the Hut. The first two weekends were fun, and we earned the great sum of eightpence each. (At that time a quarter pound bar of Cadbury's Milk Chocolate cost twopence.) On the third Saturday, however, we were undoubtedly less enthusiastic for walking one and a half miles loaded down with pebbles!

The Hut became the focal point for the island. A visitors' book was (and still is) kept there. Entries for those early years read almost like a *Who's Who* of the day. Celebrated writers of the period included John Galsworthy and John Buchan. Arthur Henry Patterson, a local naturalist and writer, who characteristically used the self-deprecatory pen-name John Knowlittle. He was a man of rare humour, and some of his cartoons are to be found in the Scolt visitors' book of this period. Patterson was good friends with another well-known local naturalist/writer, Ted Ellis, who accompanied him on many of his jaunts round the countryside. His granddaughter, Beryl G. Tooley, has recorded his life in her book *The Life of the Yarmouth Naturalist.*

Artists who stayed on Scolt at that time included Peter Scott, whose first visit in 1933 is marked in the visitors' book with a fine drawing of three brent geese in flight. Beneath it he has added his own critical comment 'heads too big'.

Roland Green, one of the most successful bird artists of the inter-war years also left behind in the Scolt book a whole page of pen sketches for us to admire.

Among the naturalists who stayed here in the early years, Miss E. L. Turner, the original watcher, also left the first entry in the visitors' book. She also made, subsequently, a permanent record of her two years here in her book *Bird Watching on Scolt Head.*

J.A. (Alfred) Steers, later Professor of Geography and President of St Catharine's College, Cambridge, first visited Scolt in 1924. On arriving at the Hut he heard shots and went to investigate the cause.

On the beach he discovered Miss Turner, pistol in hand, firing at a target she had set up above the shingle ridge to the rear of Hut Hill, where there are high dunes facing north. Having introduced herself, she explained that friends had suggested she take a pistol with her to the island, for her own protection. 'As I'd never fired one,' she added, 'I thought I'd better practise with it. This seemed the safest place.'

James Fisher is perhaps primarily remembered as a pioneering wildlife broadcaster. He was, however, also author, schoolmaster, secretary for the British Trust for Ornithology and a one-time employee of London Zoo. He stayed on Scolt in 1939. In this year Dr Julian Huxley's work *The Living Thoughts of Darwin* was published – a work on which Fisher had collaborated. Dr Huxley stayed on Scolt with members of the British Association in 1935.

Politicans visiting Scolt in those years included Malcolm MacDonald, a cabinet minister and son of Labour's first Prime Minister. E. Hilton-Young (later Lord Kennet), the stepfather of Peter Scott and a naturalist/author in his own right, was at the Hut in 1924. Subsequently he became a Minister of Health. Sir Geoffrey Shakespeare, MP for Norwich and Under-Secretary at the Admiralty, first visited Scolt in 1935. It was the start of a long association with the island for him and his family. His son, Sir William, still visits annually. During the early years nearly all brought a cook with them. When they went out for their walks around Scolt and luncheon or dinner was virtually ready, a bell would be rung to summon them.

This was, in fact, a big ship's bell which had come off of HMS *Snapdragon*. It hung from the Hut veranda and would be rung to herald lunch within ten minutes. On a normal day it could be heard up to half a mile away.

From April 1 to October 1, while visitors were staying at the Hut (and during the winter, when Dr Long was there) the warden had to make a daily trip – seven days a week, including Sundays – with stores. This was regardless of weather and tidal conditions; so when the tide was out this entailed a long trudge on foot, carrying the provisions.

One of Scolt's most memorable visitors in those early days was undoubtedly the Duchess of Bedford, a celebrated lady aviator, whose last visit to the island was in July 1936. Meeting her as a child of ten for the first time proved to be a great disappointment. I had conjured up a mental picture of someone entirely different. She was nothing like I imagined a 'flier' and a duchess to be. Perhaps it was the clothes she wore – a tweed suit and a masculine felt hat with the brim cut away in front (not unlike a German steel helmet).

Later Father recalled meeting the party on its arrival on the ten thirty ferry, spending the morning looking at tern nests and young, and watching the adults fishing – both out to sea and in the harbour – and returning with fish to feed the young.

They then walked to the Hut along the north shore and, because it was such a lovely day, decided to have lunch sitting on Hut Hill. Father had carried the hamper the three-quarters of a mile from the ternery and was relieved to reach the summit. (On opening the hamper, he claimed he could have eaten all the food and would still have been hungry!)

From the highest point of Hut Hill the view is fantastic – there is no lesser word to describe it – virtually the whole of Scolt and a general view of the harbour and coast for miles around. When conditions are right one can pick out the old lifeboat house at Blakeney Point and dunes to the east, Spurn Point (Lincolnshire) and King's Lynn to the west. Naturally, Father pointed out all the interesting features on Scolt and gave the visitors a general rundown of his work and involvement.

The Duchess said, 'This is certainly a fantastic view, and a lovely spot. I can understand why you love and enjoy your work so much. However do you keep in touch with all the numbers of nesting birds and the general happenings on the island, with such diverse terrain?' Father answered, 'The only way is to walk.'

The Duchess paused before saying, 'I know what you need, a horse.'

'That would be practical, but I can't afford to feed a horse, let alone buy one!'

Without any hesitation she said, 'I'll see you get one.' Father's impression was that she meant what she said.

In September that year the Duchess's aeroplane was reported missing. It was believed to have crashed in The Wash. Her de Haviland Gipsy GAAO wouldn't be seen again flying along the North Norfolk coast...

Famous writers and artists, baronets and peeresses were certainly not the greatest 'rarities' on Scolt. My first sighting of a really unusual bird there came in 1938. I was walking across Long Hills with Father one morning at about half past eight when he suddenly exclaimed, 'Hello, what have we got here?' There were some strange-looking footmarks in the sand – great big ones, like a chicken's.

We had a running dog (lurcher) called Fly with us. Father said, 'That's not long since it was here – look at the oul bitch !' She was getting excited – she could smell the bird. He kept calling her back.

'That'll go in a minute,' he exclaimed, obviously knowing what it was that had made those footmarks. I had no idea what it could be.

When we got onto lower and flatter terrain, Fly started to run. When we looked, there was this biggish bird (I can still see it, in my mind's eye) with a long grey neck and a mahogany brown back. It took off slowly, clumsily. If it had been at all slower the dog would have had it. It bent round to the east and flew towards the mainland. Of course, that was a great bustard – possibly the last in Norfolk.

CHAPTER THREE

Schoolboy at Burnham Deepdale

My academic standard was never very high. Any 'qualifications' I acquired were at Burnham Deepdale Church of England School. (The school and the village itself, which adjoins the eastern boundary of Brancaster Staithe, were later transferred to the parish of Brancaster.) Like most of the local children I failed the 'Eleven-plus' examination and completed my schooldays there. There was an alternative – Wells Central School, eight miles away. This boasted a higher standard of education than Deepdale.

My sister Daisy was one of half a dozen from our school who transferred there. That was how I was aware of the effort it involved. Attending the Central meant getting up at seven o'clock, putting on a suit and tie in school colours, and cycling the three miles to Burnham Market railway station in time to catch the eight o'clock train to Wells. The train returned at five fifteen - then it was cycle home in all weathers. This was not for me!

I could not be persuaded to change my mind because, apart from the travelling involved, I would miss out on my shooting during the winter months - especially the woodpigeon shoots. For years a national campaign had been waged to reduce the number of pigeons. Commencing February 1 and continuing to the end of March, every Wednesday and Saturday a chosen few 'locals' were allowed to shoot the pigeons in the woods as they returned to roost.

At the age of ten my father bought me my first shotgun – a single-barrelled bolt action .410. It could kill a rabbit or woodpigeon at a distance of twenty-five yards. At that time there was no age limit to carrying a shotgun, and a licence was needed only for carrying one on a public highway. I was the only local boy of my age to have a shotgun. Carrying it I would ride, proud as Punch, through the village on my bike, with the dog running alongside me. I was given my 'stand' (shooting position) in a particular wood at this 'tender' age, thanks to a great friend of my father, the gamekeeper, Billy Daniels. As this was a great privilege, I did not want to lose it by not being home from school in time.

On reaching the age of eleven and not choosing to go to Wells, we automaticaly graduated from the infant room to the 'Big Room', where we were taught by the head teacher, Miss Kaye. She was a forceful little lady – she had to be, with us boys to contend with. (There were never any masters at the school.) She stood no more than five feet four inches tall, while some of the boys in her charge were eight inches taller. They were big boys, ready to leave school at fourteen and go to work on the land. But she would control all of us, She was keen on all sports and used to instruct us boys in football, cricket and shinty (a rudimentary hockey-like game). She would sit at her desk looking at the class. (There would be some thirty-five to forty pupils in each of the two classes.) If someone was up to no good she would just lower her glasses down onto the end of her nose and look at you. Her eyes seemed to bore right into your brain. I always felt she knew what I was thinking.

'Bobby Chestney, I wouldn't do that if I were you!' she would say. How the hell did she know what I was going to do?

School restricted my other, and to me more important exciting and worth-while activities. If there was the remotest chance of escaping from the classroom or of not going there at all I took it. Who wanted to be stuck indoors when a good bird migration was taking place? And spending so much time with Father certainly did not improve my enthusiasm for school. Perhaps, even in those early days, his aim was to prepare me to follow in his footsteps at Scolt.

While 'rabbiting' on the island in the winter he was able to observe and record what was passing through on migration or stopping over. From the age of twelve I got the bird watching 'bug'. He would say, 'You ought to have been with me today,' and would reel off a long list of birds he had seen. Then he'd add, 'I reckon it'll be the same tomorrow.'

What a thing to say to a budding ornithologist! Naturally I would ask if I could go with him the next day. He never said yes straight away, but, 'Better have a look in the bird book, so if you do come you'll know what you're looking at.'

I would study each species from the list he gave me, so that I knew all their main features. The strange thing was that I could retain all this information without any trouble – it was the only thing I could! I knew the size, the weight in grammes (a unit we never used at school) the main identifying features, call and country of origin of all these birds, and of any species with which they could be confused.

Next morning Father would go outside to look at the weather, note the wind direction, come back in and say, 'I bet there'll be some good stuff moving today.'

'Can I come with you ?' I would plead.

'You'd better ask your teacher.'

Each day Miss Kaye would pass by the top of the village green in her car at approximately twenty minutes to nine. I would be watching out for her at a quarter past eight, just so I didn't miss her. When the car stopped she would say, 'Going to Scolt Head with your father today?'

As he would not let me pretend to be sick in order to miss school, I replied that he had told me there was going to be the best migration for years.

'I don't want you neglecting your schooling. This will encourage the other boys to take days off.'

'How can it, if they aren't interested in bird watching?'

'Well, all right, off you go.'

Obviously Father 'knew' his birds, and therefore had a good idea of what we would see on the day. He would occasionally misidentify a bird, however. If it was a 'new' one to me, he would look through his binoculars and say it was a so and so. Every bird he pointed out I would carefully check. When I studied it I would discover that it was in fact a similar but different species from the one he had told me. He continually kept me on my toes with these 'mistakes'.

This happened when I saw my first velvet scoter (an uncommon species of sea duck). We were both looking out to sea through binoculars and Father was listing all the birds in sight – brent geese, eider, common scoter by the buoy, and a great crested grebe behind. I noticed that the 'common' scoter had a white patch on the wing.

'That's not a common, it's got to be a velvet scoter!' I cried excitedly

Looking at it again, he said, 'Blast me, so that is! However did I make that mistake?'

I couldn't wait to get home to tell Mum that Dad didn't know the difference between a common and a velvet scoter! Mum said innocently (she always played along with him in these games) 'Why, Charles, Bob is getting better at identifying the birds than you are.'

Next day at school, before the start of lessons, Miss Kaye would make me tell the class about the birds I had seen. I took delight in this, and went into great detail, especially when I had seen a new species. When I had finished she would tell the others to carry on with the essay they had started the day before. I would have to write about my excursion to Scolt Head, which I found much easier.

Otherwise much of my time in the classroom was spent looking out of the window.

Next to the school was an overgrown garden, ideal for nesting and migratory birds. One day, while I was watching a hedge sparrow struggling to feed a very late-hatched cuckoo, something appeared out of the low cloud overhead. It was huge and shaped like a silver cigar.

As it came nearer I realised it was an airship – something you did not see every day! (Later I discovered it was the German *Graf Hindenburg*.)

I shouted, 'Cor blast, that's an airship,' and dashed out onto the playing field in time to see it quite clearly as it passed almost directly overhead. I could hear the engines purring quietly as it slowly continued eastward. In the meantime, Miss Kaye had assembled the rest of the school and had walked them to the playing field just in time to see it disappearing into the mist. When I returned to the classroom I was severely reprimanded for leaving the room without permission; but who cared about that – I was the only one in the school who got a fantastic view of the Zeppelin!

Before mains water came to the village (in the early 'fifties) communal wells and pumps were the only source of drinking water. People living near the seashore collected theirs from freshwater springs actually on the edge of the creek, because any wells sunk near the high water mark were permeated with salt water, which rendered it unfit to drink. Spring water was collected when the tide was out. The water was kept in a pail in the pantry. Sometimes when going there for a drink I would find that someone had left the lid off the pail and there was a mouse swimming round and round. Scooping it into the cup of my hand, I would discreetly deposit it outside.

Our doctor came through the village every day in one of the few motor cars to be seen locally. When he was needed a red flag was placed on a pole in the garden, and on seeing this he would know who wanted him. A visit would cost two shillings and sixpence (12½ pence). Medication cost extra. You could not afford to be ill in those days!

After examination, if medicine was needed, he would take the 'cure' from his bag. For coughs and colds it was a brown liquid which tasted of aniseed and mothballs, each bottle being a quarter full and topped up with water from the pail in the pantry. A white mixture was produced for stomach disorders or a general 'out of sorts' feeling. This tasted of school chalk and stale water. The bottles were given a good shake and labelled 'One tablespoonful to be taken after meals until finished'.

When tonsils needed to be removed, the kitchen table was scrubbed and, before you knew it, they were out!

The doctor knew that money was short. His usual advice, given free, was, 'Take a good dose of Epsom Salts in the morning and one of Syrup of Figs at night.' This must have been sound advice – within a few days people seemed to be as good as new!

'Progress' caught up with Brancaster Staithe in the mid-'thirties, in the form of electric power. The erection of the poles and fixing of cables took most of the summer. On my way home from school I found it exciting to watch the men putting the poles into the big holes they had dug. It was also fun to roll the huge empty wooden cable reels to the dumping point – a pastime stopped when one of the lads received badly crushed toes!

When the power was finally switched on there was great excitement. No more filling the paraffin oil lamps and trimming the wicks to make sure the glass chimney didn't soot up – all that was necessary now was to flick a switch. Instant light!

That same November, one of our school lessons was about the South American gauchos, who used a bolas – two stones strung together, swung round the head and hurled to entangle the legs of cattle or other running animals. I decided to make my own bolas.

This was achieved by removing the handles from my sister's skipping rope and increasing its thickness. We tried it out on the bullocks in the meadow and it worked OK. (The most difficult part was removing it from the animals' legs!) On my way to school one wet afternoon I was practising throwing my bolas at telegraph and electric light poles with considerable success. One of my friends bet that I could not reach the next pole, a distance of some twenty-five yards. This was a red rag to a bull!

Whirling the bolas around my head with all the strength I could muster, I let it fly. Unfortunately, however, it flew higher than I had intended, and wrapped itself around the power cables. When they came together there was a terrific blue and orange flash. Badly scorched, the two balls fell onto the path, but there was no sign of the rope. I looked to see if anyone had seen what had happened. Not a soul was in sight. So, grabbing the balls, we ran off, each of us swearing not to mention the incident. The next day we watched as a new transformer was installed, just above the school playing field. I had 'blacked out' the entire village!

From the age of twelve I spent many happy hours with Billy and Aggie Daniels. I helped Billy with rearing and feeding the pheasant chicks and with the twelve hives of bees he kept. I enjoyed extracting the honey from the comb (this is done by turning the handle of the spinner) filling the pound jars and sticking on the labels. The odd sting was expected, especially when collecting a swarm of bees. The most stings I had was fifteen, when collecting one in thundery conditions, which bees don't like. When I got home that particular evening I could hardly see out of my eyes, my chin was swollen onto my chest – I looked like Elephant Man!

Although I felt totally 'at home' with Billy and Aggie, there was no way they could persuade me to stop for a meal. Whatever the weather, come meal times I would jump on my bicycle and ride home. The round trip was four miles, and I would be back within the hour!

I was less 'comfortable' with many of my own relatives. My Uncle Simon, who was local and virtually lived with us, was the only one outside the immediate family whom I got to know. I must have been fourteen years old before another of my father's brothers caught up with me. This is how he told the tale:

'Bob was out in his rowing boat. I waited for him to come ashore. He moored his boat, and as he came up to me I said, 'Aren't you Bob Chestney?'

'What's that got to do with you?'

'I'm your Uncle Jim.' Putting my hand in my pocket, I brought out a half crown (12 pence) and offered it to him. A half crown was a lot of money to a young lad, but he looked at me, then at the coin, told me what I could do with it, and ran off.'

I hated (and still do hate) to be given presents, as I did not want the embarrassment of thanking the giver.

The first boat my father had used when he had become warden, to get to and from Scolt, had been the old Jessie, a heavy 14 ft clinker-built rowing boat which he had rigged with a lugsail. Now unseaworthy, she was permanently moored in a side creek at the harbour. My pals and I had many hours of fun playing at 'pirates', and pretending that we were at sea. (We didn't care that she leaked like a sieve and only floated on certain tides high enough to reach her.)

Harry Loose was one of the few fishermen who found time to talk to us boys – probably because he had no children of his own, he and his wife having lost twins at birth. One day during the summer holidays Harry stopped to watch us playing on the Jessie. After some moments thought he said, 'What you boys wanta do to stop har a-leaken like that is to get a bucket o' that there ooze from Ooze Point, an' smear that into har cracks. That will stop har a-leaken, at any rate on that theer tide.'

The ooze in question was a soft grey-blue clay, a glacial deposit from the last Ice Age. A seam of it is found low down the beach at Thornham and Titchwell, from whence it runs east, taking the same line through Brancaster harbour.

The ooze is covered by a layer of peat four to five feet deep, in which is embedded sizeable oak and other trees – living vegetation some thirty thousand years ago. In the past it was found to be an ideal substance ("the texture of stiff dairy butter", according to one description) to render newly excavated ornamental ponds and pools. A two inch rendering stopped any seepage, while it remained wet and undisturbed.

Naturally, we were keen to stop Jessie's many leaks since if we hadn't continually bailed out she would have sunk. So at low tide we cut slabs of ooze out of the bank with our pen knives. (We had also used this ooze bank for many years as a slide into the channel at low tide.) The major cracks sealed we waited for the tide. The operation proved most successful and after a few more tides we knew every leak and marked them for future reference. Now the Jessie was 'seaworthy' at least on that one tide! – we could venture into the main channel.

The following day all the leaks were sealed. As soon as she floated, it was 'up anchors' and away. Amid great excitement we rowed into the main channel. As always, Father got to hear of our little adventure. The next day, when we were out in the channel, he made a point of catching us and explained how dangerous it was to play around in a boat of the Jessie's condition. We pointd out that it was now safe and that we rarely had to bail any water out.

'Come and join us and see for yourself!'

After rowing for over an hour, the boat having shipped virtually no water, we returned to the side creek.

We pointed out to Father that she was quite safe in the channel for a short time. After some thought he agreed to let us continue, providing we did not venture further down the harbour than a particular buoy. Strange to relate, there were no mishaps, at least as far as the boat was concerned. However, while fishing from her one day, Alf Burton caught a huge eel. While he was trying to take it off the hook, it wrapped itself round his left wrist. A second hook became embedded in his thumb. As quickly as I could I cut the line close to the hook. The eel, now free, dropped to the bottom of the boat.

Alf wanted us to take him home, as the hook was well and truly buried in the fleshy top of his thumb; but we had no intention of doing this – the fish were biting too well. So we tried to remove the hook. The barb would not allow this so I said, 'I shall have to cut it out.'

A good fisherman always carries a sharp knife and a piece of string. Luckily for Alf the knife was very sharp. While one of the lads held his thumb tightly, I probed for the barb. They must have heard Alf shouting a mile away on the mainland!

The hook finally came free, and I gave the thumb a good douching in the tide. Someone joked, 'It's a good job there aren't no sharks about,' as the blood spread over the water. Alf sat in the boat holding the painful thumb as I baited a new line for him. In less than five minutes he had hooked a huge dab – the largest of the day – and in the excitement of getting it aboard entirely forgot about his painful injury!

As the holidays progressed we grew bored with just rowing and became envious of the passing sailing boats. Father had taught me to sail early on. Now, at the age of twelve, without wishing to sound too conceited, I was fairly good at it. Knowing that the Jessie's mast and sails were stored in the barn I thought, why not get them out and see if we can fix them up?

Apart from the odd wormhole the mast was reasonably sound, but needed re-rigging. The tan sail was rotten and past any repair. When Father came home that evening I told him what we had done, and asked if we found a sail could we then use the boat for sailing. He laughed, saying, 'Of course you can.'

We jumped with joy, unaware in our excitement that we should be most unlikely to find a sail of any description. I lost no time in asking the fishermen and the sailing fraternity; but with no success. Feeling downhearted, I thought that was the end of our sailing venture. Then I had another idea. So I asked a pal, whose father worked on a farm, if they could acquire four sugarbeet pulp sacks, in good condition. These were made of closely woven hessian and when opened at the seam each measured aproximately five feet square. Therefore if four were sewn together, the result would be a reasonably sized lugsail.

The following day my mate delivered the sacks. I set to hand sewing them together. When I had finished I persuaded Father, before his nightly pub visit, to lay the hessian square out on the kitchen floor and draw in chalk the shape and size of the proposed sail. Then I carefully cut along the chalk lines, before going to bed.

After hurrying home from school next day, I set to hemming by hand the cut edges – a long and laborious task which took me two evenings to complete. The sail finished, Father said he would 'rig and step' the mast and fasten it on the gaff (spar) ready to hoist and set sail.

I could scarcely wait for Saturday's tide – a neap (small) tide flooding slowly at around one o'clock, which gave Father ample time to rig the Jessie, and for us to collect the necessary amount of ooze to seal all the leaks (by now we knew every one) plus a bucketful in reserve, just in case. Just before the boat floated, Father again instructed us in how and where to tie the rope on the gaff that hoisted the sail, and how far we could venture down the harbour, adding, 'If she looks like sinking sail downwind to the nearest shore, then wait until the tide goes out before you attempt to walk home.'

The boat finally floated, the sail flapping in the light south-south-westerly breeze. Father asked, 'Are you ready?' In great excitement we all yelled, 'Yes!'

Pushing the boat through the wind, the sail filled and we slowly headed against the tide down the harbour. Not far from the shore we waved to the onlookers, who had gathered to watch this amusing sight; but little we cared what we or the Jessie looked like – we were sailing! Later we celebrated by sharing a bottle of Vimto.

We sailed every possible day, mending the sail when necessary. Frequently we forgot to allow sufficient tide to return to the Hard, and had to 'abandon ship' and walk home. When left overnight in the channel the depth of water at low tide would be the same inside and outside the boat, due to the ooze coming adrift.

It eventually dawned on us that by placing the anchor away from the channel she would settle directly downtide of it and become high and dry at low tide. Any water gained while afloat thus leaked out, leaving her ready to be re-oozed before another day's venture.

The following summer we were using the same sail, which by now needed constant repair. Just before the school holidays, Harry Southerland gave us a cotton lugsail. This increased the Jessie's sailing performance and reduced the amount of rowing we had to do. It was now possible to sail much nearer the wind, which helped to increase both our sailing expertise and enjoyment.

My sailing pals still remember those summers. It certainly was an adventure, sailing off on our own for the very first time. I am sure it increased everyone's patience, perseverance and our comradeship – something which would stand us in good stead in the years ahead.

It wasn't only sailing at which we became 'expert'. With transport to and from Scolt Head virtually non-existent, St Catharine's College acquired its own boat, in order to transport the geography students in the charge of Alfred Steers back and forth. This was named the Tyke, and had an American Elto five-horsepower engine. When the college didn't need it Father had the privilege of using both the boat and engine, which he taught me to operate when I was twelve years old. The ignition was battery driven, so he showed me how to connect the batteries up and how to start the engine. There was a special technique. Since there was no pull-cord you had to swing a flywheel by means of a handle on top of it. When there was enough momentum to take it over top dead-centre it would fire.

Usually by Guy Fawkes Night (November 5) it starts getting colder and wetter – conditions which I considered to be more suitable to life in the classroom. As work was slack on the farm during the later part of the year, there was time then for thrashing the corn stacks – and from the classroom we could hear the arrival of the steam engine puffing and rattling as it shunted the threshing machine drum and the elevator into position, ready to start thrashing the following day.

The average stack represented a day's work,. and would usually be completed between three thirty and four o'clock. This gave us time to dash from school and assist in killing the rats and mice that had made their homes in the stack.

During my final two years at school I adopted a more – or slightly more! – responsible attitude. I persuaded Miss Kaye to let me have time off on a Wednesday to shoot pigeons, and was allowed to leave school at quarter past three instead of quarter to four. Perhaps she saw this as an inducement to make me work harder. In retrospect, this may have succeeded. My report at the end of term 'slightly' improved. I should add, however, that in return for the favour of letting me off early on a Wednesday, Miss Kaye received, each Thursday morning, a brace of young woodpigeons, plucked and ready for the oven.

I remained 'accident-prone', however. Country folk say that mishaps come in 'threes'. Mine certainly did.

After lots of practice I could ride my bicycle facing the opposite direction. I could also get up speed and stand on the saddle, guiding the bike with my body – riding with 'no hands' was a bit tame! Father pointed out that it might be very clever, but that sooner or later I would come a cropper. Needless to say his prediction was right. The inevitable happened.

Doing my balancing act I hit a pot-hole in the road. I was thrown over the handlebars and landed on my right arm. The pain was so terrible I could not get my breath. The whole village must have heard me howling in pain. Leaving my bike lying in the road, I walked the half mile home. The family certainly heard me long before I got there. Mother met me at the door. She asked me what was the matter. Through my tears I said, 'I've hurt my arm.'

In fact it was broken, and had to be set in plaster of Paris at the Norwich hospital. Within three weeks, however, I was riding my bicycle again (unknown to Father). The biggest punishment I got from breaking my arm was not being able to join my mates chasing rabbits in the harvest fields. The weight of the plaster when I was running put too much tension on the arm. (But it would have made a good cudgel!)

One evening, hot and sweaty after leaving the harvest field, the lads decided to have a swim, as the tide was high. My sisters and some other children were having fun running along baulks of timber moored in one of the creeks. These were thirty feet long by eighteen inches square and had been there many years, having originally been salvaged from a wrecked wooden sailing barge.

In the term prior to the summer holidays we had been reading about

Canadian lumberjacks and how they manoeuvred logs by spinning them with their feet into the main flow of water. I had been fascinated by the pictures of them illustrating this technique.

Unfortunately, I could only watch my friends' antics as they played.

Father landed close by, home from Scolt. As he walked past he stopped to say, 'I'm glad you've enough sense to keep on the shore. You stay there – with that extra weight of plaster, if you fall into the water you won't be able to swim.'

'All right,' I agreed; but as he walked away I thought 'silly old bugger!' I watched him go for his usual pint at the 'White', and when he was round the corner of the Green, I thought it would do no harm just to have one run down and back on a baulk. I ran to the end with no troubler and turned to run back, but two of my mates had followed me. The baulk began to submerge and at the same time roll. I heard Eileen shout, 'Be careful, Bob!' But the warning was too late. Losing my balance I fell into the water.

I tried to swim to the surface, but found it impossible. I felt my feet on the mud bottom. Even with a superhuman effort it was no good. I could see the sun on the baulks of timber and even the ripples on the surface. As I struggled my lungs felt as though they would burst. Lights started to flash and my head began to pound. I continued to fight towards the surface. Then everything went black.

The next thing I became aware of was Eileen's voice, from a long way off, saying, 'It's all right, it's all right.'

I could see her through a 'fog'. I felt terribly cold. I was coughing and being sick. I became aware of scores of people around me. Although I tried to get to my feet my legs were like rubber and would not support me. Eileen helped me up and virtually carried me home. Mother had seen us through the kitchen window, which overlooked the harbour, and met us at the back door.

'What's happened this time?' she asked. Eileen told her the full story. I lay on the couch, still wanting to be sick. I felt more dead than alive. Mother said, 'Oh well, we'd better take those wet clothes off.' But I was more concerned with what Father would say when he found out. After a cup of tea it was suggested that I go to bed before he came home. I didn't need to be told twice!

He didn't visit me that night as far as I knew; but I got little sleep – mainly due to my aching arm, but also over worry over what was in store for me in the morning. Reluctantly I went down to breakfast. Not a word was mentioned until it was over. Then he said, 'What happened to you after I went out last night?' I gave my account of the incident as I saw it. He replied, 'Oh ar? What am I going to do with you? I wish you would heed the advice given to you.'

I wondered how he had known and said, 'I suppose the girls broke their necks to tell you?'

He laughed and answered, 'What makes you think that? I get to know most of the naughty and stupid things you get up to nearly before you do them. I wish you'd use a little more common sense, instead of learning the hard way!'

The third time I nearly came to grief was soon after my arm was out of plaster. In early October I decided to go shooting rabbits on Scolt with my dog. By catching the last of the tide down the channel in Father's rowing boat I could moor in the channel and thus return home on the very first of the flood tide, around five o'clock. The day was warm and sunny. So, before returning to the boat, I decided to have a swim in the warm water on Scolt's north beach, where it had run over the warm sand.

Afterwards, I arrived back at the boat and had to wait for the first of the tide. Being impatient, as soon as the tide reached me, I decided to walk with it. It was a three-quarter spring tide, flooding quite quickly. Walking at the bow of the boat it was possible to pick out the deeper part of the channel ahead, drag the boat over the high parts and jump on the bow in the deeper water, as the flooding tide carried the boat forward.

I had done this many times before; but this particular day was almost the last time.

Reaching a part of the channel only four hundred yards from where I had been moored, the boat grounded. Unknown to me, I was standing on mud-capped dead spring, or 'quake'. As I pulled my weight went through the mud crust, and soon I was waist deep in the mud.

The tide carried the boat forward over the top of me, the keel scraping my head and shoulders. It seemed an eternity before my head broke the surface. Gasping for breath I tried to free myself from the quake, but the suction was too great. I tried pushing myself free with my arms; but that meant my head was under water.

I realised that I was not going to get out without help so started screaming. Then, above the sound of my own voice, I heard someone shouting, 'Hold on!'

Looking towards the sound, I saw Harry Loose running across the marsh. From the edge of it, in only four or five long strides, he was within an arm's length of me. In water deeper than his pulled-up thigh boots, he stretched out his hand. (I remember how huge it seemed – no doubt the result of years of hauling whelk pots from the seabed.)

'Stop yer hollering and struggling! You want to get out, don't you?'

Holding my hand tightly he pulled. I thought my arm would come out of its socket. But slowly I felt my legs sliding through the porridgey mud, as Harry gradually tugged me out onto safe ground. He helped me up the bank onto the marsh. All he said was, 'That was a near 'un. Now you gotta retrieve yer boat!'

By this time it had been carried by the tide well past the point where I intended to moor. Thanking Harry, I ran as fast as my lungs and strength would allow. Arriving totally breathless at the boat I threw out the anchor and waited until I got my 'second wind' before making any attempt to row to the mooring position. The dog had remained in the boat, wagging its tail excitedly – no doubt wondering what the fuss was all about!

After mooring I washed the mud from my legs and clothes, before wearily making my way home. When my father asked me why I was soaking wet I told him what had happened. He slowly shook his head and said, 'That's the third mishap in less than three months. Let's hope it's the last – at least for a little while.'

CHAPTER FOUR

Learning the Hard Way

It might seem strange that I was brought up to be a wildfowler – a 'shooting man' – when my father was warden of Scolt Head nature reserve. However, he had lived partly by the gun from the day he was big enough to shoot, and for pioneer wardens like himself one of the tasks was to control predatory species, plus the rabbit population. Thus a gun was an essential part of a warden's 'working kit'.

Many accidents in the shooting field are the result of lack of instruction and guidance when first acquiring a gun. There is a code of practice to follow every time you pick one up. This was instilled into me by my father. Frequently, on the spur of the moment, he would tell me to recite the well known shooting code: A Father's Advice To His Son.

He had his own ways of making sure I kept all the safety rules. For instance, he came home late one afernoon and I had just returned from school. The weather was frosty with the odd squally snow shower. He said, 'You ought to be up Mow Creek – there are scores of ducks flighting.'

The creek, relatively close to Dial House, contained several freshwater springs, used by birds to 'water and wash' – especially by gulls returning to the coast to roost after spending the day feeding upland. (The name is spelt Mow or Mowe, and is the Swedish for gull.)

With no more ado I grabbed the gun from behind the kitchen door, put on my shooting gear and filled my pockets with cartridges. The dog was already waiting at the back door and I couldn't get out fast enough! Before I could open it I heard Father call out, 'Come back! Where d'you think you're off to?'

'I'm off to Mow Creek to shoot those duck.'

'No you're not, put the gun away.'

'Why?'

'You should know why. What should you have done first, when you picked up the gun? You always check to see if it's unloaded and therefore safe. Did you do that?'

I had to say no, but added that I knew it was unloaded, as I had made sure it was empty the day before when I had put it away.

'How do you know I haven't used it myself today?'

What could I say? I saw his point and, in spite of arguing and shedding a few tears, I could not persuade him to let me go shooting that evening, or for the next few days. From that day onwards whenever I picked up or was handed a gun, if only a minute had elapsed, I automatically checked to see if it was loaded. After satisfying my father that I could meet his strict safety criteria I was eventually allowed to shoot the marshes without his guidance.

I had one hair-raising experience with a young novice wildfowler which even today gives me the shudders when I think of it.

From Monday to Thursday I had seen thirty or forty grey geese flighting in at dusk onto the 'fresh' marshes to feed. As I made my way home I thought I would try and shoot one on Friday evening. (I had only ever shot two grey geese before.) Since the fresh marshes were privately owned my safest bet was to wait until virtually the last minute before quickly covering the four hundred yards to a clump of reeds growing in the dyke over which I had seen the geese pass on the previous four evenings. It would have to be a quick shot, then out and back to the sea wall.

As I waited for dusk I saw someone walking towards me along the sea wall. A local lad, he stopped and asked if I was waiting for duck. I said I was, hoping he would continue on his way. Instead, he asked if he could stay with me, adding, 'I haven't shot a duck all week.'

I didn't really want him with me, but hadn't the heart to say no. I then had to tell my real intention, emphasising that if he came with me he must do exactly as instructed.

Soon it was time to cross the marsh. We headed for the clump of reeds I had marked out, positioned ourselves and waited. It was not long before we heard the geese calling in the distance. The calls got louder and louder. Then – there they were! My heart began to race with excitment. This was going to be my third goose.

Crouching side by side in the reeds we watched as the birds, still honking, passed a hundred yards to our left, then turned into the wind and headed straight towards us. I whispered, 'Don't move an eyelid. We're in luck! As they come into range I'll give the countdown to fire. Get ready.'

Suddenly there was a most terrific bang. The earth on the side of the bank about three inches from my waist erupted, showering down over me. The charge from my companion's gun had blown a hole three inches wide and the same deep. Naturally the geese shot skywards, turned tail and headed into the dusk. Turning to him, and not feeling too pleased, I said sternly, 'What the hell happened?'

He was speechless, and even in the poor light I could see a very pale face with popping eyes and a 'frozen' expression. More calmly I said, 'Unload your gun.'

He seemed in a daze, so I took his double-barrelled gun from him, broke it open and removed the spent and live cartridges. Giving it back to him I suggested we get to hell out of the marsh before someone came and caught us for trespassing and poaching!

While we rested on the sea wall I again asked what had happened. He said, 'In the excitement and tension as the geese came closer I must have pulled the trigger by mistake. I didn't mean to. I thought I'd shot you in the back, and that the soil that spattered over me was bits of you!'

I realised then what a close shave I'd had.

Life underwent a dramatic change when the British government declared war on Hitler's Germany on September 3, 1939. Three days previously, Sir Geoffrey and Lady Shakespeare and their son William, who had been staying at the Scolt Head Hut, had departed. I was quickly despatched by Father to break the news to the people who had replaced them.

The Hut was closed the same October and sealed for the duration of hostilities – except for one notable exception which we shall come to.

To the considerable glee of us youngsters, rumour soon became rife that food would be in short supply. Together with my pals I decided to breed rabbits. (I had kept them before.) Most of my friends worked on local farms and therefore had a good idea where food for them could be obtained without cost!

Dial House, with its walled garden and many outbuildings, was an ideal place for rabbit breeding. My pals, in their farm cottages, were not so fortunate and had to make hutches. So I suggested that we all went over to Scolt in my boat, to collect suitable driftwood from the shoreline for them – and in four weekends we had gathered enough wood.

Our rabbit numbers soon multiplied. There was no problem with food supplies during the summer months; but as the green vegetation died off, the winter nights had to be spent scrounging for hay, straw, turnips, swedes and so on. We collected for one another in turn, keeping a watchful eye out both for the local constable and a very keen special constable.

The quantity of straw, hay, turnips and swedes the farmer was losing, as our rabbit population increased (mine alone was in excess of a hundred) became so obvious that he decided to put a stop to the pilfering. The police were asked to keep watch, though luckily it was not one of us who was caught. The culprits were duly prosecuted; but justice had come a mite too close to us for comfort. This little brush with the law effectively put an end to our rabbit breeding.

Anyone in our village who had a room to spare had to take one or two evacuees. My mother started with two boys, brothers of ten and eleven. They arrived one September afternoon, about four o'clock, having travelled by train from London to King's Lynn and then on to us by coach. They had never even seen the sea before.

Mother gave them something to eat and then, thinking they must be tired after the travelling, round about eight o'clock she thought she would put them to bed. She took them upstairs and showed them the beds, saying, 'I'll come up later and see how you're getting on.' In the event, however, it was Eileen who went up to make sure they were all right. She couldn't find them; they had 'disappeared'. Their beds hadn't been slept in. Coming back downstairs, she told Mother the boys had gone.

'Don't be stupid.'

'But they aren't there,' Eileen insisted.

Up they both went. The boys definitely weren't there. Mother and Eileen were both greatly puzzled by the mystery. What could have become of the little cockney evacuees? Had they run away? If not, then why weren't they in their beds?

Suddenly, a voice said from under the bed, 'Hey, we're here!'

Mother said sharply, 'What the hell are you doing?'

'This is where we sleep,' came the reply. 'Mum and Dad sleep in the bed, and we sleep underneath.'

There were always plenty of reminders of war for us, even in this remote corner of England. In late November 1939, two Blenheim fighter bombers were returning from a reconnaissance mission to their base at Bircham Newton (seven miles away). Unable to locate any of the local airfields because of thick fog they decided to head back to the coast. The fog was less dense here and they would be able to make forced landings on the foreshore.

One of the pilots knew the coastline and beaches from Wells to Thornham reasonably well. Apart from regular flights over this area, he had also accompanied Father on wildfowling missions. Most importantly, he knew it was free of land mines. Picking out the coastline and recognising the features of

Scolt Head, they landed on the firm sand. Luckily the tide was out. They taxied the aircraft to the edge of the dunes, knowing this to be above tide level. Having completed this dangerous manoeuvre, they now faced the difficult task of reaching the mainland across the creeks and marshes in the fog.

Two days later the fog cleared. Father organised transport to ferry an RAF rescue team and sufficient fuel for the aircraft to return to base. Naturally I took the day off from school to be in on this operation – I couldn't let such an opportunity pass me by! I shall never forget climbing into the turret gunner's position, at the invitataion of the sergeant armourer (who had made the guns 'safe') and looking through the gunsight.

That same year, in late December, another Blenheim force-landed on Scolt, virtually in the same spot and in foggy conditions. This time the pilot did not taxi his aircraft above the high tide level and the plane was totally immersed by the incoming sea.

Father ferried the RAF inspection and salvage team and accompanied it to the aircraft. He heard their decision (which he privately thought was outrageous). Since the plane had been immersed in salt water it was not serviceable for future missions and would have to be scrapped – buried on site.

At that time the government had a campaign to persuade people to give their aluminium pots and pans to the War Effort. Here was an instance where many tons, in the shape of a complete plane, were to be buried! Father decided to contact a farmer who owned a Field Marshall, the most powerful tractor in the area, and explained to him the Air Ministry decision regarding the aircraft. At low water they surveyed the beach from Brancaster golf clubhouse across the main harbour channel. The farmer agreed that there would be no difficulty in towing it to Brancaster beach – the sand was firm all the way. There it could be dismantled and the parts recycled to make a new aircraft. Father told the Air Ministry that for the sum of £100 it was feasible to do this; but they turned down the proposal in favour of going ahead with their original plan.

War or no war, Father insisted the aircraft be buried above high water mark, in the dunes, where it would not pose a hazard to local fishermen. This would also limit the chance of it being uncovered. As it was winter and there were no visitors on the island, the Hut could be used as accommodation by some of the salvage crew (if they could be called that, in this instance!). It was obviously going to be a mammoth task, the aircraft was approximately four hundred yards west of the Hut, while there were very low dunes a further hundred yards to the west. The salvage section MV Cambridge recorded in the visitors' book:

Collected crashed aircraft 6644 Blenheim bomber. Arrived January 1, 1940. Completed task February 20. Number of RAF personnel involved 36.

Their first task was to manhandle the plane along the beach to the edge of the low dunes, drain fuel from the wing tanks into cans and then remove the wings from the body. Next they had to dig a hole, and it isn't difficult to imagine the size needed to bury a twin-engined fighter bomber!

It was over a week before this hole was completed. A mountain of sand and shingle surrounded it on three sides. I watched the fuselage being manhandled over the dunes, some of which had been cut away to make the job easier. The weather was cold, with sharp frost at night and frequent snow showers, so it was several days before my next visit, by which time the aircraft had been pushed into the hole. The final task was to fill in the hole with shovels. Due to the overnight frost, every day two or three inches of sand and shingle had to be broken before work could proceed – all this to the acompaniment of squally snow showers. By February 20 the team had, as far as it was concerned, completed the task. Everyone was only too glad to return to base.

With the thaw the aircraft was seen to be far from buried. The section of the body containing the gun turret remained totally exposed as the snow melted. Father informed the Air Ministry of the situation. Their reply was that they regretted that they had no one available either then or in the immediate future to complete the job, so if he liked to recruit local labour they would bear the cost. A working party was recruited and the burial completed.

In the winter months we lads had time on our hands for roaming the street or killing rats that had moved into the corn stacks for warmth and food during the winter. All that was needed for this was a stick and a torch. Going from stack to stack, we could kill twenty to thirty in one night.

Occasional nights would be spent with catapults after pheasants roosting in the trees. We were probably a general nuisance, but nothing more. However there were complaints to the police that 'something must be done about these local lads who were getting out of hand'. Unfortunately they decided to act on his information.

No mention of this was made to my father, who was a special constable. The regular police and other specials were asked to keep the operation a secret. One of the specials, Charlie Croome, however told my father what was afoot. That night, about eight o'clock, a black maria (police prison van) would be coming through the village. Any youth – and they meant ANY youth! – would be picked up, regardless of what he was doing.

I had already gone out, at seven thirty, to meet my friends. Father thanked Charlie and set off to find me. We had not all arrived at our meeting point. I had to call for Billy Matsel, who lived in the middle of the village. As we came out onto the road we met Father who said, 'Go home as fast as you can – there's trouble!'

I started to ask why.

'Do as you're told, both of you.' Taking off his cap, he gave us both a clip round the ear. 'Don't stop running until you reach home!'

This warning was repeated to the other lads, who lost no time in getting home. We knew something had to be seriously amiss for him to act like this.

The black maria arrived at eight o'clock, but we were all safely indoors by this time. Father let it pass. Ten minutes later, as it slowly returned, he stopped and asked the sergeant what was going on. Reluctantly the latter gave the reason for the visit and also said who had been responsible for the night callout.

Later that night my father met up with him. I should like to have been there! Two nights later, just before he left for the White Horse, a knock came at the door. The same man entered sheepishly, apologised and offered Father a bottle of Johnnny Walker whisky. Father looked at him and said, 'You know what you can do with that! The boys deserve an apology. They could easily have been sent to borstal [corrective training centre] thanks to you.'

I have no doubt that the reason for Charlie Croome's tip-off that night was connected with an incident some years previously, in which Father had attempted to save Charlie's son from drowning.

Even at the 'advanced' age of sixteen I did not escape punishment when I deserved it. One time, however, I received a hiding literally for nothing. It was to prove a turning point in the relationship between my father and myself.

One particular late September evening Father was on his way out for his pint and game of solo when he was accosted by a Mrs Thompson. She alleged that I had placed a pile of bricks on her doorstep, knocked on the door and hared off on my bicycle. As she had rushed out of the door to see who it was, she had fallen over the bricks, grazing her leg and bruising her arm quite badly. My father asked if she had positively identified the boy as me.

'I know it was that little bugger of yours.'

He knew Mrs Thompson did not like us boys. (She was always reporting us for something or other. We would get back at her by riding our bicycles over her doorstep just after she had whitened it.)

I was made aware of what I had supposedly done when, instead of continuing to the pub, he was back home within half an hour very upset and asking me what the hell had I been playing at and why had I done such a stupid thing. I naturally denied all knowledge and said it certainly wasn't me who was responsible for it.

'Don't lie to me. She recognised you as you rode away.'

This was one of the few times I couldn't convince him I was telling the truth. I received a thrashing and was sent to bed. Arriving at the White Horse over an hour late and not in a good frame of mind, he was greeted with the comment, 'Overslept in the chair then, Charlie?'

'I'll kill that little devil of mine!'

'What's he done this time?'

Father related the incident. Little Bob, one of the solo school, said, 'Charlie, I can vouch for the fact that it wasn't your son. There were no bricks on the doorstep when I passed. A minute later a boy on a tradesman's bike tore past me. At the same time I heard a cry and looking round saw Mrs Thompson sprawled on the pathway.

'She got up and returned indoors. I shan't tell you who the culprit is unless the matter is taken further, when I should 'bear witness'.'

I heard Father return and come upstairs. Before switching on the light he said, 'I have made a terrible mistake. I punished you for something you said you hadn't done.'

He put the light on and held out a bottle of Bullard's light ale and a glass. As he poured the beer he said, 'It will never happen again. I'll make it known that in future if you do anything wrong it is up to the person catching you to give you the thrashing! You can get up if you want to.' Then, giving me five Woodbines, he added, 'Don't smoke them in bed!'

I was not aware that he knew that I drank the odd pint and smoked the occasional cigarette.

Perhaps even more remarkable was the fact that he had foregone his solo game that night in order to square the injustice he had done to me.

When the Scolt Head warden's job had originally been advertised, the control of rabbits had been in the contract. Proceeds from catching and selling them represented part of the wages. When the rabbits had been reduced to only a breeding stock on Scolt Head, therefore, my father found time to help Billy Daniels to reduce them on the estate. I was brought up in this environment, helping both of them. In addition I helped to shoot or scare crows and pigeons feeding on crops on the farm. It was hardly surprising, therefore, that my ambition was to be a gamekeeper and on my leaving school at fourteen, in 1940, I started in that line.

This job ceased because of the war. However, Billy was aware of a vacancy coming up locally for a pest officer. Knowing the regional pest control officer he put my name forward and I got the post. The job involved rabbit and rat control on land, following complaints from neighbouring landowners. The wage of £6 a week was not bad for a fifteen-year-old. Conditions of employment stipulated a minimum of ten rabbits a day, delivered to the local butcher, from whom I had to obtain receipts.

I found this arrangement most satisfactory until, after two winters, I became redundant. This compulsory service at no cost to the landowner ceased. In future there would be a charge per hour for the pest officer's time. Landowners found it less expensive to employ their own rabbit catchers.

One day in late September 1942 I was helping my next door neighbour, Stanley English, to thatch two wheat stacks on the local farm to make them waterproof. He was experienced in all types of farmwork – a 'jack of all trades'.

The ground the stacks stood on overlooked the village, Scolt Head and most of the Wash from Hunstanton to Holkham. There were four operational airfields within ten miles of Brancaster Staithe and at that time it was an everyday occurrence to see a Lysander aircraft towing a target (drogue) a hundred yards behind it. This would be fired at by various training aircraft.

While on top of the stack we heard gunfire half a mile landwards and saw two aircraft approaching. As they came nearer (not a quarter of a mile away, and travelling very fast at some one thousand feet) I remarked to Stanley that I couldn't see any target.

As the leading plane passed over us, the rear one fired another burst. We actually heard the bullets striking. The leader banked to the left and started to climb and we suddenly realised it was a German, with a cross on the fuselage. (It turned out to be the latest radar equipped Dornier.) Another burst of gunfire came as both planes headed out to sea. They were now flying at some three thousand feet. We heard more gunfire and the Dornier started descending at a forty degree angle, continuing until it hit the sea about a mile offshore.

Three weeks later – three days of onshore north winds having brought some duck in – I thought I'd go shooting. I reached the marsh at Scolt an hour before flight time, so decided to have a walk along the north shore to kill time. Looking to see what had been washed up, I noticed something fairly large just below the receding tide level. Through my binoculars I saw that it was the tailplane of an aircraft with the rear wheel uppermost. When I was eventually able to reach it I found three aluminium plaques, three-and-a-half by one-and-a-half inches, riveted to different parts of the wreckage. Type and serial numbers and the maker's name were inscribed in German. Realising that this was probably the plane I had seen shot into the sea, I prised the plaques off with my knife. Later I put them into my souvenir drawer at home with all my other 'treasures' and thought no more about them.

Two days later, two high-ranking intelligence officers came to the house to talk to my father. I was told to amuse myself for an hour as they had a top secret matter to discuss. Over the next three or four days they and our local constable made several more visits. Each time I was told to 'go'. It wasn't until a week later that my father openly discussed the matter with my mother, while I was in the room.

'There's got to be a fifth columnist somewhere in the area, to have removed those identification plaques. It must have been done at night, otherwise the coastguard would have seen him at the wreckage.' (There was a coastguard lookout concealed on top of the Head, keeping twenty-four-lookout in case of invasion. I found out later that the afternoon I had been there they were asleep!)

I asked Father what these missing plaques were like. Then, going to my little private drawer said, 'You don't mean something like this?'

'So you've got them!'

We had no telephone, like most people in those days, so he jumped on his bicycle and rode the two miles to the local policeman's house. The latter then informed the RAF.

The same RAF officers returned and put me through a form of the 'third degree'. After answering their questions I signed a statement saying that I was the person who had removed the three plaques, that no other person had seen them and that I had told no one else of my discoveries. By this time I was fairly frightened, but before they had finished with me they scared me even more by saying that I could have been sent to prison for this offence.

I thought that when they had gone I'd get a good ticking off from Father. However the only remark he made was, 'Don't worry, it's all, over now. But if anything like this happens again, tell me first.'

The bodies of two Germans, believed to be from the crashed Dornier, were washed ashore on Scolt in November. Both had been shot dead before the crash. Strapped to the thigh of one was a compass which my father removed and gave to me saying, 'Here you are old mate, you've got something out of it after all!'

I still have that compass.

In October 1943 a horticultural job turned up locally which turned out to be most satisfactory for me. The local farmer, who lived in a large house standing in approximately four acres, had turned over two of them to growing vegetables for the war effort. I started as odd job boy, looking after the boilers which supplied hot water to the house and mowing the grass (the mower, although motorised, was pulled by a Suffolk Punch horse, petrol then being rationed).

Then, on reaching seventeen, I became the milk delivery boy for houses of estate workmen on two farms. I had been driving a Morris van on the farm next door at harvest time since the age of fourteen and thought myself a competent driver. I was given a test by the retiring milkman. This turned out to be a 'once round a field and you'll do' affair, so off I went. (In retrospect I'm glad there was little traffic on the road!) After completing these chores I spent the remainder of the day working in the garden.

The cultivated area ran alongside a large wood and was netted in to keep out rabbits – not in hundreds, but thousands. The old 'keeper, who should have retired years ago but who was still retained, had put on weight over the years. Weighing twenty stone, he could hardly walk, let alone be capable of reducing their numbers successfully. They were always getting into the garden, eating and damaging a high percentage of what was being grown for sale.

Harry, the old gardener, also past retirement age, was most sympathetic towards us young teenagers who worked under him. I had not been there long before I found out that he and I had much in common – he was the biggest old poacher out! As the rabbits were such a problem, I offered to control them and go half-shares with the money we received for selling them. He agreed to this but told me to be discreet, as it would not be wise to let the boss or the gamekeeper know.

I got to work straight away and the project proved most satisfactory, both in the decreased amount of damaged produce and in the small monetary bonus for us, which supplemented my twenty-five shillings (£1.25) weekly wage.

Time for me, however, soon ran out. I was eighteen years old on January 19, 1944. I had already passed my medical examination ('A1') and my country needed me. On St Valentine's Day (February 14) I received my call-up papers. I had to report to the Britannia Barracks, Norwich, on March 16. Next day I told my boss, The Rt Hon William Borthwick, that I was giving in my notice, as I was joining the army.

He had been very badly wounded in the 1914-18 war. Both his sons and a daughter were serving in the forces at the time but he said that he might possibly get me a temporary deferment, due to my being in a food-producing section.

When I got home that evening I told my father about this. He was sitting in his armchair and, after thinking for a short while, replied, 'I'll leave it up to you.'

I knew what he meant.

The following morning I informed the boss that I was enlisting on March 16.

He said, 'I'm sorry to lose you. Good luck. When you finish work today go to the office; your money will be made up to the day of your enlistment. Have a good holiday!'

CHAPTER FIVE

Into Battle

I reported to Britannia Barracks on March 16, 1944. After drawing my kit I was assigned to Billet No 4, and spent the following five weeks with thirty-two other raw recruits.

The old saying 'the army has them all' is perfectly true. The good, the bad and the indifferent come to it from every walk of life and from all parts of the country. My platoon contained a small contingent of old-timers – 'desert rats' who had been transferred from the artillery to the infantry (imagine their attitude of 'indifference'!)

Fred Early was one of these and he took us young 'rookies' under his wing. Having been in the army since September 1939 he was an expert on its ways. He had twice reached the rank of sergeant; but for reasons he never would tell us had been stripped of his stripes both times. It was Fred who taught us some of the 'wrinkles' which made army life more tolerable. For example: when not on duty always walk about with something in your hand – it didn't matter what – brush, shovel, bucket, anything would do.

One Saturday, while off duty, some of us were talking outside the NAAFI (canteen). The duty officer, spotting us, came over and asked what we had to keep us busy. The reply was, naturally, 'Nothing, sir.'

He ordered the others to go with him, but, looking at me and my shovel, told me to get on with my 'duties'. The others made an expert job of scrubbing out the NAAFI!

Fred would volunteer for cookhouse fatigues, especially on a Sunday. (If you volunteered when it suited you, you weren't pressed into fatigue parties when it didn't.) I soon found out that on Sundays most of the barracks was empty, especially at teatime. Fewer pots, pans, 'dixies' and the like needed to be cleaned – this was always a salad meal!

Usually only one ATS NCO cook would be in charge of the cookhouse. Fred would say, 'We're nearly finished; we can get our own supper [or tea]. We'll finish here – you go and meet your American boyfriend.'

When all the washing up was done we would have our own meal. There was no rationing for us on these Sundays – we didn't go to bed hungry!

After completing our five weeks' primary training we moved to Nelson Barracks close by. Here we had to do an additional advanced training course before joining the regiment. This was to make us proficient in the use of all the weapons used by the infantry.

After much sweat, swearing and occasional blood-letting, the advanced training was over and we were assigned to the First Battalion, The Royal Norfolk Regiment. Before leaving for Germany we saw that volunteers were wanted for the Paratroop Regiment as glider pilots. My mate, Geoff Buckley, and I decided to have a go.

Extra training was necessary, so we had to forego our leave and were sent to a training centre in Shropshire. After spending four days here we were told that we had to be nineteen before we could become glider pilots. We were then sent to another barracks in the county to complete a further ten weeks of training.

This was the toughest yet – the previous fifteen weeks of infantry training seemed like a holiday by comparison. We became proficient in maintenance of the three-inch mortar bren-gun carrier and in wireless communication, after which I went home to Norfolk for a well-deserved fourteen days leave before returning to Nelson Barracks to rejoin the regiment. Within a week we were sent to Germany. On arriving at Tilbury docks we boarded an LST (a so-called Landing Support Transport, shaped like a bath-tub – though the latter might well have proved a better craft!) Our departure was delayed for three days because the previous convoy had been badly damaged by German E Boats (motor torpedo boats).

When we eventually did sail a strong north-east wind was blowing. The LST could make no more than four knots and rolled like a pig in the water, with the result that most of the men were seasick. Besides us, our craft carried three-ton trucks on deck and tanks in the hold. When after some four hours the wind freshened and the sea worsened, the craft bucked and rolled. On deck the trucks, and in the hold the tanks slid from side to side (how they didn't crash through the ship's side I'll never know).

After a most cold and unpleasant trip we finally docked at Ostend and boarded a train which was nearly as slow as the boat. The winter stayed cold as we travelled across Belgium to join the First Battalion Royal Norfolk Regiment at Helmond, on November 8.

As the month progressed the weather grew even colder. There were sharp frosts at night and, by the second week of December, heavy snowfalls.

The battalion was part of 185 Brigade, an independent reinforcement brigade, at this time dug in along the River Meuse. Our platoon occupied a small derelict village in range of enemy snipers and mortar fire. Fires could only be lit at night or during the daytime when visibility was poor (fog was very welcome!) Any activity attracted a hail of mortar fire and the ration trucks often failed to make it safely into the village.

Food supplies became unreliable; often the soup and food were stone cold before they reached our forward positon. When the company runner was injured, I was detailed to take over. This was where my simple country upbringing came into its own as I now had the chance to scout around for something extra to eat. On my travels I saw footmarks in the snow, to and from an old barn; but there was no sign of livestock during the day. It seemed possible that these animals, which I knew to be pigs, only visited the barn at night. If so, pork would soon be on the menu!

At dusk I positioned myself just inside the door and awaited my dinner. The moon was over a quarter full and its light, reflecting on the snow, made visibility quite good (it reminded me of duck shooting at home). It was very cold and I was about to give up when I heard grunting and squeaking. Revealed in the moonlight and making straight for me, were an old sow and her piglets. I waited until she and most of the youngsters had passed me before diving and catching one by the leg. It let out a terrified squeal and the rest bolted into the night.

Back at company HQ, having frequently helped out the butcher at home, I soon had the piglet prepared for cutting up; I jointed it up on the table. Everyone gathered round to watch, saying, 'We aren't going to eat that!'

As the pork slowly cooked, pepper, salt and onions (acquired on one of my earlier travels) were added. The smell wafted out. Officers, NCOs and privates all came to look.

'Don't smell too bad!' was the general comment.

I said, 'It will taste equally good. Come back in about one-and-a-half hours.'

I allowed it to cool a little before shouting, 'Come and get it!' The half I had cooked soon disappeared. When you're hungry roast pork and army biscuits go down a treat.

Time passed. That winter turned out to be the severest for many years and many of us caught 'flu and earned short but more than welcome spells in the warm before returning to the humdrum life of mine-lifting and patrolling near enemy lines.

Christmas came and went, as did my birthday. The Meuse remained frozen over, and we stayed on the western side of it. Little activity broke the monotony. However, one day shortly after Christmas I had to accompany Lieutenant Smith, Major B—, our wireless operator and a rifleman named Darwood to a forward outpost to see what – if anything – was happening. It was a drear, foggy day and bitterly cold. We wore white suits, to blend with the snow, instead of the usual khaki issue.

Darwood was ordered to remain behind while the rest of us went forward. It was my job to run back with a report if anything of note was happening along the line. Suddenly we heard an explosion about fifty yards behind us, but couldn't see what had happened because of the thick fog. We duly completed our mission and made our way back. When we returned to pick up the rifleman he wasn't there; it was assumed, I think, that he had wandered off of his own accord.

The following day Geoff Buckley and I were on duty manning a brengun. As it came daylight we saw someone creeping through the snow. I said to Geoff, 'It must be a bloody Jerry, trying to sneak up on us. Give him a burst on the old gun.'

'Hang you on, Bob. Don't get too excited. What's he doing here in the daylight?'

Geoff's remark seemed to make a valid point – the enemy should have used darkness to cover any such attempt at ambushing our position. We held fire. The man kept putting his hand up and falling down in the snow as he crawled towards us. We drew lots to see which of us should go out and take a closer look. I don't know whether I won or lost, but it fell to me to go.

All I had was a .38 revolver – being company runner I didn't have a rifle. I was apprehensive (to use an understatement!) but when I got to the man I recognised our missing rifleman, Darwood.

He gasped something unrepeatable when he saw me. He was in a bad way. The explosion we had heard the previous day had been this poor devil stepping on a mine. He had had one foot blown off and the other badly damaged.

I don't know how he had survived – he had been out all night in the snow. His hands had balls of frozen snow as big as chickens' eggs attached to them, from crawling. He was as good as dead. I shouted to Geoff, who came running. Between us we managed to carry poor Darwood back to our position, from where I ran to fetch the stretcher bearers. This was about eight o'clock – we were then being relieved, so we gave the stretcher-bearers a hand to carry him back to the bombed-out place we were using as our base.

The platoon officer said, 'Give him a drink of whisky.'

Darwood was delirious. We gave him a bottle of whisky and he drank two-thirds of it, as if it were water. Then he collapsed.

Afterwards I found out that he lost his left hand due to frostbite, in addition to the losses sustained from the explosion; but he lived.

We were pulled back for a two-week rest in a small town, Leuven, where we found what passed as the local 'night-life' – a seedy cafe with an even seedier proprietress, whose daughter also blended well with her surroundings. As a result of trips here, some of our less discerning comrades kept the medical officer busy for some time afterwards!

On returning to the forward positons we awaited an improvement in the weather before advancing. It finally came on March I 1945, the day which was without doubt the most memorable of my army career. It was to change my entire life and remains with me still.

The usual procedure is for an artillery barrage to be made upon the enemy forward lines, to 'soften them up' in order to assist the infantry in its advance. The artillery spotter was with our platoon in the forward position, relaying range and pinpointing targets. We heard him giving the necessary details to his ranging guns, then the command to fire, followed by 'Get down!', a second before the first of the ranging shells from his twenty-five pounder dropped slap bang into our positions. The actual target was two miles in front of our lines.

I shall not repeat the artillery officer's remarks back to his battery! The bang and blast resulted in deafness for two hours and, at the time, it felt as if the air had been squeezed out of our lungs. It was not a good morale booster – but luckily no one was hurt. The next salvo of shells passed safely over our heads, and landed on the target.

The private soldier makes no decisions; he does as he is told. Our instructions were to take the town ahead of us, called Wilhelmena, and hold it in readiness for crossing the Rhine.

As night slowly turned to day we could see our objective and the terrain we had to cross to reach it – flat, with few trees and white with snow. It bore an uncanny resemblance to the saltmarshes back home. I said to our sergeant, 'I don't like the look of this. We'll all be picked off like rabbits before we reach the town.'

He said reassuringly, 'Don't worry, we've had worse. When we advance this time there'll be six Churchill tanks supporting us.'

It was indeed reassuring to hear them revving up in front of us. The order came to 'move out'.

At that moment I could have put a Rizla cigarette paper in my mouth, rolled it around, removed it and found it as dry as when I put it in! We advanced approximately three-quarters of a mile; all was quiet. In front was a dyke twenty feet wide and six feet deep. On reaching it the tanks dropped into it and were unable to get out. Totally stuck, but with their gun turrets just above ground level they were still able to fire.

The water and the dyke's banks were frozen hard with a covering of snow, making crossing on foot very difficult; but we managed it somehow.

Once across, advancing without our tank support made us 'sitting ducks'. We had only covered a short distance when we came under heavy fire. Shells and mortar bombs burst all around us. The crack of bullets filled the air. This is when death is close. We passed about twenty cattle that had been caught up in the barrage. Some were dead, some badly maimed. The rest just stood there, too dazed to do anything. The farther we advanced, the worse the bombardment became.

We were frightened, yes; but the remarkable thing was that no one panicked. (Strange as it may seem, my pants remained 'clean' – at least at this point, though later I am not so sure!) I heard the wireless operator on my left give out a yell and saw him pitch forward. I nipped across to him. He was still alive, although in great pain. He asked me to remove the 18 set (large wireless set) from his back. This weighed twenty-eight pounds. I took it off and placed it in front of him, hoping it would give him some protection.

In the meantime my section had moved on. I ran and caught up with them. The ground continued erupting all around us. I was within ten feet of our sergeant when he dropped forward at an unnatural angle. Experience distinguishes between a trip and being hit: he had been shot in the head.

Within seconds our platoon officer went down screaming. He was a man we were particularly proud to be serving under, having been made up from a sergeant to full lieutenant in the field. He had also won the Military Medal in an an anti-tank action with a private known as 'Basher' Bates. The latter, who had been killed in the action, was awarded the highest British military honour, the Victoria Cross.

Smoke was belching from under the officer. I ran to him, wondering why. He was lying on his face, so I rolled him over onto his back. The Veery Light cartridges in his pouches had been ignited. On contact with more air they burst into flames, burning my face and hands. The heat was so intense I could do nothing for him. When his screaming stopped I was certain he must be dead.

By the time I caught up with the survivors of this onslaught, only a lance corporal remained with about a dozen men from the thirty-two who had started off. He coolly shouted, 'We can't advance against this lot. Take cover and await further orders!'

I was probably the first to take his advice, jumping into a shellhole. (We had been told in training that shells rarely drop in the same place twice.) I removed my tin hat, to wipe the sweat from my burnt face, which was stinging.

It is impossible to describe what happened next. I thought one of the cattle we had passed earlier had kicked me in the back, leaving its red-hot foot behind! The pain was terrible (though that is an understatement). The army are great ones at giving advice to the wounded: 'The initial pain soon goes and numbness takes over.' However I can state categorically that this isn't quite correct – the word 'soon' is wrong!

It might sound strange, even naive of me, not to have realised that I had been wounded. However it did finally sink in and I managed to remove my FSMO (full service marching order). I tried to move, to see what was happening around me, but found that I was paralysed from the waist down. This really frightened me as I thought my spine had been smashed. I could feel warm blood running down my back and round my waist. In fact, I had been hit just below the left shoulder-blade, the shrapnel passing through my kidney, spleen and part of my gut.

How long I lay there I do not know. The pain had become less intense, but I had begun to feel a terrible deep cold. Then I heard voices. Two of our stretcher-bearers stood there looking down at me. One said, 'Is he alive?'

I blurted out, 'What the hell are you talking about? The buggers can't kill me!'

They lifted me onto a stretcher, belly down (very painful) and I was carried to a waiting jeep. Bullets still cracked past. My feet hung over the end and I clearly remember saying, 'For Christ's sake take off my boots!' They had become heavy as lead.

As the jeep moved out I began to hear beating drums. Multi-coloured lights flashed before my eyes, and my body seemed to weigh a ton. Then everything went black.

When I came to I was in hospital. I could see an array of bottles above my head, with tubes leading down. I followed these with my eyes, to find that one was attached to my arm and one to my leg. The third, which went up my nose and into my stomach, made me begin to choke; so I pulled it out. The man in the next bed turned and looked at me.

'Where are we?' I asked.

'Nicht verstehen,' he replied.

Thinking I was in a German hospital, a prisoner of war, I lost my cool.

Struggling in an attempt to get away, I found I could hardly move. I began to shout and yell (to this day I don't know why). A nurse quickly arrived and calmed me down by telling me I was in a Canadian hospital, in Belgium.

The next thing I remember was the padre sitting by my bedside, asking how I was feeling. I replied, 'Awful!'

'Would you like to send a letter home to your parents?'

I saw him write the hospital address and the date – March 14. Why, I thought, the fourteenth and not the first?

CHAPTER SIX

Hospital and Slow Recovery

The padre repeated, 'Today is the fourteenth of March.' He then went on to explain, 'It is two weeks since you were wounded.'

I had 'lost' two entire weeks from my life.

After another month in hospital I was considered fit enough to be sent back to England. I was taken by ambulance to the airstrip. Every bump felt like a knife in my back. Then they loaded me aboard a Dakota (Douglas DC-3) aircraft and flew me to Wroughton in Wiltshire.

Despite a perfect landing, every crack in the runway seemed like a 'sleeping policeman' to me. An ambulance took me the hundred yards to the hospital – another painful experience. I was allotted bed number seventeen in a ward of twenty beds. I didn't realise that when you reached bed twenty the mortuary was the next stop – much later I found out that very few patients ever came out of this ward, all the critical cases being assigned here.

I didn't realise how ill I was. Time was totally lost; night and day became one, and it was impossible to register how long I was awake or asleep. In a state like this you experience many illusions, so real that at the time they seem to have actually occurred. (The painkilling drugs no doubt contribute to these sensations.) On waking up one day I thought I saw Mum and Dad sitting there, but rejected the idea out of hand. I was convinced that to come and see me all the way from Norfolk was out of the question (my father hated travelling). So I closed my eyes and went back to sleep. On reawakening, I was amazed to find them still there. They were not an illusion!

'Whatever made you come all this way to see me?' I asked.

Father answered casually, 'There wasn't much doing on Scolt Head or Cley Marshes [he was looking after both reserves, as the Cley warden, Billy Bishop, was in the navy] so Mum and I thought we would visit our new grandson in London. (Eileen, now married, had given birth to a son, Roger.) Being near we thought we'd better come and see you, too.'

To me this was a perfectly acceptable reason at the time, though later I learned differently. I was told subsequently that the War Office had informed my parents that my condition was critical, due to a relapse. After a fortnight I improved sufficiently for them to return home.

I still remember how old and drawn they looked, though at the time I little realised that I was the reason for this.

I have no recollection of how long I stayed at Wroughton Hospital. At some stage I was transferred by ambulance (and what a journey!) to Kewstoke, near Weston-super-Mare in Somerset. I admit I was most relieved to get away from Ward 20 and its horrific sights and sounds.

However, I had not been at Kewstoke many days when for the second time my condition became critical. As if being wounded were not enough, my lungs collapsed, due to pneumonia. This was followed by empyema – a condition where pus fills the pleura, the membrane surrounding the lung. This pus had to be removed by a syringe, inserted through the chest wall twice daily; but even this could not keep up with the build-up of pus.

By this time, I had become familiar with some of the medical terms and eavesdropped on the doctors discussing my condition. It didn't sound very good!

'The only alternative is to insert a tube through the back and remove the fluid.'

Then, after another short consultation, 'We'll have to operate.'

Within minutes I was wheeled to the theatre and prepared for the operation. The surgeon explained why he needed to operate, but not how he was going to do it. However, he did add that King George V had been the first person to experience this particular operation, which had since become standard practice.

As he talked the nurses laid me on my right side and strapped me by my legs and waist to the operating table. When finally secured I was given an injection somewhere near the spine. The surgeon, scalpel in hand, said, 'I'm making an insertion. It won't hurt, you'll only feel a tickle.'

This I did feel, but demanded, 'Aren't I having an anaesthetic?' He replied, 'Your lung condition is such that a general anaesthetic would cause irritation.'

I noticed that he was holding what looked like a pair of parrot clippers – the kind we used in the garden for cutting back the twigs of fruit trees.

'This might hurt a bit. Don't be afraid to yell if it does!'

What an understatement! I heard a crunch, and felt the pain. My brain could not pass the message 'scream', let alone 'yell'.

However, I did eventually let out a scream. Perspiration ran off my face in a shower. As he chomped through another rib the pain was repeated; but this time it proved too much and I passed out.

Later I found out the full details of the operation. Approximately one and a half inches (36mm) of bone had been removed from two of my lower ribs. (This is where the parrot clippers came in – to chomp through the bone.) A tube with a flange two inches long could then be inserted into the lung cavity to drain the pus.

When I awoke I was back in the ward, with the tube attached to a bottle. This stood on the floor with its syphoning apparatus already working efficiently.

Over the next five weeks I had to spend part of each day in an 'iron lung', to reinflate and improve my lungs. At that time the apparatus was like a coffin. My body except for the head was completely inside the box. A diaphragm operated by a motor increased and decreased the air pressure inside the box at a controlled rate, so my lungs had no choice other than to react to the changing pressure.

On my first visit to the 'coffin' a nurse came into the room, had a chat with 'my' nurse, and said to me, 'I haven't seen you in here before. There's nothing to be afraid of.' She gave me a big kiss and then off she went. While I lay in the lung, ten more nurses came in and did and said exactly the same thing. Needless to say, I didn't raise any objections to this 'treatment'!

As I was wheeled back to the ward all the nurses and doctors I passed laughed and remarked, 'So you have had your first visit to the iron lung.'

I couldn't understand how they all knew. On reaching the ward the sister said, 'I see you have been installed and received into The Order of the Iron Lung.' Then she let me into the secret. When a fresh customer went there all the nurses deliberately applied excess lipstick, so that when they kissed him most of it was left on his face.

'Let me see myself in the mirror,' I demanded.

'No,' was the curt reply. 'I'm cleaning it off. Then you must rest.'

Unknown to me, mirrors were banned in my ward. Later I found out the reason for this.

As our ward nurse was celebrating her birthday the following day, I asked her to take ten shillings (50 pence) from my wallet and buy herself a box of chocolates. To do this she needed my pay book, as I was entitled to sweets or chocolates without 'coupons'. Picking up my wallet she looked at a photograph in it, and asked, 'Who is this?'

'Guess who?'

'Is it one of your family?'

'Sort of.'

'Your son?'

'No.'

'Your brother?'

'No.'

After pondering, she said, 'Who is it then?'

I said, 'That's me.'

'It can't be, you're much too old.'

'How old do you think I am?'

'Fifty to fifty-five.'

'Take out the photograph, and read what is written on the back.'

'"Bob aged eighteen, March 1944." It can't be you!'

My army paybook confirmed that it was indeed me. Sitting on my bed, she burst into tears.

When Dee (my sister Daisy) who was in the WAAFs, visited me at Kewstoke, she didn't recognise me either. I looked like a wizened little old man – bald and thin as a skeleton. I weighed about four stone. Even weeks later, on seeing myself in the mirror it was like looking at a complete stranger.

Slowly, day by day, my condition improved. My thighs, which had been reduced to the size of my wrists, began to fill out. The two bedsores either side of my bottom, as large as old pennies, at last began to heal. (At one time the pain from these had been worse than that of my wound.)

Another sign of an improvement in my condition occurred one sunny day when we called the nurse and asked her to draw the ward curtains. As she reached up the sun shone through her thin cotton uniform, to reveal the outline of a trim little figure. Naturally, it took several minutes before we were satisfied with the position of the curtains. The instructions went something like this: 'Just a bit more to the left', 'Little more to the right', 'Too far to the left' and so on. No doubt she had cottoned on to our little game, though she never let on. At the time it boosted our morale, and was something to 'ooh' and 'aah' about for a while!

What a relief it was when the tube was removed and replaced with one much smaller in diameter. This drained into a dressing strapped to my back, making it possible to move more freely and lie more comfortably in bed. After twenty weeks I was once again capable of shaving myself. On VJ Day (Victory Japan Day, June 8) came the final ceasefire. The war was over, and to celebrate I was determined to get up, to look out and see the sea. The doctor finally agreed that I could have five minutes sitting in a chair by the window.

I expected to be able to cover the ten yards from my bed to the chair by myself. How wrong I was! My legs, still like matchsticks, had a will of their own and couldn't hold me up, let alone walk me to the window. Carried there by two nurses I saw, not two hundred yards away, the beach and the sea. I must admit I had a good cry. Within minutes my back was killing me, and I was thankful to get back to bed.

Each week I became stronger, and by the end of the month, encouraged by a physiotherapist, I was taking my first steps (between parallel bars) unassisted by human hands. Now the urge to get out of bed became of the utmost importance. From my bed I could not see the sea, but I could smell the salty breeze when the wind was onshore. Homesickness was creeping over me. I was determined that as soon as I was strong enough I would go for a paddle. Every day I increased the distance I could walk and at the end of ten days I 'made' the seafront. Although, due to the tube in my back, swimming was out of the question, I was determined to paddle next day. Just to get my feet wet would be heaven itself!

The following morning dawned fine and sunny, with only a light wind. After lunch I told the ward sister of my intentions, and eventually convinced her that I was not only determined but also quite capable of making the journey to the beach and back.

I made my way slowly to the sea, resting on bench seats on the way. Walking against the light wind tired me, and on reaching the high tideline I was glad of a rest for several minutes, before attempting to go into the sea. Then, taking off my PT shoes, I rolled up my trousers and waded into the water. What a refreshing feeling, and what a marvellous salty taste as I scooped up a handful of water.

Waves rolled lazily to the shore. Children were playing twenty yards from the edge, in no more than six inches of water. I walked out, taking care not to get my trousers wet. Suddenly I heard a scream of delight from the children, and saw a wave much larger than the rest rolling towards me. I knew I could not make the shallow water before it overtook me.

Although, as it passed quietly by me (it was only six inches higher than the previous waves) it nearly washed me off my unsteady feet, wetting me above the crotch. I waded ashore and collapsed on a seat to let my army trousers drip dry (they now weighed a 'ton' and were most uncomfortable).

When sufficiently dry I started on my return journey to the hospital, which now seemed miles away, up a slight incline which looked more like a mountain to me. Halfway I felt extremely tired and stretched out on a bench to rest.

With the sun pouring down and the sound of the waves in the background, my thoughts turned towards home, and to what I might be doing there on a day such as this. I must have slept for some time, before being awakened by the ward nurse asking if I was all right.

I said I was OK, and not to worry – there was no need for a wheelchair, I could walk the rest of the way. So off I started up the steepest part of the incline; but no more than twenty-five yards from the main gate I could go no farther. I had to admit defeat and ride in the wheelchair. Once back in the safety of the ward, I collapsed on the bed.

By eight o'clock I had recovered sufficiently to eat a good supper. The only drawback to my adventure was a sunburnt face (it must have caught the sun when I was asleep on the bench). It was painful and the skin soon peeled off, but it had been well worth it!

When I eventually felt able to visit Weston-super-Mare (the sanatorium was at the southern end of the town) I was accompanied by two wounded comrades. Roy was a lieutenant in the Hampshires and David a sergeant in the Beds and Herts. Because we were in a civilian hospital we did not have to wear the blue military hospital uniform.

David's sternum and part of his ribcage had been shot away. He was supported by a corset and brace and bent even more than Roy and myself did. As we walked along the seafront, we noticed our reflections in the plate glass window of a shop. We stopped to view ourselves and couldn't stop laughing. Our damaged shoulders drooped about four inches. With a forward lean and large dressings on our wounds we looked like three Quasimodos!

Roy and I were standing together. We thought that with David in the middle our group would appear more 'balanced'. So Roy moved to the left and I to the right. Unable to stop laughing – although this was still a painful experience – we acted even more stupidly. (What we looked like I hate to think.) Two dear old ladies passed by. We heard one say to the other, 'They shouldn't let them out.' Obviously they thought we were from Kewstoke mental hospital!

We left the shop window and had only gone a few paces when a jeep roared up and stopped short. Two military policemen jumped out. The sergeant shouted, 'Whose army do you think you're in, you horrible little men? You're improperly dressed – where are your caps?!'

Roy remarked quietly, 'The last time I saw mine it was covered in blood and mud.'

'Where's your AB64?' (the book which held all one's army particulars).

Roy produced his and handed it to the MP. On reading it he looked at us for several seconds (our laughter could not have helped matters). Then the penny dropped. Springing smartly to attention, he saluted, said, 'Sorry, sir,' jumped back in the jeep and drove off. We often saw them after this encounter, but they never glanced our way again.

My next goal was to return home – at least on leave. I felt fit, and was itching to go; but the doctors considered that I wasn't ready for the long journey from Somerset to Norfolk. I explained that I had a sister living in London who was a qualified nurse. She could attend to my dressing and clean my drain tube. A visit to her would break the journey nicely.

It was early September before I was allowed to go home for two weeks. Eileen came and collected me. We discussed past experiences, and then talked about what I was going to do in the future. I said that I should be glad when I could start my gamekeeping.

Eileen said, 'That won't be yet awhile. Perhaps your wounds will prevent you from doing any type of manual work. It might be too much for you.'

'I can't see why, when I'm fully recovered.'

She paused, then said, 'Haven't they told you the result of your gunshot wound?'

'No.'

Eileen started to explain. It didn't sound too bad, at first. 'The fourteen inch scar on your stomach will appear less severe over the next twelve months, and will eventually reduce in size.' She paused.

I looked at her, waiting for the rest of the 'good' news. She let me have it.

'You've lost your left kidney and spleen, and you have some gut damage. The two lower rib sections that had to be removed will always leave a weakness on your left side.' For the first time, I realised the seriousness and the likely consequences of my injuries. I was totally 'floored' by my sister's disclosures. It would be a long, long time before I would recover from the shock.

CHAPTER SEVEN

Recuperation and Back Home

After spending one week with Eileen in London, I returned home for a further two weeks. One day, while waiting for Father, as he moored the boat, I was sitting on the end of a boat down the harbour. I saw a Mrs Sunderland-Taylor – whom I had known for many years – approaching me, so called out, 'Hello, how are you getting on?'

She replied 'All right,' and carried on. I watched her go up to Father and overheard her say, 'I understand Bobby's coming home.'

'Yes, that's right. That's him over there, on the end of that boat, in his shorts and pullover.'

'I've seen that fellow,' she retorted quickly, 'and that's not Bob. That's not Bob.'

Father said, 'It is. You'd better come back and have a word with him.'

When they came over, Mrs Taylor looked at me and burst into tears. She said, 'I'm sorry, Bob, I didn't recognise you.'

After returning to Kewstoke I was transferred to the Royal West of England Sanatorium, just down the road at Weston-super-Mare, where I stayed until my final discharge in November 1945. It was like a second home to me. I got to know and admire the nursing staff. The staff sister, in particular, made an impression upon me – not only was she very like my mother in her ways and personality, but even looked like her!

Of course, although my state was a terrible worry to my parents, they were not alone in their anxiety. The war affected all layers of society equally, from the poor up to the very rich. This was brought home to me very vividly by an experience of my father's.

The shipping, coal and oil magnate, Sir Geoffrey Cory-Wright, had a house in Brancaster, which he visited towards the end of the war. He was, in addition to being a highly successful tycoon, also a very keen ornithologist and photographer. The family had regularly spent holidays at Brancaster during the 'thirties, and he had visited Scolt Head on numerous occasions.

Sir Geoffrey and my father had known each other over a period of time. One of the former's business interests was the Cunard White Star shipping line, which used for the front cover of one of its menus a colour photograph he himslf had taken at Scolt Head, of a common tern alighting at the nest.

He had five sons, the eldest four of whom all served in the war. One of them, having accquired a pair of German binoculars, had given them to his father. This particular son was subsequently reported missing in action – either taken prisoner of war or, possibly, killed. No news was received by the family of his whereabouts for a long time.

One day, Father and Sir Geoffrey were walking together on the beach at Scolt Head. At that time I was in very poor condition after being wounded, and the two of them were no doubt attempting to console each other in their anxiety for their sons.

Father said that he thought the war must soon be over and that Sir Geoffrey's son would return home safely. Sir Geoffrey said he felt certain that my condition would improve, adding, 'When I know my son is alive, I shall present you with these binoculars, Charles.'

Father replied, 'If you do, I should accept the gift.'

Not many weeks later, Sir Geoffrey came down to see my father. His face showed great relief – though he had already lost two sons in action. The son who had given him the glasses had been reported alive, being held as a prisoner of war.

'There you are, Charles,' he said, handing him the binoculars.

"C. Chestney" was engraved on the top of the case. (Of course, I still have those glasses.)

Eventually, as predicted by Sir Geoffrey, I was sent home – although the doctor told me it would be another three months before the drain in my back could be removed. I arrived home feeling pretty grim. Arrangements had been made for the local nurse to call daily, and my disability pension was increased from seventy to a hundred per cent. I was not to work for six months and had to take things easy.

In fact, the tube was removed in time for Christmas. I could at last have a bath! Everyone around me was making 'whoopee' at the festive season. The lads came to see me and tell me what ducks they had shot and what was about. Father, on returning from Scolt, where he'd been rabbiting, would tell me all about his day's activities. That was all I could do – just sit there and listen, and watch everyone but me have a good time.

I really was feeling low. By the end of winter I felt like doing myself in; I couldn't even go pigeon shooting – something I hadn't missed since the age of eleven. I had been told I couldn't take on the gamekeeper's job I had set my heart on, and that I would never do any manual work. I just couldn't see a future for myself. In this feeble physical and mental condition, as I lay in bed turning things over in my mind, all I could think was: 'Cut down in my prime!' I was only twenty, after all.

As summer approached, there seemed little improvement, either in my condition or my prospects. My depression if anything deepened. I wasn't strong enough to do any physical work – even swimming was a big effort. I couldn't chase a rabbit – my lungs hadn't opened up enough for me to run about. Any extra effort tired me and I got dreadful backache. However, I needed something to do to occupy both my time and my mind, as well as supplement my two pounds five shillings (£2.25) per week army disability pension.

Though I didn't sense it, there must have remained considerable anxiety at home as to what I was capable of doing. It had to be something light and not too demanding. Apart from my time in the army I had never eaten out with anyone. However, I was invited to tea with Billy and Aggie Daniels, and driven to Keepers Cottage by a friend (cycling was still out of the question). During my visit we discussed past events and what the future held for me. Billy came up with the suggestion that I keep bees.

'I've got more hives than I can look after,' he added. 'You can start with two of mine.'

Suspecting that this was a 'put-up job', and that it was merely a way of finding something for me to occupy myself with, I felt I had to say yes. Next evening, after all the bees had returned home, two hives were delivered to my father's allotment. Despite my initial misgivings I soon found that beekeeping was an interesting hobby even allowing for the odd sting or two! Regular attention is paramount during May, June and early July, otherwise the bees swarm. They fly off, leaving the hive in a weak condition, thus greatly reducing the honey output and their chances of surviving the winter.

Under Billy's watchful eye, and with his help, I extracted fifty-eight pounds of honey that first year and increased the number of hives to four (eventually this became twelve). I continued beekeeping for a number of years, until I became warden and could no longer find time during those crucial eight to ten weeks.

1946 was the first summer that the reserve was open to the public since being requisitioned by the Ministry of Defence in 1940. Sometime during the middle of May my father came home and announced that it looked like being an exceptionally busy season, both with the birds and the visitors. He would have to employ extra help – at least while the tide was in. I jumped at the chance, saying I could do the job. Father hesitated slightly, then, to my relief, he agreed. (Little did I realise at the time that the job had been specially created for me!)

So that summer I spent a considerable time at the ternery with him, meeting the visitors and helping him with the wardening duties. At the same time he was filling me full of information and explanations of the 'what' and 'why' questions which visitors endlessly asked.

I had never before realised what an interesting and satisfying job it was. Although I little realised it then, my father's ambition must have been for me to follow him as warden of Scolt Head. As a child and teenager I had never been keen on following him in his profession. What had discouraged me had been the long hours he worked in the summer. He left home early in the morning and returned late at night. I had hardly seen him, only heard him tell my mother of the trials and tribulations of the particular day.

The following year my father, Uncle Simon and Harry Southerland thought it would be possible for me to operate a ferry to Scolt during the summer months. No regular ferry had, of course, operated since the outbreak of war. Harry being in the boat business, it was decided that an old motor boat belonging to my father would be repaired and be made 'shipshape'. This boat had an old Morris thirteen, horsepower engine, complete with straight-through gearbox and clutch. The only problem was that it required crank starting, so that if it stopped I couldn't start it again by myself – I had to wave somebody down or get one of the passengers to help me.

The arrangements were that Simon would be at the land end, to crank start it for me, and push the boat off when the passengers were safely on board. My father would meet me at Scolt landing point. Their roles would be reversed on the return journey. I was to be skipper and also have the profit from the venture as my wages. For both my father and uncle it must have been very time-consuming; but nevertheless the set-up did work satisfactorily all that summer.

There were hitches, of course – notably due to the difficulty in starting the engine. I remember one instance because the person involved was Lord Alanbrooke (General Sir Alan Brooke, Chief of the Imperial General Staff) who was staying with Sir Archibald and Lady Jamieson at Thornham. Their son, Major David Jamieson, had been awarded the Victoria Cross, following action in the breakout from the Normandy beaches in 1944. After climbing onto a tank to direct it away from enemy fire, and being wounded, he had withdrawn his men from a forward position to one of safety.

Lord Alanbrooke had been up to Fetlar filming and had come to Norfolk both to show this footage and also to film the terns on Scolt. Being the important person that he was, Father ordered me to take him and his wife over to the island and bring them back alone. One particular time doing this I ran over a buoy, fouling my propeller with the rope, which stopped the engine. Feeling apprehensive, I said to my passenger, 'Ah, I've got a bit of a problem.'

'What is it?'

'I can't start the engine,' I replied, explaining about my wounds.

'I can't see it's really a problem.' His tone implied that he had been in worse situations. I put the engine out of gear and he started her up. He could have been anybody, lending a hand.

Many other visitors were once again coming to see the colony of breeding terns. Now there was a far wider cross-section of the public than before the war, when the gentry had been in the majority, with the occasional visit by the 'Bob Chestneys'. The privileged few could have my father's undivided attention for several hours.

He was expected to show visitors the nesting birds and to tell them about the island, in the hope that this would encourage them to give money to or join the Norfolk Naturalists' Trust or National Trust, which jointly managed Scolt and relied on donations for their main sources of income.

As the season progressed, discontent was expressed by some of these visitors because they were no longer receiving all my father's attention, as part of his time now had to be spent with the newcomers. This undoubtedly worried him and was reflected in a mood we had rarely seen before. We were having a flask of tea after a very trying day, near the end of the season, when he remarked, 'I don't want too many more days like today. I've got to do something about it.'

By the end of the season, however, he had arrived at what he felt was the solution: to continue giving the oldtimers all his attention when they were on their own, but if the party were a mixture of old and new he would have to keep them as one big party. Undoubtedly, having given the matter a great deal of thought, he was aware of the resentment he would cause in his regulars, resulting in a reduction in both tips and prestige. It would also reduce the amount of donations towards the upkeep of Scolt.

I understood the predicament and totally agreed with this new approach. The change in social attitudes resulting from the war made the old pre-war warden/visitor relationship no longer acceptable. By the season's end we had fully covered and discussed all aspects of wardening Scolt Head. It was the first time I had listened to him talking about the many facets of the island.

I now realised what a profound knowledge he had of the subject, in particular of the terns. I could also see for myself their struggle to survive, and watch how they reacted and coped with the many setbacks they encountered, and understood why Father spent those long hours at the ternery in the breeding season. The terns were without a doubt the 'star attraction'. To see and hear the thousands of birds take to the air, screaming as they wheeled overhead, was a fantastic experience. With the continuous daily visits by parties of humans it was no wonder they became aggressive. Frequently they dive-bombed the intruders, striking them on the head with their sharp bills and – as they had me when I was little – even drawing blood in an effort to drive the threat away.

By the end of the season I realised what a fulfilling job Father had, why he had become so involved and why he had encouraged me from the time I was little, hoping that I would follow in his footsteps. In a way, it was a stroke of luck for me, being wounded – instead of being a gamekeeper, I was proud to follow my father's tradition.

The warden's duties included maintaining and cleaning the Hut, and transporting visitors there by boat. The next season it was decided that an engine with a self-starter was essential. Being one hundred per cent disabled I qualified for a grant and, after much form-filling, was given £150 to purchase a new eight-horsepower Vedette self-starting engine. By now I was much strongerI and could operate the boat single-handed. The number of visitors increased but petrol rationing limited the number of trips I could make.

Among my passengers to the island that summer was Hugh Gaitskell, later leader of the Labour Party, but at that time Minister of Fuel and Power. Being aware of this, I quickly informed him of my circumstances and petrol problems. He appeared to show no interest in my plight during the journey home – I felt most discouraged.

Less than two weeks later, however, I received a letter from the local office of Fuel and Power saying: 'We have been instructed to increase your fuel allowance. Enclosed please find supplementary coupons for July, August, September and October, an additional twenty gallons per month. If and when additional fuel is necessary please contact this office immediately.'

These coupons were valid for private use, not 'dyed red' (red coupons could not be exchanged for petrol for private use, and were issued in an attempt to control the blackmarket). Of course it soon became known that Bob Chestney had a supply of undyed petrol. The price offered me per gallon was staggering – but who would be chump enough to kill the goose that laid the golden eggs by selling? Not Bob C!

Every year prior to the war two sisters, a Miss Edwards from Suffolk, and a Mrs Metz, married to a German and living in Germany, had come to stay at the Hut as part of the latter's holiday in England with her sister. The party had always consisted of these two and Mrs Metz's two boys. It had been something they had all looked forward to. These visits had ceased with the war but recommenced in 1947. The two families made a special trip to Brancaster Staithe to renew their friendship with the Chestneys.

Doubtless they felt apprehensive about the reception they would receive. Mrs Metz asked my father about staying in the Hut and going sailing, fishing, swimming and bird-watching again. She was worried about my attitude after my experiences at the hands of her husband's countrymen.

My father answered, 'I can't speak for Bob, but I'm sure it will be OK by him, as it is by me. He's just landed – the best thing is for the boys to go and meet him.'

I saw two young chaps walking towards me and recognised them before they reached me. I was genuinely pleased to see them again and shook hands. I felt no animosity at all. After a long chat we joined the rest of the family and made arrangements for their stay in the Hut. I would arrange the fishing bait, rods and nets, and give them the use of my sailing boat.

These annual visits continued a further six years.

My physical condition was greatly improving, and I had even become interested in the fairer sex. Prior to this I had taken very little interest in girls – having three sisters probably caused me to be unimpressed by their charms!

In those days we youngsters did not have cars or motorbikes. The only form of motorised transport locally, for our use, was the bus. On Sundays this left Brancaster for Hunstanton at three thirty. It returned at nine thirty. Most of us went on it, one of the main attractions the other end being the Capitol Cinema. One particular Sunday a friend arranged a 'blind date' for me. I was to meet the girl concerned on the bus. We were to go to the pictures together.

The girl's name was Phyllis Irene Rutland, and her family was from Titchwell. She was sixteen at the time and, unfortunately, things didn't get off to a very good start between us. As this was in the winter shooting was in full swing and after a couple of meetings I told Phyllis I could only see her on a Sunday (shooting not being allowed in Norfolk on the Christian sabbath). Then, because I always seemed to have other things to do, I told her we had better dissolve our friendship. Nevertheless, after not seeing one another for a while, we did meet again and our relationship started up anew. Phyllis's family didn't think too highly of me for a start. A 'well-wisher' had come round to see her Mum when she was pegging out washing in the garden. They were having their customary washday natter together, when this person said, 'I understand your daughter is going out with that Bob Chestney.'

'Yes.'

'Well, you know he was very badly wounded in the war. There are rumours that he's not really a man.'

When her Mum told her, Phyllis replied, 'I'm not really interested in what people say, I'm going out with him, and I'll make my own mind up!'

Phyllis used to work in Brancaster, at Groom's baker/grocer's shop. Wednesday was her 'half-day', and we would catch a private bus which collected people wanting to go to the Cosy at Burnham Market. This returned at nine thirty – so, on frosty moonlit nights, I was still able to shoot duck after saying goodbye to her. (She, of course, continued on the bus, home to Titchwell.)

However, much of the magic of shooting had gone!

Phyllis's home was always neat and tidy. What a contrast when I first took her to meet my parents, at Dial House. Six geese were fast asleep in front of the black-leaded cooking stove, their heads resting on the fire curb. Two dogs, asleep on the couch, woke up when we came into the room, wagged their tails and went back to sleep.

Mother laid her *Woman's Weekly* on the table, and got up to say hello. However, there was nowhere for Phyllis to sit – the other easy chair was occupied by the cat. Mum suggested that we all go into the lounge to meet Dad. He was sitting in an easy chair and had been asleep. (The indication of this was that he always twiddled his hair with his fingers into 'horns' that stuck out.) I knew that he was only pretending to be asleep now, but went through the motions of waking him. He slowly turned his head, opened one eye, squinted at Phyllis and said, 'Who are you?'

She was speechless.

I said, 'Come off it – you know who she is.'

He opened the other eye, looked Phyllis – who was a 'petite' girl – up and down and said, 'You aren't very fat, you haven't come here to eat our grub!' (Food was still rationed.)

I said to poor Phyllis, 'Sit down and take no notice of him.' I could see she was most uncomfortable so at nine thirty decided to take her home. Hardly a word was spoken as we cycled the three miles to her house when we were indoors I could see she was nearly in tears. I had to say something. It came out a bit like this:

'It wasn't a very good impression you got today, for your first visit to my home.

But take no notice of my father's behaviour – he was teasing you and testing you out. He knows all about you, otherwise his reaction would have been entirely different.'

Phyllis replied, 'I am not going to your home ever again. Your father is horrible. I hate him!'

I laughed and said, 'When you get to know him you will look back and laugh at tonight. Tomorrow he'll tell me what he really thinks of my choice of girlfriend.'

The next evening, before his visit to the 'White', he said, 'What about this young girl you brought home last night? Are you serious about her?'

'I think so.'

'You want to be sure. She's a nice girl and not to be messed around – you know what I mean.'

'Yes, I do.' I told him of her impression of him, and that she wouldn't be coming home with me again.

'She's an intelligent young lady. She'll soon forget about that little incident.'

By the following Sunday I had persuaded Phyllis that the way Father had behaved was all nonsense and that the family was expecting her for tea. Fortunately she agreed to accept the invitation and Father behaved sensibly and within a short time she was totally at home, realising that Father really did have a devilish sense of humour.

With my commitments in the summer, our time together was limited. I was running the motorboat and, according to tides, I might be finished at six o'clock, or I might not start work until four or five o'clock and finish at nine. Although she wasn't really a seafaring type, Phyllis either had to come with me to Scolt on her afternoon off or wait for me to finish work. She didn't like swimming (which I adored) but she did like coming over to the island and being with me – I guess she must have been fairly keen!

After we had been courting for about two years I persuaded her to go duck shooting with me. (Shooting was allowed then in the Cockle Bight.) I got a bag of marram grass for her to sit on and we settled down to await the duck flighting in. Patience was soon rewarded. As they came in on the flooding tide I shot four or five wigeon. Suddenly Phyllis gave a yell.

'Shut you up, the ducks ull hear yer!' I growled.

'I'm getting a wet bottom!' she wailed. The tide had been creeping up and had penetrated her sack of grass.

That was the one and only time she ever went duck shooting with me! However, after three years of courtship, in October 1949, we became engaged.

The following July Father was diagnosed as having incurable cancer. This put a great strain upon my mother and Eileen and her family came to stay with us on holiday at Dial House.

One particular day during this stay the tide was out from 5 pm onwards, and it was a good time to go 'butt-stabbing'. This method of catching flounders ('butts') involves slowly walking along the edge of deep pools looking for pairs of eyes and mouths not covered by sand (while the fish are feeding) and then spearing them with a cod hook straightened out and lashed to a long thin pole. Twenty to thirty fish could be caught in less than an hour.

When we left Dial House at seven our instructions were to return, with the fish gutted and cleaned, not later than nine o'clock. Eileen would have started cooking the chips, thereby reducing the time we should have to wait for the meal.

She saw us coming from the kitchen window and turning to Dad she said, 'You've time to walk to the Jolly and have a drink. By the time you get back dinner will be ready.'

Mother said, 'I'll come with you.' (She had rarely been known to visit a public house before, although she did like an occasional glass of sherry at home.)

The fish and chips were cooked and keeping hot in the oven. Hearing a knock on the front door I went to open it. There stood, not Mum and Dad, but my pal Ernie Loose's father, Ernest Loose Senior. He said gravely, 'I have some terrible news for you.'

I said, 'What's Father collapsed and died?'

'No, it's your Mum. She's been knocked down by a motorcar. She's lying on the pavement outside my house. I think she's dead.'

I asked Mr Loose to tell the rest of the family what had happened, and ran the two hundred yards to where Mum lay.

She looked like a rag doll that had been thrown to the ground, lying there in a pool of blood. It was nearly dark. I couldn't see the extent of her injuries, so put my hand under her head, to lift it into a more comfortable position. It was then that I realised it would make no difference. Mr Loose had been right. She was dead.

For a few moments I felt totally stunned. Then a car travelling from Brancaster stopped and a lady got out. 'We thought there had been an accident because we passed a car parked with its lights full on not half a mile from here. A man was doing something to the front wing. It looked suspicious.'

She had had the presence of mind to write down the car's registration on the only thing she could find in her handbag to write on – her food ration book.

While we were talking Mr Loose returned home. He told me that Father was at his house and that he would ring the police. There was nothing I could do for Mother. I asked the lady if she would wait for the police and tell them what she had seen and the number of the car. I went home with Mr Loose. Father was sitting in a chair. He knew Mother was dead. Eventually he managed to tell me what had happened. The car had been travelling very fast through the village towards Brancaster. It had been weaving from one side of the road to the other. When not more than twenty-five yards from them it had again crossed the road. Mounting the pavement it had literally taken Mother off Father's arm. Without stopping it had sped on, with a loud chaffing sound. Mother had been thrown fifteen yards by the impact.

'Why was it her and not me?' he continually asked.

I could not console him. The police arrived within ten minutes and took statements from the witnesses. An ambulance arrived and Mother was taken to Wells Cottage Hospital. The driver and his car were found five miles away, on Holme beach, at one thirty the following morning. When the constable opened the door the man asked, 'Is she dead?'

He was found guilty of manslaughter, and received an eighteen-month prison sentence. I understand that his reason for not stopping was to save his female passenger embarrassment.

CHAPTER EIGHT

My Destiny Unfolds

My mother's death shattered my father. From then on there was only one purpose left in life for him. He was determined to live until October 19, when the Committee met to decide who would be the new warden of Scolt Head. Not everyone was in favour of my appointment, although this was in fact carried through, thanks to the support of Professor Steers and of Mr N. de Basil Corbin, the Eastern Area agent for the National Trust. Father heard the news that I had been appointed and died later that night, a happy man.

Burnham Deepdale church was packed for the funeral service. People from all walks of life made up the three hundred strong congregation. For me there was just one sour note. As both my mother and father had been cremated, I had wanted their ashes scattered on Scolt Head. I was certain that would have been the wishes of them both. The family, however, preferred to bury the ashes in Deepdale churchyard and to erect a headstone over them.

It fell to Ted Ellis to sum up what must have been the feelings of a great many of my father's friends, and of Scolt visitors in general who had met him over the years. The following is the obituary Ted wrote, and which was published in his regular 'In The Countryside' column in the *Eastern Daily Press*:

"An Old Friend…"

From a hilltop on the North Norfolk coast this afternoon I looked out towards a hazed grey line of sea and all that lonely stretch of dunes and saltings lying between Brancaster and Holkham of the darkling woods. Away over the big creek the marram-tufted bluffs and ridges of Scolt Head Island were visible only as a yellow-brown dappled and scarcely definable smudge, with the little observation hut almost merged into the general drabness of the landscape. In the stillness of shadowy autumn it was not easy to recall earlier memories of that wild and beautiful realm of sea birds and flowers, of pied oystercatchers piping on shingle, of terns wheeling in a blue sky in their screaming thousands, of foam blowing across the great beds of sea lavender, of baby seals dozing on the beach, of shelduck marching across the green samphire flats.

But I had cause to remember these glories especially today, for in a little while I was to bid farewell to an old friend in whose gallant company I had tramped the island in fair weather and foul through all the years of our acquaintance. Mr Charles Chestney was to relinquish his wardenship of the sanctuary. I feel that I must pay tribute to the selfless enthusiasm with which he has carried out his work for the I National Trust through the years, and to the kindly help he has given to all naturalists, young and old, whenever they had come to share the delights of his kingdom by the sea.

Father's wish had certainly been for Phyllis and I not to wait but to get married as soon as possible. In his own words, 'You have known each other for four years, you should know your own minds by now.' Although Dee had helped out with Phyllis while Father had been ill, it was obvious that, as warden, living on my own in Dial House would be impractical. I had always been looked after, always had someone to help me. I've always liked company, and I now felt totally alone. Above all, I had no-one to explain things to, or to listen to me.

Phyllis and I were married on December 3, 1950. Due to our Scolt Head duties the ceremony had to be fitted in on a Sunday afternoon – the only 'free' time available to us. There were flurries of snow as we left Brancaster church for the wedding reception at the Sailing Club. This continued throughout the day and overnight. By morning it had drifted up to a foot deep in places. We learned later that many of our wedding guests had had to stay in hotels overnight, because roads had become impassable. Two parties had been hospitalised, due to injuries sustained when their vehicles had left the road in the treacherous conditions.

Phyllis and I just took over from my parents at Dial House. On the Monday morning I went out to the island and started wardening, as Father had done. There was no time for a honeymoon – it was straight into the job. Phyllis automatically took over looking after the students and the running of the house, plus everything associated with it.

Even in those days, Dial House was really an information centre. People would enquire, 'When are the boats?', 'How are the tides?', 'What shall we see?' She had to know all these things, as well as cope with me coming home at unsociable hours. In fact she managed it all most expertly – she was a 'brick'! I think visitors hardly realised that Mum and Dad had died. Things ran along smoothly, as they had always done!

Our 'honeymoon' was postponed for eighteen years – 1968 would be the first time we should be able to get away together! And the first time the whole family would manage to get out together would be even further in the distant future – in 1974.

Life would not be easy for us, but it was what we wanted to do.

CHAPTER NINE

Magical Little Seabirds

I have already referred to Scolt Head's star attraction being its terns, and it seems appropriate at this juncture to fill in a few more details about these 'magical' little seabirds.

Terns differ from their close cousins, the familiar black-headed gulls of beach, field, garden and town parks in a number of significant ways. They are more lightly built and have narrower and more pointed wings; their tails are forked like a swallow (hence their old country name, 'sea-swallow') with long 'streamers'. Like the gulls which are found nesting with them nowadays in Norfolk terneries, their heads have black 'caps' in summer; but the flight of the tern is so different – so much more buoyant and graceful.

Unlike the gulls, which will as soon scavenge for food on inland rubbish tips as from the surface of the sea, terns cannot feed away from water. They locate their food by hovering over water, and dive to catch the prey they have selected. Each species seeks its own fish size and diving depth, which are relative to its own size. Three species form the bulk of terns nesting in Norfolk. The smallest is aptly named the little tern (in Britain – least tern in North America). Not much bigger than a swift, it has a yellow bill, tipped with black, orange or yellow legs and a black cap with a white forehead.

It feeds mainly in shallow water, especially in harbours when the tide is out, on fish trapped in shallow pools. During severe wind and rough seas food becomes scarce and it is common to see twenty to thirty little terns at one time hovering just above the waves, dipping and taking plankton and minute sea animals (no larger than a pinhead) from the wave tops and water surface. At other times, diving to a depth of three to four feet, they feed on round fish, shrimp or similar tiny crustaceans, sand goby, whitebait and sandeel.

The 'middle' size of tern, the common tern, is smaller than the black-headed gull, but half as big again as a little tern. The red bill is tipped with black, the legs are red and it has a wholly black cap in the breeding season. Like its larger relative the Sandwich tern, it feeds principally on the flood tide at sea. However, when fish are available in the harbour it can be seen hovering and diving there on the flood and threequarter ebb tides.

The food of the common tern in Norfolk is principally whitebait (mostly young herring) caught up to a depth of four feet. Feeding mostly takes place at sea; although (prior to 1957) when food was abundant, feeding was common in the harbour on the flood and ebb tides, virtually throughout the summer. Birds could be seen there in great profusion – I have seen 2000 diving for food at one time. One of the many highlights when visiting Scolt was the boat journey from Brancaster Staithe, through the many hundreds of terns, diving and catching the small fish which had come into the harbour on the flood tide. Often birds would only miss the boat by a few inches, as the shoals of fish moved with the tide.

The Sandwich tern was named for the town in Kent where it was first identified as a distinct species in Britain. Apart from its comparatively large size and its much whiter appearance, it is distinguished from the other terns by its black bill – tipped with yellow or horn-colour – black legs, and by the feathers of its black cap (in the breeding season) being frequently seen raised, in display or aggression. In North America it is known as Cabot's tern.

Sandwich terns fish in the open sea when they first arrive and can dive to a depth of six feet. If they are seen in the estuary, later in the season, it is usually a good indication that hatching has commenced. Sandeels appear to be their main food, but gluts of whitebait during the breeding season are utilised. Fish size can be up to 23cm (principally sandeel) and under extreme conditions birds can and do make a round trip of eighty miles to obtain a single fish, when feeding young.

Common and little terns have nested in Norfolk since the early 1700s. The Sandwich tern was a much later arrival; the first authentic record was in 1903 when one was shot by a 'local'. The first Norfolk breeding record was for Blakeney in 1912 – the year the Point was officially established as a nature reserve. It has nested in the county every year since, numbers increasing slowly, assisted by protection. The first nesting record for Scolt was 1923 and by the mid 'thirties the Norfolk population was estimated to be 1500 breeding pairs. Although fragment groups did nest spasmodically at two other sites

(Salthouse and Stiffkey) the main bulk of birds stayed at Scolt and Blakeney Point.

Two other species of tern have bred at Scolt Head this century. The very rare roseate tern (similar in body size to the common but with much longer tail streamers) nested in small numbers both here and at Blakeney Point. Scolt's last nesting pair was in 1949. Arctic terns, distinguishable from the common terns principally by their all-red, untipped bills, shorter legs and longer tail streamers, still breed in Norfolk in small numbers.

The three main species need different habitats for nesting. The little tern mainly chooses open beach among 'egg-size' shingle, or shingle and sand. It is therefore found nesting low down the beach on habitat highly vulnerable to flooding. When northerly winds increase the height of the normal spring (large) tides – an annual occurrence – little tern nests are often lost.

At one time the common tern was the most abundant tern species not only on Scolt but generally along the North Norfolk coast. It nests in a variety of habitats on an open beach, on or among the younger dunes or the associated shingle, not as low down the beach as little terns. It is therefore less vulnerable to flooding by forced tides.

Sandwich terns are the first to return from their wintering quarters to Norfolk, the earliest birds being expected back about March 22. These are mainly males. Before starting their ritual of displaying and pairing they rest for five to seven days. (They are also geared to depart before the females.)

In some years, however, the very first arrivals start displaying immediately and I suspect that these have wintered in the Mediterranean. Having a much shorter distance to travel than the bulk of birds from Africa, and feeding en route, they arrive in good condition and are thus able to display straight away. These are also the more experienced birds.

Although terns pair for life, the pair bond is broken outside the breeding season. In order for terns to return to the breeding colony, the pair bond must be reinforced prior to their departure from the breeding site; and therefore, at the end of the breeding season, there occurs an intense five-day air and ground display and nest establishing.

When the terns return to breed, numbers increase until the nesting area is 'alive' with displaying pairs. Displaying, courtship and mating are followed by a precise positioning of the nest. Nesting sites that were successful in previous years are preferred to untried or unsuccessful ones – particularly by common and little terns, as well as ringed plover and oystercatcher and, to lesser degrees, redshank and black-headed gull.

They usually return to the successful breeding site of the previous year (I consider 'success' to a bird to be hatching eggs) and take five days to re-establish the site. This also stimulates birds which have failed elsewhere and are searching for a new site. The female, principally, incubates for the first fourteen days, being fed by the male. The procedure is reversed until two days after the eggs have hatched. Then it is 'all systems go' to satisfy the ever-hungry young!

Between 1940 and 1945, when the reserve was closed to visitors by the Ministry of Defence, there had been a noticeable improvement in tern fledging success. The area of sea adjacent to the ternery had been a practice area for aircraft firing at moored targets.

In 1944 a coaster, the *Vina*, approximately three hundred feet in length, had been moored a mile out to sea off the west end of the island. Destined for the breakers' yard at the outbreak of war, she had been moored at the mouth of Lowestoft harbour, ready to be used as a 'block' ship, to be sunk in the event of invasion. Off Scolt she was to be used as a floating target; but her career proved to be short-lived. During a gale she had dragged her anchor and had ended up on the outer harbour bar with a broken back. Several tons of steam coal of very high quality remained in her bunkers – a bonus for us locals in those days of coal rationing!

Here she continued to be a target for Blenheim bombers and rocket-firing Typhoons. After the war various salvage companies attempted to recover her for scrap metal; but the cost was higher than the expected return. Today all that remains of the *Vina* are the bow and stern sections; the sides of the hull are missing to sand level, exposing the remains of her steam boiler. Obviously she is a great attraction to holidaymakers – but a word of warning! To reach her you have to cross the main harbour channel. The distance is greater than it appears, and it's easy to be cut off by the fast-flowing flood tide. We have rescued a considerable number of visitors marooned on the Wreck Sand and, sad to say, scarcely a year goes by without somebody being drowned.

During the war years nesting terns paid little attention to the noise of low-flying aircraft and gunfire. During those years, Father only visited the ternery occasionally during the breeding season mainly for recording purposes – when firing practice was not in progress. Their breeding success had never been better – a surprise, considering that, in addition to all the military activity, there was no control of natural predators. With peace and the reopening of Scolt, human visitors returned. Tern breeding success dropped to the pre-war level.

My father had discussed this with me at great length. Having eliminated the predatory factor once again, he had been sure that the human factor must in some way be responsible for the high chick mortality, though he had remained puzzled as to its exact contribution. Low fledging success of common and little terns in the 'thirties at Blakeney Point and Scolt had been (and still was, at the time of my appointment) commonly accepted – even by the Scolt Head Committee – as 'typical' of these species and was attributed to them being 'bad parents'. Sandwich terns were considered 'much better parents', as their fledging success averaged forty per cent, compared to the others' ten per cent. What had given my father food for thought was that during the war years common and little tern fledging success had risen to between forty and fifty per cent, while Sandwich terns had reached a peak of seventy per cent. A further striking factor was that the latter had also successfully hatched clutches of two eggs (clutches of three are exceptional); previously one of the chicks would have died in the shell – most just on the point of hatching.

Both at Blakeney and Scolt human disturbance had always been discounted by the 'experts', although – depending on the tides – on some days it continued an entire six hours. Therefore no control of visitors had been deemed necessary. To Father's knowledge, the effect of continuous disturbance, particularly during the incubation period, had never been studied. He had brought this to the attention of the committee; but they had all agreed that there was 'no reason for his concern', the human factor not being considered detrimental to tern breeding. Furthermore they stated that, despite increasing visitor pressure, breeding tern numbers remained constant. Therefore there was no reason to change the management policy.

This conclusion was, of course, strongly influenced by the fact that Scolt relied mainly on the generosity of its visitors and the general public for its financial support. Their priority was to experience the thrill, the pure 'magic' (there is no other word for it) of walking through a large colony of breeding terns and of being able to examine the eggs and young on the ground, close at hand. My father, being on the spot, had been the only one to see and really understand what was the success or failure at the ternery. He couldn't accept that it was 'natural' for the chicks to die even when weather and food were favourable. He had also pointed out the stupidity of the experiment carried out in the 'thirties: some terns had been shot to prove that they were responsible for the decline in flatfish at Blakeney; stomach contents examined had proved negative. No-one involved in the experiment had realised that the protective bone protruding from these fish made it impossible for young chicks to swallow them!

Unfortunately my father had died before he could put his findings into practice. When I took over I was thankful that I had not read any scientific material concerning tern behaviour. I was aware of what he had had in mind and decided to implement his ideas. I also appreciated what a task I had ahead of me, following him, and resolved that if through my new approach I didn't get any improvement in fledgling numbers at the end of five years I should give up wardening. I had the backing of Professor Steers, who as chairman of the committee had been instrumental in my being appointed warden. I could not let him down.

I established one landing and departure point for visitors, met every boat on arrival, conducted each group through a limited nesting area and answered questions on site. We finished the tour away from but overlooking the main nesting area, where people could stay as long as they liked, before continuing over the rest of the reserve if they wanted to. No unauthorised person was allowed into the restricted area unless accompanied by me and I erected boundary posts to separate the ternery from the unrestricted area to the east of it. Marker posts along this route – which would become known as the 'nature trail' – pointed out the return path to the departure point, so that visitors avoided the ternery on their return. In 1951 eight hundred people visited the ternery (by 1960 this figure would total 3,000, and by 1966 6,000 – each receiving my undivided attention!) I knew it would not be easy to restrict visitors at all – let alone overnight! Few restrictions had been imposed on visiting parties or photographers outside the breeding area.

In introducing my ternery management plan my intention was to keep as many visitors as possible happy without disturbing the entire ternery. Firstly, though, it was important to explain to local visitors and the committee why the restrictions were necessary. For generations access to the island had been unrestricted. Fishermen collected driftwood from the shoreline, among the nesting birds, for the copper fires upon which they boiled their whelks. Locals landed and walked anywhere without interference. So why should they stop now? Nobody likes change!

However I was convinced that my father had been right and that good fledging success at Scolt depended both on my ability to gain local and visitor support for my scheme. As I gained knowledge about tern behaviour and the effect of disturbance, I realised that I had to spend longer and still longer hours at the ternery during the breeding season. I had to ensure that positively minimum disturbance, both from humans and predators, took place.

June weather in Britain can be extremely varied, even on the comparatively dry North Norfolk coast. True to the 'inconsiderate' natural laws governing these things, inclement weather usually prevails just as the tern chicks are hatching. Two or more days of wet and cold conditions at this critical period result in an increased chick mortality – a trend exacerbated if adults are disturbed from the nest. The local ferrymen continued their visits to Scolt Head irrespective of weather conditions, the fares being a substantial part of their livelihood through the summer months.

The day in question – by no means exceptional – shows what the terns had to put up with from humans. There were prolonged heavy showers all day, the temperature rose to no more than 50 degrees Fahrenheit (10 degrees Celsius) and the wind was fresh south-westerly. Nevertheless three elderly ladies braved the elements. I met them on their way to the ternery and introduced myself. As with every party, I asked them the purpose of their visit.

They replied, 'We have come to see the nesting terns.'

'Not the ideal day to visit a colony of terns just as they're hatching young,' I remarked.

'Our friends came last week and talked so much about it that we decided we must see for ourselves,' one of them retorted, adding, 'We have come all the way from Norwich, and we are members of the National Trust.'

'There's one question I must ask you – are you bird lovers?'

'Oh yes,' they all agreed.

'Well, in my opinion, you are no such thing!'

GASP!!!

'What bird lover would dream of disturbing birds with very small chicks in this weather?' I asked; but it made no difference to their attitude – my 'subtle' plea had fallen on deaf ears.

'All right then,' I agreed reluctantly. 'But before I take you into the ternery and disturb them there are certain things you must agree to. First, off with your coats!'

'But we shall get wet!'

'That's right. Why should you stay dry and the tern chicks get wet. It's raining fairly heavily and they won't have any protection from the rain when we disturb the parents. Are you still positive that you want to see the tern nests?' I repeated.

They were most adamant that they did.

'All right, I will take you. But when we reach halfway there will be no turning back.'

I gave no further explanation and we started to walk along the specified route. This area, which I had set aside to minimise disturbance to the main colony, held four hundred nests of varying species, compared with over a thousand within the restricted area.

On reaching halfway we came to the area where nests had been hatching for four days. The more active chicks had instinctively scurried away to hide, the moment their parents rose from the nests. However the newly hatched chicks were still in the nests, dry and fluffy, being brooded by their parents. The ladies remarked, 'Aren't they lovely!'

We soon found the older youngsters. Running through the wet grass they had quickly become wet, cold and bedraggled. It was heart-rending to see these pathetic little creatures, looking like wet sponges covered in sand, on their backs and kicking their little legs in the air. They were making weak little calls. With great concern the ladies asked why they were in this sorry state.

'Mainly due to us,' I replied. 'Because we have put the parent birds to flight. The only protection they have against the weather is their parents brooding them.'

As we continued we came across several more chicks that were past the point of no return. By this time the ladies were in a great state of distress, and one of them actually burst into tears, saying, 'Oh my God, what have we done? We must turn back.'

Despite this outburst of remorse, there was no way back now. 'I knew that you didn't grasp the significance of my earlier remarks,' I said. 'We cannot turn back. To do so will send the adult birds away again, and the chicks already subjected to the wet and cold won't have sufficient time to get dry and warm. Prolonging the situation will almost certainly increase the chick mortality.'

Now all three were in tears. All they could say was, 'What have we done?'

'The best thing for us to do is to get away as quickly as we can,' I said, hurrying them from the nesting area to where we could cause no further disturbance. As we walked towards the departure point I explained what a difficult job it was to satisfy visitors who had no idea of the fine balance between the success or failure of nesting terns. This included members of the National Trust, I added.

It had rained virtually all the time since we had started out until we reached the spot where the ladies had left their coats. Needless to say they were pretty wet. As they put on their coats I said, 'Now you know what a wet tern chick feels like.'

We walked on to the departure point to await the ferryman. Jokingly I said, 'I haven't seen your membership cards.'

One lady opened her handbag and taking out her card handed it to me. It was two years out of date!

After a pause I said, 'I agreed to take you into the ternery only because you told me you were National Trust members.'

They looked shamefaced as I went on, 'I suggest you write to the Trust at Blickling Hall, telling them what has happened here today. Pay the arrears and make sure you renew your membership each year in future. Tell all your friends who want to visit Scolt that the terns have made Bob Chestney their chief spokesman, and they have told him this: 'Visitors are welcome, but only when the weather is fine. Please keep away at other times. This also applies to Trust members. We terns rely on the general public for financial support, the National Trust and the warden for our survival, and we hope that none of you will let us down.' I added that due to the war many subscriptions had lapsed, resulting in loss of income badly needed to support properties such as Scolt for future generations.

The following day I saw the tragic result of our visit and it convinced me that such an occurence would never happen again – not while I was warden of Scolt Head.

In August Mr de Basil Corbin came to stay at the Hut. When I met him he asked me, 'Whatever do you say to visitors?'

'Only the truth.'

He told me of a letter he had received from three ladies who had paid a visit to the ternery on a wet June day. In it they had described virtually everything which had taken place. The outcome had been that they had paid their arrears and each had donated ten pounds to safeguard the terns at Scolt.

CHAPTER TEN

...and Other Branches of Nature

U pon my appointment as warden many people had genuinely wished me success in my new job; there had been others who had given advice as to what I should or should not do.

In my third season, on the day of the committee's summer excursion to Scolt, I was asked by one of its members if I considered myself to be 'over-zealous' in the way I was protecting the terns. There had been several complaints about the restrictions, and the committee was concerned about their necessity – they had been 'most satisfied' with past management under my father. I realised that the committee members were not aware that past breeding success could possibly be greatly improved by what I was trying to do. I knew there were two members who supported me and I therefore had no intention of allowing this new Chestney approach to be 'overTERNED'!

On reflection, it was probably my simple but unorthodox method of presenting the terns' case that resulted in my not always being taken seriously – either then or now; but I had to adjust my presentation of the case to suit the level of knowledge of my audience. After predicting what an individual tern, or pair, was going to do, I was often asked, 'Do you really know what the birds are calling?'

I would say with great conviction, 'Naturally, the terns have their own language. In fact they have made me their chief spokesman and this is their message: "Our needs are few – we have the right habitat and food supply, we can survive extreme weather conditions, limited food, predation and even egg collectors. But please, Bob, don't restart those continuous daily walks through the colony while we're nesting – that is worse than all the other hazards put together."'

When asked what qualifications were necessary to become a warden my reply would be, 'As you can see, you don't have to be clever!'

I found that it is the human species which needs the most attention, as it has lost all its natural survival instincts. On the other hand the terns are the experts. They can cope when given the opportunity.

When asked if I had a degree, I would reply, 'Yes, the highest.'

'In what subject?'

'Tolerance!'

I found this to be essential in order to convey a simple message to the visitors in the short time allotted to them on the island. I tried to hold their attention by presenting the information in an entertaining manner when the main purpose of their visit was just to come and look. All I tried to do was to convey a favourable impression of my subject. My degree of success could only be measured by such comments as, 'It was wonderful, we must tell our friends.' Time was too limited to show them all the things I wanted to. With only half to three-quarters of an hour available to them after disembarking from the ferry, I had to hold their interest while conveying a limited amount of simple information about the terns and Scolt Head.

Although Scolt is especially renowned for its terns, it also abounds in other interest. Over thirty bird species have nested there, including the terns already described. Black-headed gulls nest regularly; common, herring, lesser black-backed gulls and kittiwakes have also bred. Oystercatcher, redshank and ringed plover still breed annually, and in former years lapwing nests were also abundant. Mallard and shelduck are the two 'regular' breeding wildfowl species on Scolt; but gadwall, tufted duck and canada geese have also nested. Kestrel, short-eared owl, woodpigeon, stock dove, pheasant, red-legged and grey partridges and carrion crow have all bred, as have blackbird, linnet, hedgesparrow, wren, skylark, swallow, wheatear, reed bunting, grasshopper warbler, whitethroat and yellow wagtail. Some of these species, their nesting habits and their relationships to the terns will be described more fully later on, as will many of the island's interesting and varied bird migrants.

In addition, Scolt possesses a wealth of interesting and rare plants which grow on various levels of saltmarsh, on shingle ridges and sand dunes. One of the most abundant here (though it is nationally rare) is the shrubby sea-blite, a member of the goosefoot family which grows vigorously between the tidal and non-tidal areas. As its name implies, it resembles a small shrub rather than typical saltmarsh plants such as the very localised sea heath, matted and rock sea lavenders and greater sea spurrey, which stand only an inch or two in height. Above the sea-blite level the first colonising plants another goosefoot, the prickly saltwort, sea rocket and sea purslane are common. Occasionally, sea kale and horned poppy also grow here.

There is no more beautiful a sight anywhere than Hut Marsh in July. Its higher levels become a carpet of mauve, with the flowering sea lavenders. Earlier in the year the pink of thrift similarly covers the shingle laterals. Prior to these species receiving legal protection, they were gathered for flower arrangements.

The dune sand is stabilised by a host of plants, many of them unique to this kind of habitat. Chief among them are marram and sea couch grasses, although lyme and other grasses and sand sedge also have important parts to play in this habitat. Among the colourful vegetation on the lower dunes are found the beautiful sea bindweed and sea holly – a striking contrast in pink and blue when in flower – several ferns, the strange, rare green-flowered sea spurge, purple vetches, the deep yellow bird's-foot trefoil and lemon yellow biting stonecrop, the pink of centaury and the pure white of sea campion. Less common, but undoubtedly the 'jewels' in Scolt's floral crown, are the rosy pink, green and brown bee orchids, the delicate pink to deep red pyramidal orchids and the purple sea pea.

The abundance of plants and the total absence of toxic sprays encourage the presence of many lepidoptera species. In addition to dark green fritillaries, graylings and other resident butterflies there are migratory movements of the red admiral, painted lady, peacock and clouded yellow; and tortoise-shells can arrive overnight in many hundreds, on the sea rocket. The largest concentration I have seen was of some two thousand, on an area 50 yards long by two yards wide. Although I walked virtually on the edge of the sea rocket, not one tortoise-shell was disturbed – their only interest was in feeding.

Too many moth species have been recorded on Scolt to list here; but mention should be made of the rare death's head hawkmoth. This, the largest European hawkmoth, turns up on Scolt occasionally and is one of the few moths caught out in sunlight. Those I have seen were all flying close to the Hut.

Other insects are also found in great profusion, no doubt once again due to the absence of sprays. In August millions of grasshoppers may be found in the dunes; eating sandwiches there can be perilous – one's food box becomes covered with jumping animals! In autumn, spiders' webs stretch in great profusion on the sea-blite, hardly a bush being without a fine gossamer cover glistening in the sun. One might expect to see rabbits, stoats and weasels on Scolt – even long-tailed fieldmouse and pigmy and common shrews; but more unusual animal visitors include roe and fallow deer, hedgehog, coypu, otter, fox, grey squirrel, natterjack toad and – for one day only – Mrs Carrie Raven's tomcat from Brancaster! Bearing in mind that all mammals can swim, what next?!

As I learned that there was a great deal more to Scolt than its birds, I realised I should have to not only lay out a 'bird section' of my new nature trail but also, complementing it, a means of looking at the vegetation, the beach, sea animals and so on. Before the school parties came I would send the teachers a questionnaire, to be handed on to their pupils, so that they had some idea in advance of what they would see on their visit to the island.

When they came to Scolt and reached the beach there would be sea animals, shells and other things for them to identify along the tideline, all strategically placed – skate eggs, dogfish eggs, common seaweeds, horn wrack (which is an animal, not a plant), razorshells, horsemussels, sea urchins and so forth. These had been collected in the winter (January to March) when they had been washed up by northerly winds and had been saved for the summer visitors. Having laid them out on the shoreline I knew exactly what we were going to find, of course! And, surprise, surprise, what we found corresponded exactly with the things described in their little nature trail leaflets. So the children could fill in what they saw. Naturally I didn't do this with adults – they were left on the boundary line. Off they used to go, and I would hare back to the landing point again to meet the ferry. I have often walked the quarter mile of the nature trail twenty-two times in one day with parties – and back again! – not stopping for eleven hours.

There is no doubt that seeing Scolt for the first time, especially when the birds had young, was an overwhelming experience for visitors. The nesting birds, particularly the terns, were what they remembered. The finer points went over the average person's head – he or she had neither the interest nor time to become involved. I had to put over to them the fact that these beautiful and exciting birds were fighting for their survival. Not every egg would hatch, not every chick would fly. By giving them a chance to get on with the job without too much interference from man (the warden included) many of their difficulties could be overcome.

Many visitors wanted to stay on the reserve longer than their allotted time, once they discovered so much to do there. Unfortunately for them time seems to go more quickly on Scolt than elsewhere! A group of thirty-six London schoolchildren, all totally unfamiliar with anything to do with Scolt Head, visited the reserve. As always, knowing beforehand the standard reached by each school party, I adjusted my talk and the information it contained accordingly.

Most had never seen the sea before so I started by telling them why Scolt was so important for seabirds, plants and so on. On reaching the point on the beach where I left parties I said, 'You have two hours before you have to catch the boat to do what you like. Your teachers can now take over.'

One lad said, 'Whatever are we going to do for all that time – there's nowhere to spend any money!'

'That may be so, but you will find that on Scolt Head two hours are only as long as one hour elsewhere.'

He was one of the first to return. Running up to me he said, 'You are right, Bob, two hours is only one!' He sounded so sincere when he added wistfully, 'I wish it would happen like that at school.'

Another satisfied customer!

Most of the school parties only had two or three pairs of binoculars between them. I would say, 'If you turn them round the other way you will be able to use them as a magnifying glass.'

I had discovered this effect accidentally, after I had cut my finger – looking at it through the 'wrong end' of my glasses I brought it into focus, and could see how the colour changed from the purple of the inner part of the wound to a more red colour on the outside. On one of the committee's visits I found Ted Ellis studying a mould on a shrubby seablite plant. Having discovered it to be a rarity, he was looking at it intently through a small magnifying glass.

'Very interesting,' he exclaimed upon my approach. 'It doesn't belong in this country. It's from the Mediterranean.'

I said, 'Ted, I expect that came in last July during those terrific thunderstorms we had. North Norfolk was covered in red dust that was reported to have come from the Sahara.' (We had had all sorts of things – including creatures, such as a cricket, something I never heard of before or since.) I asked him if I could have a look.

He handed me his magnifying glass.

'I don't want that, Ted. I'll use my binoculars.' I turned them round and put them to within an inch of the mould. The Committee stood behind us, laughing. Bob Chestney was 'winding them up' again – or so they thought, until I said to Ted, 'I see – it's like a lichen.'

I explained to him exactly what I could see. He said, still somewhat incredulously, 'Can you really see it?'

'Yeah, have a look.'

He had a pair of 6×35 binoculars with him. He turned them round, and focused them onto the mould. 'Oh yes,' he said. 'Yes.'

The committee members hadn't realised that I had been playing it 'straight' for once. They all had a go then!

As the seasons progressed I got to understand the general public more. I even became a little less big-headed and began to think more of what the visitors wanted to get out of their trips to Scolt. They used to come up to me and say, 'We've found a nest.'

'Oh no,' I'd say, straightfaced. 'As I have told you, every nest on Scolt is marked.'

'We can't accept that. We found one that wasn't.'

'I can't believe that! Where is it?'

They would tell me where they had found the nest, and that there were three eggs in it.

'It must be an oystercatcher's nest, then. Are you sure it didn't have a little stake by it, with a number on?'

'No.'

'Oh dear. I'm afraid that's one I don't know about, then.'

They used to go back and tell everyone that they had found a nest that the warden hadn't known about. What they didn't know, of course, was that every morning I used to nip along the beach, pull the stakes out and smooth the sand. The chances of the eggs being trodden on were very, very remote. So visitors would 'find' these nests and be as pleased as Punch with their discovery. Our motto was 'send 'em away happy'!

Every year boys from Oundle School would visit Scolt Head. There would be about twelve to sixteen of them, all as keen as mustard, in the charge of the vicar. If I kept on pointing out, 'That's a so-and-so, that's so-and-so,' they would soon lose interest – it would have been too much like a school lesson perhaps.

So occasionally I used the trick my father had played upon me when I was little. I'd say, 'Hey, there's a black-tailed godwit over there.'

In fact the bird would be a bar-tailed godwit. Someone would have to tell me that I was wrong, that it had an upturned bill, that there was no white wing-pattern, and so on. Of course there was always one little old Bob Chestney type who would stick his neck out!

'Hey, Bob [they all called me Bob], it's a bar-tailed.'

Everyone would stare at me apprehensively. Would I deny it? I'd study the bird through my binoculars. 'Oh dear,' I'd gasp, 'however did I make that mistake? I can see it is, now – I do apologise.'

One particular day we did actually see a black-tailed godwit (which, needless to say, I 'identified' as a bar-tailed) and also two Lapland buntings. So I said, 'Oh, ah, reed buntings.'

Of course the birds had lovely straw-coloured bills, instead of the grey bills of reed buntings. Someone had to tell Bob Chestney he was wrong again, and just why he was wrong. Within seconds they did! This held the boys' interest. Even at the end of the day, if we saw a bird just before we departed, I'd point it out and say, 'That's a so-and-so.' Everybody would have their 'beadies' on it, to confirm whether it was or wasn't. When they got back to school they'd say, 'Oh, Bob Chestney – he doesn't know one bird from another!'

The second year the vicar arrived with the boys he said to me, 'By the way, Bob, when you're not identifying these birds correctly it's not very good for your standing with the boys. It's not good for your own ego, you know.'

'Oh dear,' I remarked, and left it at that.

He arrived the third year with yet another set of lads. This time he had a different comment to make. 'I don't think it's possible, Bob,' he said, 'for you to make the same mistake three consecutive years, is it?'

'What are you talking about?' I asked innocently.

'You've pointed out these birds – black-tailed and bar-tailed godwits and so on – and then you've gasped when you've been proved wrong by the boys. But you're obviously making these mistakes deliberately!'

'Well, in a way.' I explained it to him.

'But you don't rate very high in the boys' esteem,' he objected.

'Does that matter?' I asked. 'Those boys were as keen when they left as they were when they came. If you can achieve that over a six-hour period then I don't reckon you're doing too badly.'

'But what about your ego?'

'Well, I never did rate that too highly anyway.'

'I don't think anyone will believe me when I tell them, ' he said. 'You don't have to tell them, do you?!'

I am convinced that some visitors lost all their inhibitions when on Scolt Head – perhaps because it is an island, cut off from the 'normal' moral conventions of the mainland. For example I escorted thirty female students who were studying the unique flora and fauna of the sand dunes and saltmarsh. They also had to give accounts of the longshore drift, the shingle rides and how they had developed.

When summing up at the end of the four-hour tour I remarked that what we had studied and seen was a lot to absorb in such a short time, but was there anything else I could do for them before I departed.

Some replied 'Oh, yes please!' (an answer I put down to a misunderstanding due to poor presentation on my part – rectified the next time round!)

Phyllis and I had no transport in those early days, and only the local shops for shopping. We worked hard and for long hours. It was expected of us – though people were appreciative in those days. Those we met were real ladies and gentlemen – from all walks of life. Their gratitude gave us the drive to continue – we felt we had to be ambassadors for Scolt Head.

Sometimes the burden Phyllis had to bear was made worse by me. Some people say I'm a 'great talker'. This is possibly true and before my departure for the island I'd tell my long-suffering wife that I would be home 'without fail' at nine o'clock. Frequently, however, I would meet someone on the way home to detain me, who might ask me, 'How are you, Bob? How's the season going on?' I would therefore be, almost habitually, late home for my meal!

At first Phyllis was a bit bewildered by this kind of thing; but she soon caught on. So if I said I should be home for nine, she would work it out to get my dinner ready for about a quarter to ten!

One of Father's sayings had been, 'Listen to what other people have to say; you are never too old to learn.' Within a few years of becoming warden I thought I knew all there was to know about terns. However, this belief was soon shattered – by a fourteen-year-old girl!

Her father asked me to accompany his family on a visit to Scolt Head, adding that he would appreciate my explaining what was happening in the ternery and the different sounds and calls of the birds to his daughter, whom I shall call Jennie. The only way she would be able to 'see' the birds would be through my eyes – Jennie was blind.

I admit I was hesitant. This would be my first attempt to convey the activities of nesting terns to someone who could not see. How should I go about it? The father was persistent – doubtless sensing my apprehension. Finally I agreed, little realising that the boot would be on the other foot. It would be Jennie who would 'see' something that I had missed.

We started the tour and approached the first oystercatcher's nest. Because the season was well advanced, I explained, the early first successful nesting pairs had young almost fully fledged.

Jennie remarked, 'What a noise they make!'

I said, 'The noisy ones are those with young. In fact this pair are about thirty paces away. Their chicks are, to them, positive things. They are mobile and need protection from all kinds of danger. Parental protection instinct is triggered off due to the period of incubation. It explodes when the adults hear chicks in the shell but wanes as soon as the young fly. On the other hand, eggs to a bird are negative to incubating birds.' An idea struck me and I told Jennie to hold out her hand.

'You can feel the size of the eggs,' I said. 'While you're doing that I'll catch two oystercatcher chicks – one fifteen days and the other three days old. You can compare their size with that of the eggs from which they hatched. 'After replacing the egg she had been handling in the nest, I gave Jennie the chicks I had caught. Without any awkwardness she examined each chick, by running her fingers over it from bill to feet.

When she had finished she exclaimed, 'Don't they grow fast. The older chick is much bigger than I expected.'

'Oystercatcher eggs take a month to hatch. Then the young leave the nest within twenty-four hours and accompany their parents to feed,' I explained. 'At four days old the young are quite mobile, searching for food in the tidal area near to the nest. They receive additional food and warmth from the adults as and when needed. They are fully fledged about five weeks after hatching.'

As we walked on we came to a common tern's nest containing three newly hatched chicks. I placed one in Jennie's hand and she again examined it carefully with her fingers. Her questions were very different from those of a sighted person. For example, 'Why is there a raised point on the tip of the bill?'

'That is a specially hardened tooth, or nail, developed and only used for the purpose of breaking the shell of the egg, thus allowing the chick to emerge when it is ready. 'Around the fourth day the tooth drops off, as it will have done its job.' I explained that on a rare occasion I had known the egg tooth fail to develop – 'Therefore the chick perishes inside the shell, because it's unable to break it.'

Until tern chicks are fully fledged they have to be patient and wait for their parents to return with food. The adults identify their own chicks by individual voice patterns – as with human finger prints, no two patterns are the same.

Even with the help and protection of a warden, the little and common tern pairs here only manage to raise on average one chick every three years. Their breeding life is between nine and twelve years. Chicks take three weeks to hatch. After a further fifteen days the soft fluffy down is replaced by developing feathers. It takes twenty-eight to thirty-three days from hatching for them to fledge.

We continued our tour, coming next to a common tern nest containing two eggs. This was a second clutch. The birds, having lost the first, had been incubating this one for little more than a week. I placed an egg in Jennie's hand, so that she could compare its shape and size with those of the oystercatcher's egg. She remarked how much smaller it was.

In the next nest, another oystercatcher's, hatching had just started. I gave Jennie an egg so that she could feel the chipped shell, through which the chick was pecking its way out.

'Put the egg to your ear,' I said, 'and you will hear the chick pecking and calling.'

After doing this she asked a most unusual question: 'Why is this egg so smooth compared with the others I have held?'

The parent birds were making a noise and fuss, because they knew the eggs were hatching. They were doing their utmost to attract us away from their nest.

Their distress made the family anxious to leave its vicinity, so they did not press for an answer to Jennie's question – thank goodness. I hadn't the slightest idea why that particular egg should be smoother than the others. I was unable to answer.

The following year, I deliberately felt scores of eggs, not only with my finger tips but with my lips – more sensitive than fingers. Nevertheless, despite all the eggs I examined, at all stages of incubating, I could not define a smooth egg from a rough one.

One evening I was out in the ternery. The first successful clutches were on the point of hatching and pairs which had been unsuccessful had virtually all relaid. The sun was low in the west, the day's bright light spent. In this dull light I saw that eggs on the point of hatching had a definite sheen. As I continued I saw that the newly laid eggs were noticeably duller, lacking the sheen of the others.

On my return I pondered this, examining closely the events that occur with the eggs during their period of incubation. When the answer finally dawned on me the answer was so simple! How stupid I had been not to have seen it sooner! Of course the shiny eggs had been buffed and smoothed during the period of incubation – sufficiently for Jennie's sensitive fingers to feel the difference. Eggs are rearranged many times during a day, to maintain them at a uniform heat. The rough and dull eggs hadn't been subjected to this process for long enough for it to have had any effect.

This simple finding gave me more food for thought. What else did I not know, or was unaware of? Thanks to a blind girl I realised I had only scratched the surface.

CHAPTER ELEVEN

The Great Flood

An eminent Harley Street gynaecologist, Mr Beatty, had been coming to stay at the Moorings Hotel at Burnham Overy Staithe for many years. Phyllis and I had got to know him well, and he had forecast that our first daughter would be born about February 22, 1952. As this had been my father's birthday we were hoping his prediction would come true. Unfortunately, however, this date came and went and there was still no sign of the baby. Phyllis did not commence labour until March 13, a Thursday. On the Saturday morning, March 15, she was still in labour. At that time of day very few people went to hospital to have babies, so two doctors and a nurse arrived at Dial House to await a complicated delivery.

That morning I had to take some visitors, Captain and Mrs Marshall and Mr and Mrs Palmer, to the island (they had all been coming to Scolt for many years) so I arranged that if the baby were born while I was away a sheet would be hoisted up the flagpole which had already been secured on Dial House.

About lunchtime we stood on top of Hut Hills looking across. The flagpole was bare – nothing had happened yet. Phyllis had now been in labour for two-and-a-half days. We continued our tour of the island, up to House Hills and then back to Beach Point. I climbed up to the summit of Long Hills and, with some relief, saw the sheet flying from its flagpole. I was a father!

When we arrived home we were told the baby was a girl. She weighed a healthy nine-and-a-half pounds. The visitors congratulated us, had a cup of tea, and then went off home.

Although Phyllis had had such a rough time with Sandra – it had been a breach birth – she was back at work within a fortnight, looking after the students and running Dial House again. That summer Sir Lawrence and Lady Bragg stayed with us. (A former Nobel prizewinner for physics, he was at that time the

Cavendish Professor of Experimental Physics at Cambridge.) Lady Bragg insisted on returning from Scolt every evening, so that she could give Sandra her six o'clock feed. She also looked quite 'at home' changing nappies (diapers) and pitching in with all the little less than glamorous chores associated with a four-month-old baby. Phyllis certainly appreciated this unlooked-for help.

This distinguished couple were typical of the fantastic people we met in the course of our lives in those early days.

The following winter disaster struck the coastal areas, not only of Norfolk but of other low-lying parts of Britain's east coast and similar areas of the European continent facing the North Sea. Holland, in particular, suffered severe damage and considerable loss of life.

The east coast flood of January 31, 1953 was the most devastating in history. Bungalows had been built south of Hunstanton, on a low-lying area behind the sea wall. Within seconds of the sea breaking over the wall they were flooded to the eaves. Two of our friends, who had moved there from Brancaster Staithe the previous October, were among those drowned.

At Cley the sea also broke over the sea wall, drowning livestock on the fresh marshes. The depth of water was so great that dead sheep were left hanging from the telegraph wires. The loss of land birds also must have been great, as they would have been roosting in large numbers in the flooded areas.

The wind was tremendous – no lesser word would describe it at all accurately. Some idea of its strength can be gained from the fact that, at its height, it was impossible to walk straight into it – we had to lean at an angle of forty-five degrees. Seagulls, blown into hedges, were impaled on the thorns.

The cause was a massive low pressure system centred to the the north of the British Isles. This produced a north-west wind which, after remaining at gale force for two entire days, reached gusts of ninety miles per hour on the third, January 31.

The morning tide – at an exceptionally high (spring) level – was unable to ebb fully. By three o'clock the sea was already at the predicted level for that evening's high tide. The wind's magnitude forced water in front of it, creating a 'wall' which surged downwind towards the east. Being unable to pass between Britain and the continent, this huge volume of water spilled over the low-lying areas, when the evening tide built to unprecedented levels.

In all 27,000 acres (mostly agricultural land) were inundated along the east coast of Britain. Eighty-five people were killed and an estimated five thousand more made homeless. In addition to the enormous stock losses and damage to property, the flooded agricultural land could not be cropped until the soil had been neutralised.

At the time there was no national flood warning system – it took this disaster to prove the necessity for one.

The surge ('a wall of water eight feet high,' according to some eyewitnesses) hit Brancaster harbour, quickly flooding Dial House despite its standing some twelve feet above the predicted level. I suppose, with hindsight, we should have been warned by the tidal situation that day. What fooled me was the slow rise in the water level between three o'clock and five. It seemed there was nothing to be alarmed about.

On checking again at five o'clock, after dark, I found the water level to be less than that of the highest of the spring tides of the March to September period. I shone my torch to the north, into the harbour. The sight I witnessed was fantastic. Huge waves were rolling up the harbour and breaking on the Hard. Boats which had broken free from their moorings were being pounded on the shoreline, just thirty yards from where I stood by my barn.

I stayed watching for a short time. Tiles, ripped from the roof by the wind, were crashing down around me. Others were being blown some twenty-five to thirty yards. Conditions similar to these had occurred in the past, flooding our outbuildings. Dial House itself had not been flooded in the twenty-four years that the Chestneys had lived there. So, convincing myself that everything would be all right, I returned indoors.

At five twenty-five I again went to check the height of the tide. Phyllis was waiting for the football results on the wireless (no television in those days!)

While I was outside, Dick English, our next door neighbour (I had been with his father, Stanley, in the Dornier episode) arrived to tell us his house, which stood at a lower level to ours, was flooded. He enquired about the safety of the pig – won by Phyllis at the village fête the previous August. She told Dick I was outside and he came hurrying to find me.

In the meantime I had gone into the backyard, where I was wading in water six inches deep, trying to reach the pig. The water was rising very rapidly.

Taking a rope from the wall I eventually managed to get it round the pig's neck, just as Dick arrived. The water was now two feet deep. The poor pig had only its head showing above the flood. However we managed to drag it from the shed across the yard. Then suddenly the water was waist deep – the six-foot boundary wall had collapsed, due to the action of the waves. As my ferret hut was attached to this wall I tried to return to save them; but the waves were too great.

With the wall gone and the wooden sides to the coal barn torn free, marsh vegetation and pieces of wood swamped the yard. Dragging the pig behind us, we battled through this debris to reach the shelter of the higher inner yard.

A pig, at the best of times, is a most difficult animal to persuade to do anything; but somehow or other we managed to coax this one along with us, and eventually arrived at the outhouse (the old brewhouse). This was at the same level as the house itself, some four feet higher than where the pig was normally kept. Of course we never imagined the water would reach here.

However just as we were drying the pig off and securing it in a corner the water came rushing through the door. We couldn't find the rope we had used earlier, so, grabbing the pig, we carried it through the house – which at this stage was quite dry. We then continued the other side of the house, across the village green to Lester Southerland's house. This was an old farmhouse whose outbuildings included a pigsty. Even above the roar of the wind the squealing of the pig could be heard. One would have thought it was being killed.

Shortly after this the water entered Dial House. Sandra was only nine months old. To her water meant one thing – bathtime. As it came under the door of the room where they were sitting she said to Phyllis, 'Bathtime, Mummy!'

I returned home to find the water two inches deep. The power points were all on the skirting boards. Knowing that electricity and water don't mix, I turned the power off at the mains, thus plunging the house into total darkness. The water, rising quickly, soon reached the fire in the Rayburn. With a whoosh of steam the fire door burst open, showering hot coals and ashes into the room.

The water continued to rise. So, with no fire and only torchlight to see by, we took Phyllis and the baby upstairs. We were closely followed by the two dogs and Jimmy the cat, who had jumped onto the sideboard to escape getting wet. Sandra was wrapped in a blanket and Phyllis was left with a torch. The whole house was freezing cold. Water was coming through the ceilings of the two north-facing bedrooms, due to spray being blown over the house. Rooms on the south side were, however, dry – thank goodness!

Leaving the family safe, dry and comparatively warm, Dick and I returned downstairs, to find the water had reached the top of the dining room table – approximately two feet four inches (the height at which it would remain in the house before eventually receding). The time was six fifteen, and by now news of the flood had spread; but friends arriving to help couldn't reach us due to the depth of water. As soon as it receded they negotiated all manner of flotsam and rubbish to climb in the lounge window. One good friend, Harry Wyatt, who lived close by, came to find out what was being done about the baby, being concerned about her above anything.

I must admit the situation was frightening. Onlookers told of seeing huge waves breaking over Dial House and thought at the time that we should be washed away. Harry insisted that Sandra be taken somewhere warm and dry. He was unable to take her to his own home because his wife was about to have a baby herself, and he was afraid of upsetting her. So he took Sandra to his next door neighbour, Ivy Nudds. We knew she would be in good hands there.

News of the flood reached the Jolly Sailors. Other friends rose to the occasion. Downing their pints in a hurry they came to offer assistance. Basil Davey – a good friend since our schooldays together – was the only one without wellies, so he rolled his flannel trousers above his knees, hung his shoes – tied by their laces – round his neck, and stayed barefoot until one o'clock the next morning helping to bale out the water, until the floor was relatively dry.

Two other friends, Bill and Gaby Adams – the local squire and his wife – arrived prepared to roll up their sleeves and get stuck in.

I suggested that we three went across to the Sailing Club, to see what we could salvage there (they were both founder members of the club). The clubhouse was about twenty-five yards from Dial House, but on slightly lower ground. As we crossed the road I shone my torch in the direction of the clubhouse. It was a converted wooden whelk house. Originally whelks had been boiled there in a copper – two bushels at a time in a wicker basket. The sail shed and store locker had originally been used for storing and tarring the whelk pots. A third shed, the same size as the other two, had been retained by the owner.

The wooden buildings had been totally wrecked and lay scattered on the high tide level. It was clear that nothing could be achieved that night, and that it would be dangerous to clamber about the wreckage in the dark. With great difficulty I persuaded Bill and Gaby to return to the safety and warmth of their own home.

Jason Borthwick sent a message to say that he would have a vehicle standing by to evacuate us if the tide looked like flooding us again. The cellar was still full of water, but that would have to wait until daylight. A very tired and cold work party had had enough. Everyone was ready for bed. It had been a traumatic eight-and-a-half hours and the time was now 2 am. Strange to relate, though, no-one – not even Basil – caught cold!

Dial House was cold, wet and uninviting. Lester insisted we spend the remainder of the night at his house. On our way we collected Sandra. Ivy and Bert were reluctant to let her go – she was fast asleep and settled (I think she was the only Chestney to sleep at all that night!)

In the morning the wind had moderated; but what a mess greeted us both inside and out. The debris around the house may have been unbelievable; but the mayhem within was devastating. Words could not describe the scene. Phyllis just stood and cried.

The floor was covered with two inches of mud. The smell of it – due to the large quantity of fine pieces of dead marsh weed in it – was indescribable. It covered everything to the height the water had reached. It was heartbreaking.

After removing seven bucketfuls of it from the lounge, it then took one hundred and thirty bucketfuls of water to remove all traces of the filth. So, gradually, we cleared and cleaned each room, sorting out what could be salvaged.

Being in part Jacobean, Dial House has walls two and a half feet thick. Water seeped from them for weeks, and the walls remained damp up to the flood level. The RAF spent a day trying to dry the place out with their hot arc blowers; but as soon as the atmosphere became damp the moisture returned. Even the heat from three fires, kept burning day and night took a week to make any noticeable impression.

The walls of the outbuildings were stacked high with all kinds of debris – tons of vegetation ripped from the saltmarsh and reedbeds. Tommy Large's old coal barn – a wooden structure one hundred and twenty feet by sixty – had been totally demolished. Its remains had ended up around Dial House, adding to the debris. It ended up in sections around the house, together with several smashed boats. All this debris piled up made it impossible to get out of the house, other than through the south-facing window.

The only structural damage, however, was to the north-facing boundary wall. How the outhouses had withstood the battering beats me! I do know that I was relieved to see the barn undamaged except for a few missing tiles as here, stored for the winter, was my motorboat.

Apart from the structural damage, the mess and the inconvenience caused by the flood, plus the loss of our personal effects, a further legacy of it was the destruction of my father's notebooks and Scolt Head records, and of many historic and irreplaceble photographs. In all, it took two weeks to clear up the mess. We were by then determined to be more prepared in future, should flooding be likely.

Scolt Head also suffered considerable damage from the flooding. Due to this one exceptional tide a minimum of twenty yards was lost from its north-facing dunes, along the entire length of the island. Approximately one-sixth of the dune system disappeared and, about 11 miles east of the Hut, a section of the low dunes was totally cut away, creating a channel for the high tides to flood through onto the saltmarsh. This area became known as 'The Breakthrough' – a name which persists to the present day. Despite this gap being sealed by the (then) Norfolk River Board, subsequent wave action undermined the 'fence' and eventually some 600 yards were totally eroded. With time, however, a natural shingle movement up the beach took place, partly compensating for the earlier losses, increasing the land height at the Breakthrough sufficiently to stop all but the highest spring tides from flooding over it.

CHAPTER TWELVE

Views on Rabbits

The short sea crossing to Scolt Head – tranquil most of the summer – at times held its own perils. The season following the flood Alfie Chilvers started operating a ferry to Scolt Head. He had acquired a twenty-four foot motorboat for the purpose. On June 2 – Coronation Day – the wind reached gale force and the rain bucketed down. Nevertheless, eight people insisted on visiting Scolt. 'Don't take them, Alfie' I advised.

'I gotta,' Alfie said. 'They're booked up.'

So away we went. It was bad enough in the harbour but when we turned the corner conditions worsened considerably. Green water was breaking over the bow and the boat was filling up to the floorboards. It was frightening, with the waves coming at us some four feet high and four to five feet apart. However Alfie kept chugging on.

'Alfie, turn her round,' I pleaded.

'I'm too frightened to turn her round!' he protested. Suddenly, though, there was a bit of a lull. Pulling him to one side I grabbed the tiller and put it hard over, to go downwind with the waves. Just as I turned, however, one came rolling up on the quarter. We hadn't fully turned to run with the waves, and we caught it, shipping several hundred gallons of water. The boat just stopped dead, wallowing there. Then, eventually, she started to pick up again, and off we went. When we got back safely all Alfie could say was, 'I'm glad we di'nt go all the way across!'

We used to do the bookings for him, as I had operated the boat prior to this time. People would ring us up to book and it worked to my own advantage. I knew everyone who was coming.

The resources of the Norfolk Naturalists' Trust and National Trust jointly responsible for the financial and administrative costs of Scolt Head and Dial

House, and for the warden's wages – had become greatly depleted. The structural stability of Dial House itself had been weakened by the January floods, so I was relieved when the situation was resolved. Professor Steers approached the Nature Conservancy – a government-funded body recently set up to promote nature conservation and to establish sites of scientific interest – to take over both Scolt and Dial House. After negotiations were completed, the Conservancy took over in October 1954. The Scolt Head Management Committee ceased to function as such, but remained intact as the Scolt Head Advisory Committee.

As the renovations at Dial House would take twelve months to complete, we moved out to my sister-in-law, Betty Rutland's house. Other changes to our way of life were occurring during 1954 too (not all of them to our benefit). The same month that the Conservancy took over the management of Scolt Head a fresh disaster – not, I am certain, connected with the change! – hit Scolt Head and me personally. Myxomatosis had already virtually wiped out the mainland rabbit population. It now arrived on the island. Rabbits were part of my wages – as they had been in Father's time – and my financial status that winter suffered acutely.

The disease is transmitted by fleas commonly found on rabbit ears, which are held there tightly secured by the proboscis. While the rabbit remains alive the flea stays attached; but immediately the rabbit is dead a change of blood temperature occurs. The flea unlatches, to seek a new live host. Crows and gulls can easily become the new hosts (for how long I cannot say) while eating the dead carcasses, and I assume that this was how myxomatosis arrived at Scolt.

Doe rabbits average four young per litter between March and September. Before the disease the Scolt rabbit population was estimated annually at some eight thousand on October 1.

Views, including those of the committee, were divided about rabbits on the reserve. Conservationists and ecologists argued that they were a beneficial species. By grazing the vegetation, especially on the dunes, they encouraged a greater variety of plants to flourish (including 'ecosystem' species, early in the year). During late summer the shorter vegetation also reduced the fire risk. The grazing of saltmarsh (the main feeding area and food source throughout most of the year) also resulted in a larger variety of plants retained longer over the years. Botanists saw rabbits in a different light. Some advocated extermination, others strict control. They argued that grazing of the dunes resulted in erosion, and in areas becoming 'mobile', so that natural plant succession could not develop.

I attempted, as my father had done, to maintain a reasonable balance between the two extreme views, thus hoping to keep both parties happy.

My father had introduced tame rabbits to add new blood to the original stock, as it had become closely interbred and undersized. Following the arrival of myxomatosis, does produced young virtually throughout the year – litters of six to eight being found commonly each month. These were thought to be the result of reduced pressure on the does, due to fewer bucks being present, and also to reduced stoat numbers – in turn because of the myxomatosis destroying their food.

Possibly to alleviate the loss of young to stoats, doe rabbits on Scolt (and probably elsewhere) have them away from the main warrens. These nursery stop-holes are usually fleet (shallow) and no more than two metres in length. Each time the doe feeds the young the hole is opened, then totally sealed on her departure. Material from the excavated hole is spread, flattened and firmly packed. It takes an experienced eye to detect a stop-hole but stoats and weasels become experienced in finding the entrances. I do not think it is the scent given off by the young which betrays them but that deposited by the doe during the packing down of material in sealing the hole. I have yet to discover where a stoat has entered a stop-hole except by the front entrance.

On Scolt the majority of these nursery holes are made between the winter storm and low spring tidelines. When strong north-northwesterly winds occur during the period April to June they increase the height of the tide beyond the norm. The stop-holes are flooded and virtually all the young rabbits are drowned.

Five hundred does could produce litters of four young each month. By the first week in July the young would also be breeding, and so on. Imagine, then, the rabbit explosion by the end of September! Such a large concentration of rabbits obviously supports predatory species in particular the stoat. (Foxes were 'discouraged' from staying on the reserve. Those that succeeded in reaching the island had a very limited stay, since a vixen at a certain time of the year would soon attract dog foxes.)

The annual stoat population prior to myxomatosis was estimated at between fifty and sixty – twelve to fourteen per mile – on October 1. There was no reason to reduce stoat numbers to any degree, as they played an important role, especially in rough winters, when I was unable to visit the island to maximise reduction of rabbit numbers myself.

Stoats were, however, controlled at the ternery during the breeding season, and trapped at random along with rabbits throughout the winter. These two forms of control proved satisfactory prior to myxomatosis, maintaining a reasonable balance between rabbit and stoat populations.

The first sign of myxomatosis was on October 20, 1954. Within six weeks the disease had spread over the entire reserve, virtually wiping out the rabbit population. By December I thought that every one had died. Even footmarks were absent from the sand. On January 6 and 7, after an appreciable fall of snow (which remained for four days), I decided to cover everywhere I should have expected to find rabbits.

I discovered evidence of a single rabbit in twelve different areas, recording in my notes at the time: "I bet the total rabbit population of Scolt does not exceed twenty."

Over the same two days I was also able to estimate the stoat population, by noting footmarks in the snow. It did not exceed ten. In addition, two weasel tracks were seen, leading to a well-used hole surrounded by mouse and shrew remains. (Weasels had always been a rare species on Scolt – their increase in the following few years would lead to the highest figure ever recorded there. A decrease, to between four and six across the entire reserve, would correspond with a fresh increase in stoat numbers.)

Subsequently rabbit numbers would slowly increase to between 2000 and 2500. Myxomatosis would reoccur periodically, reducing them by varying percentages up to 90%. The stoat increase would prove slow, and eventually reach a fluctuating number between twenty and thirty. One year short-eared owls killed at least five, without eating them.

CHAPTER THIRTEEN

Egg Thieves and Diplomacy

Phyllis's lot in those days was no easy one, especially where looking after the students was concerned. Cooking was done on Mother's old black-leaded coal stove and, as there was no bathroom, she not only had to carry all the water upstairs but also to cart the slops down again. She had shopping to carry home by hand, plus a baby to manage. As I have said before, I returned home at ungodly hours for meals. So Phyllis was 'tied' to Dial House and I was in a similar situation in the summer at Scolt Head. We were never seen out together, and many people thought she was an unmarried mother!

Fortunately she had two staunch helpers – her Mum and Betty. The three of them certainly made a formidable team. Gran would do the washing and prepare vegetables in the kitchen, while Phyllis and Betty did the clearing out, feeding and waitressing. Without Betty, Phyllis believes she would have been unable to cope. Their *pièce de résistance* was undoubtedly a party of twenty-seven students from Lancaster University. Twenty-seven packed lunches were required, on top of twenty-seven breakfasts and twenty-seven dinners. Phyllis refused point blank to get up at five thirty in the morning to prepare the lunches single-handed. So three girls (different ones each day) would be got up to assist her.

At times like that Phyllis thought What am I doing here? This is madness!

Our second daughter, Catherine, was born at Dial House on October 13, 1956. Unlike Sandra's birth this was, fortunately, a normal, straightforward event.

One year I was in bed with quinsy. This was in the middle of summer, which was certainly not an ideal time to be laid up! All hell was let loose in Dial House. Phyllis had to cope with everything and everybody. Not having mains water we relied solely upon our own engine and well, and had to pump water up. There was no way Phyllis could manage this. Fortunately, the six students we had staying with us at the time were in the charge of Professor Steers.

'Right boys,' he commanded. 'Every night we'll have one hundred turns each on the handle, to get Mrs Chestney enough water to last her the next day!'

Later on the students would change, both in their attitudes and manners. They would be less appreciative and forever demanding. They wouldn't change for dinner, just come in in dirty gear and loll around the place. They were a different class altogether from those boys of the early days. We wouldn't have changed those times – there was always a house full of laughter. We had a wonderful time.

Many of those students from the early days kept in touch. Often they would turn up years afterwards and say,' Do you remember me – I'm so-and-so?' And they would feed back information to me from, say, the Ministry of Agriculture before it became published, knowing that it would be of interest to me.

The cross-section of people I met as warden certainly made me see humans in a fresh light. There were always the clever ones, for example, who knew it all and needed no advice from the warden. I reacted differently, according to each individual group.

I had had a good tutor. My father had taught me the 'tricks of the trade' while discussing the many awkward customers he had encountered. It had been his philosophy to wait for the know-all to make a fool of himself (after being set up for this purpose). Then he and the rest of the group would cause no further trouble. One should never appear too clever with know-alls. It was often an advantage to appear 'thick'; with a Norfolk accent it was possible to achieve the impossible! My father and I considered ourselves to be showmen – we had the greatest show on earth. Despite originally believing that everyday happenings were common knowledge, it eventually dawned on me that this was not so.

With the exception of Professor Steers, even the Scolt Head Committee was not totally aware of what it was all about. When they came on their annual visit to the ternery each summer I gave them a run down of the happenings and details of progress from the previous year. I expected them to be up to date with the information given in previous years and from the annual report. Rereading my annual reports today, there seems little indication there of what success the terns achieved thanks to the new management at Scolt; so perhaps I was to blame in expecting the commmittee to grasp the information and be up to date with events.

Ted Eales, warden of Blakeney Point (who, like me, had followed his father in the job), couldn't understand why there were nests at Scolt later than at Blakeney. Thinking he was in the know, I explained to him that when virtually all the nests on the 'route' had hatched I made up dummy nests by using eggs which had been flooded by the high tides of late July. These remained for visitors to see, until the terns that had successfully nested moved off with their young.

This system worked satisfactorily. School holidays did not commence until August 1 – by which time there were few, if any, genuine nests with eggs. Having noted both children's and parents' disappointment I felt there was no harm in 'extending' the season by another two weeks for their benefit. Perhaps, if I could 'send them away happy' they would, like the terns, return in future years.

This slight deception also helped the ferrymen financially. When the breeding season finished the number of visitors to the island had formerly dropped considerably. By working in close cooperation with the boatmen I could better ensure that they continued to use a single landing and departure point for the passengers, thus in turn helping me keep disturbance of breeding birds to a minimum.

The first week in the August following my chat with Ted Eales a group of passengers landed. On meeting them I was asked, 'How many nests shall we see?'

'Although the season is well advanced there are sufficient nests remaining to make it worth the trip.'

They roared with laughter, and I began to suspect that something was amiss. I asked if they had visited Blakeney.

'Oh yes, we know Teddy very well.' (Knowing that only Ted's relations and close friends called him that, I suspected he must have given my secrets away.)

We stopped at one of the two genuine nests in the twenty that were strategically placed for visitors to see. I said, 'This is a common tern nest – one of the few remaining. The eggs will successfully hatch in the next two days.'

Before I could say any more they were laughing their heads off again. One of them slapped me on the shoulder and said, 'We know all about your little tricks!'

I picked up one of the eggs (previously examined, so that I knew full well that it was 'chipped') and placed it to the ear of one of the women. When she heard the chick calling inside she told the rest of the group. They had to listen.

We continued the tour. I pointed out the dummy nests, but didn't stop to examine them. We eventually came to the second genuine nest, which we carefully examined. Once again they could hear the chick calling and the bill tapping the shell as it struggled to emerge. They asked why 'Teddy' had told them they would see only dummy nests.

'I haven't the faintest idea,' I replied airily.

What they said to Ted on their return and what his explanation was I don't know. Next time I saw him I said, 'Your family thought they were going to have a good time at my expense when they came to Scolt; but I have a suspicion that the laugh was on them!

Although the Bird Protection Act of 1924 had given nesting terns legal protection from egg collectors, it had been several years before this was accepted by the local people. Understandably so, since seabird eggs provided not only a modest income, when sold to hotels, but also a source of food in the summer and winter (when pickled in water glass). I must admit they are most palatable, especially when hard-boiled!

During my years as warden, however, the threat to the eggs came not so much from those wanting to eat the eggs, or to sell them for small amounts to hotels to supplement their meagre wages, but from collectors augmenting their cabinet displays.

The dodges used to obtain them were limitless, although in the majority of cases the collectors gave themselves away. Tern eggs were (and still are) among the most sought-after by collectors, despite the high fines now imposed. Sandwich tern eggs were the most highly prized. Their colour range is vast – I have seen eggs ranging from totally black to all-white – with markings representing butterflies, ducks, sheep and even, in one instance, of an elephant, as clearly marked as if painted by an artist. Even the 'ordinary' type of Sandwich tern egg would sell for a pound, in the 'fifties, while a more unusual type could earn the thief £20 or more.

The professionals were relatively easy to pick out from the father who just wanted an egg for his little boy. Usually they arrived in pairs. Their uniform tanned outdoor appearance, rucksack or dufflebag (though I didn't overlook handbags, and I even caught one young couple concealing eggs in their child's beach bucket!) and binoculars, which always remained in the case, marked them as a 'species' apart.

On landing they separated themselves from the other visitors and showed no interest in the terns flying overhead or along the shoreline. Being met at the noticeboard by a grinning warden they had hitherto purposefully ignored was no doubt something they hadn't bargained for. They had expected to wander among the nesting seabird colonies as they did on other reserves.

As I gained knowledege, experience and understanding not only of the wild species but of the human one too, I found the latter to be the more cunning, devious and unpredictable.

I regarded egg collecting by boys as a phase, like collecting stamps, cigarette cards or steam engine numbers – something they would tire of. In some cases this childhood hobby did in fact serve as an introduction to natural history. (Two lads whom I caught collecting eggs on Scolt in the early days are today doctors of zoology.) However, most egg thieves showed in an exchange of glances that they considered us too 'thick' to have recognised their characteristics. So the game was to play along with this assumption, without revealing any suspicions. I discovered that egg collectors came from all walks of life including titled persons.

I rarely prosecuted, preferring to discuss the ethics of the hobby; but one time, knowing that two Leeds University students had taken some, I stopped them on the way to the departure point and asked for the eggs they were carrying in their binocular cases. Of course they swore that they hadn't taken any. I asked four other visitors to stay, as I needed witnesses if I searched the students. One burly gentleman remarked, 'If you think they have eggs in their possession go ahead and search them.'

After much protest they handed over their binocular cases. I found six little tern and two oystercatcher eggs in one case, while the other held four little tern, three common tern and four redshank eggs. After taking their names and addresses I escorted them to the ferry. I did prosecute them, and they were each fined £25.

On another occasion a couple started to wander off on their own; but after I had explained the procedure they decided to remain with the party. The husband said he was an ornithologist and would like to be put in a position where he could watch the terns. This I did, and then continued with the rest of the party. On my return I stopped to chat with him and realised that he couldn't tell a tern from a bull's foot! (I found that few egg collectors knew anyhing about the birds or the eggs they collected.) As we chatted his wife said she wasn't interested in our bird talk, so she would go for a walk. I explained why the ternery was restricted to the general public and pointed out the boundary, clearly marked with white posts, adding warningly, 'I hope I don't catch you in the restricted area.'

As she walked away her husband positioned himself so that I had to turn my back to the ternery in order to talk to him. About ten minutes later I heard common terns calling from the east boundary line area. About thirty birds were circling high over their nests inside the restricted area. From my position I was unable to see the cause of the disturbance as low dunes obscured my view.

I said to the man, 'Stay here while I check on the cause of that disturbance.' (I already had an idea of what it might be.)

When I got there it was no surprise to see his wife a hundred yards inside the restricted area. Approaching from behind I put my hand on her shoulder. With a start she dropped the tin she was holding and looked round. I picked up the tin and inspected its contents. Concealed in cotton wool were two common tern eggs. I escorted her out of the ternery to where her husband was waiting.

'I had no idea that my wife was doing such a stupid thing,' he said. 'Come off it,' I retorted. 'You came here prepared with a tin full of cotton wool. You didn't think your little ruse would work did you? We wardens aren't idiots – you should never go by looks! Please follow me – I want you on the next ferry.'

Alfie remarked as he landed the ferry, 'What, another two, Bob?'

'Yes,' I answered, 'they never learn!'

Another encounter was with a young lady whose sole possessions seemed to be her bikini and dufflebag. As she approached within some two hundred yards of the ternery she took the bag off her shoulder, did something to it on the ground then replaced it and continued walking.

I told some friends with me, 'That's the prettiest egg collector I've ever seen!'

They were sceptical; but later I caught her red-handed, with some Sandwich tern eggs. It transpired that she was stealing them for a male friend whom she had left on Brancaster beach. The business with the dufflebag – which she had been preparing to receive eggs – had given her away at the outset.

The ruses egg collectors thought up were many and varied. One day eight people landed by ferry. One man hastily approached me saying, 'I'm a keen ornithologist and photographer. I should like to visit the ternery on my own.'

At the same time he reached into his pocket, took out a fiver and offered it to me. I ignored it.

'Visitors have two choices during the breeding season,' I told him. 'One is to accompany the warden on his conducted tour of the nesting area; the alternative is to go off on their own and to keep outside the ternery.'

'If I go on my own, shall I see Sandwich tern nests?' he asked.

'No.'

He decided to join the main party. Several times he repeated, 'Shall we see Sandwich tern nests? Shall we get near them?' – questions which the average visitor doesn't ask. I also noticed that although he had a camera he made no attempt to take any photographs. However I kept cool and answered all his questions in my usual matter-of-fact way.

We arrived at the nesting group of some 150 pairs of Sandwich terns. No eggs had actually hatched; but many were chipped, and the young could be heard calling inside the shells. I showed each of the visitors in turn the little white egg-tooth on the top of the bill, working away to chip out, and told them to listen to the chick calling. I explained that within a week all the eggs in this group would have hatched, thinking this might deter my suspected egg collector. As we moved away he asked if he could remain to take a few photographs.

'Certainly,' I replied. 'But don't be long.'

The rest of us carried on; but I was keeping my 'north eye' on him. He at least went through the motions of taking photographs. Then he took a handkerchief from his pocket to wipe the lens. With it still in his hand he knelt down, as though to get a close-up of the eggs. After looking my way and obviously believing I was occupied with the rest of the party, quick as a flash he picked up an egg, placed it in the handkerchief, stood up again and wiped the camera lens. Then he replaced the handkerchief, plus egg, in his pocket.

I was the only one to have witnessed this action. Not wanting to let him know that I was aware of what he had done I said nothing as he rejoined the party. Ten yards further on I stopped and said, 'Listen!' (The birds were returning to their nests.) 'Can you hear that one call above all the rest?'

Everyone agreed that it was different. With apparent conviction I said that the bird was telling me she had no eggs to return to.

Turning to the group I asked everyone to check the soles of their shoes, to see if someone had trodden on an egg. Naturally, they were all clean; so I said, 'Then someone has taken an egg.'

I asked several of the party if they had taken an egg. Receiving a negative reply from each of them, I then turned to the man whom I knew to have the egg and asked, 'Have you taken an egg?'

His answer was also a curt, 'Certainly not!'

I reminded him that he had been the last person at the nest site, and therefore had had the best opportunity of taking one. I told them all that I should soon find out who did, in fact, have it. My next ruse was to ask the suspect to walk back towards the nest site. As he approached the birds they took to the air. Not surprisingly, as they flew over his head one bird dived at him, repeatedly calling at him in aggressive fashion.

'Right, you – back home!' I shouted. 'That's certain proof that you're the culprit.'

He returned to the group. I told him he had two choices: he could give me back any eggs he had taken, so I could return them to the nest, and I should then escort him to the departure point to catch the ferry; or, if he insisted that he'd not taken an egg, then, as a special constable with the 'power of search', I should indeed search him. If I should find an egg in his possession I should not hesitate to prosecute.

For several seconds he remained speechless. One woman said, 'Give Mr Chestney the egg, you scoundrel! The bird has proved you've got it.'

Putting his hand in his pocket, he took out the handkerchief containing the egg and handed it to me. Most of the others gasped when he produced it. I heard one of them say, 'The birds were right.'

I replaced the egg in the empty nest cup. When I returned to the party the culprit was totally deflated. All his 'bounce' had disappeared. With no further ado I escorted him to the departure point. Before he boarded the ferry I said, 'People like you aren't welcome on Scolt Head. Don't come back while I am warden!'

The voice of the 'robbed' bird remained a topic of conversation among that party for the rest of their stay on the island. What they didn't know, however (and I certainly wasn't going to tell them) was that it had actually been a male bird, with a more guttural voice than the others, anxious to get back to his chipping egg! To me this had been no unusual call.

Egg collectors really were a nuisance; outwitting wardens became as important to them as obtaining eggs. If it was a challenge to them to get the eggs off Scolt, it was also one to me to prevent them from doing so! I had to catch them in possession of eggs – if they suspected my intentions, incriminating evidence was quickly disposed of. I have, purely by chance, approached people who, on seeing me, have dropped eggs onto the ground and walked away. I have searched them, to reinforce their belief that I was aware of their activities; but in such a situation it was a complete waste of time. Without eggs actually on them there was no case to answer. Perhaps not all collectors who took eggs from Scolt were caught but I am confident that not too many succeeded.

One group of young egg thieves, however, does deserve special mention – if only because of the important role one of its members in particular was to play later on in the Scolt Head story.

I first met Gordon Howell in 1956 when he was fifteen. He was in the forefront of the beatnik trend, with long hair reaching halfway down his back. His mates had nicknamed him Rajah – no doubt due to the genuine Pandit Nehru-style jacket he always wore and which, from its appearance, he also slept in.

As a small boy he had spent a considerable amount of time in the company of his grandfather, a retired naval petty officer. His grandmother was related to four or five different local families; but for some reason of his own the grandfather didn't get on with any of them. There is no doubt that Gordon was greatly influenced by him and not always for the best. He was, in fact, a tearaway and a loner.

He was with his brother David and two friends, Mike and Colin Softley, when I apprehended them egg-stealing. In previous years they had collected eggs over a six-mile radius of Scolt, and few species were missing from their collections.

Sandwich tern was one of them. I was certain that they had been responsible for taking common tern eggs from the ternery earlier in the season.

Eventually I did catch them taking Sandwich tern eggs. They stood there shamefacedly, not saying a word. Then Mike blurted out, 'What are you going to do with us?'

I replied, 'As you know, the National Trust as guardian of Scolt Head and its nesting birds considers this to be a very serious offence. But it's up to me what measure should be taken. First, I want your assurance that you will all keep out of the ternery during the breeding season. I am prepared to teach you about and show you all the terns and the variations and range of eggs, if you are genuinely interested. If you agree to my conditions I'm prepared to drop the egg-collecting case.'

Without hesitation they agreed. I didn't see them again that season; but the following year, before the birds had even started to lay, I saw them walking across the harbour towards the ternery. When they arrived at the notice they stopped. I made them wait half an hour before joining them. From then on they came virtually every day that it was safe to walk across the channel. During the season I took them into the restricted area. By the end of the summer they had learned to appreciate all the setbacks nesting birds had to overcome, without humans taking their eggs.

They became very interested, were soon good ornithologists and in the autumn further extended their knowledge by helping me with the mist-netting of passage migrants. We all became very good friends and they helped me in my many duties, becoming expert in the tidal and boating aspects of the job.

Local inhabitants had never been orientated towards terns. The old fishermen continually claimed that although they had nested on Scolt for years, since it had become a sanctuary there were nothing like the numbers there had been 'in the days when they were boys'.

I approached each fisherman in turn, explaining the reasons why I thought it necessary to restrict visitors and locals alike. If they could refrain from collecting driftwood from the time the terns arrived until at least mid-July, this would be an advantage not only to the old birds nesting but also to younger nest-prospecting birds.

However I received no positive answer from any of them. All they managed to convey was that they felt this restriction was 'the thin end of the wedge' and that it would be followed by further restrictions and eventually lead to them losing all their rights and privileges regarding Scolt Head.

I could only reply, 'While I am warden here it won't happen. Remember I am also a local person; without your help I certainly cannot achieve what I have set out to do.'

Being single-handed on the island meant things were fairly tough for me. I was already working an eighty-hour week during the season; but even more time needed to be spent there in order to maintain vigilance at all times of the day. Proof that the new management plan was working could be seen in the increase in the number of chicks successfuly fledged at the ternery, however, so in 1957 I finally persuaded the Nature Conservancy that an assistant was warranted. I told them they must first advertise the post locally. One person only answered the advertisement and he was to start on May 1 for a period of eight weeks.

I contacted him one week prior to this starting date to explain his duties when I had finished he said, 'I have decided not to take the job.'

Slightly taken aback I asked why, adding that it wouldn't interfere with his swinner (shore crab) catching (they were used to bait the whelk pots). 'Or your collecting brood mussels,' I added. (These are small mussels not yet of saleable size which are put in beds, or lays, to grow big enough to sell.)

He replied, 'It's got nothing to do with that. I would have to stop local people – many of them my own relations – from doing the things they've done for years. I've been persuaded not to take the job.'

As there was now a rush to find another warden the job was advertised nationally. On May 12 the successful applicant arrived. He was Jim Kinnis, who had just finished his National Service in the RAF. His parents had divorced, his uncle was a doctor and he hadn't an idea in his head about birds – literally unable to tell one from another. He had no notion of conservation – though he was eager to learn and was, at least, good company! When he first came he couldn't even swim; but I did manage to teach him that! He was employed during the eight weeks officially only when the 'tide was in'; but even he, though somewhat divorced from the reality at Scolt, realised within two weeks that unless he covered the maximum time possible (ie the hours of daylight) it would be a total waste of time.

It took most of the eight weeks to familiarise him with the basics, let alone for him to become capable of operating a boat in all weathers, understanding the tides, getting to know the reserve and appeasing visitors who still resented the restrictions. What he did learn obviously took up my time and I argued strongly that a permanent summer warden would be the ideal answer.

However this was not to be – not for another four very trying seasons. Next year I had Peter Mountford for the first of the two seasons he spent with me. Like Jim he stayed with us at Dial House, so Phyllis now had someone else to look after on top of the students; and she had to cope with two of us coming home at all hours.

My next assistant was Ken Spenser, a good ornithologist and conservationist who had written a book on lapwings. Paul Leitzer whom I had got to know over a period of some years followed Ken and was my fourth assistant in five years. Still only sixteen with a public school education, Paul was quite experienced with boats, having his own small dinghy with an outboard which he operated from the harbour. A great asset to me was the fact that he was also a keen ornithologist; so I recommended him to the Nature Conservancy.

Of the thousands of people I spoke to on Scolt I came to know few well. Having a lot to do I couldn't afford the time to get involved with hangers-on, as they could be difficult to discourage. I suppose that in a funny sort of way I resented people coming to Scolt. In the early days I had let all and sundry know about any rare bird that turned up on the island. After a week all the fuss would die down; but I just couldn't afford a whole week to give birdwatchers my undivided attention. So people, for much of the time, became incidental.

One man visited the reserve every year for more than ten years. I recognised him each year, as I took him on the conducted tour, by several rather unusual characteristics. Firstly, he always wore a thick tweed suit, collar and tie and stout leather shoes, even on a boiling hot day. Secondly, he had a pronounced North Country accent.

'Hello, Mister Chestney,' he'd say, on meeting me. 'There's soom little ringed ploovers on t'beach, Mister Chestney.'

'I think you mean "ringed plover chicks",' I would correct him.

'Oh aye, that's right, Mister Chestney!'

I'd watch him go into the Cockle Bight in his swimming trunks and, because he failed to wade out far enough into deeper water, get himself covered in mud! This was evidently the highlight of this man's holiday. Who he was I shall never know; I knew nothing about him, except that he came to Norfolk every year and stayed in Hunstanton. One year he failed to arrive, though I shall never know why.

Another visitor came to the island for many years without my having an inkling as to his identity. On completion of the tour on what proved to be his last visit, I accompanied him to the departure point. While waiting for Alfie Chilvers we chatted. I said, 'After all the years you have been coming to Scolt I don't even know your name!'

'Farnon,' he replied. 'Sir William.' He explained that he was staying at the Moorings. 'I love this part of Norfolk, ' he said, 'and in particular Scolt. It was during one visit that I had the inspiration to make the design for the threepenny bit reverse a spray of thrift.'

I discovered that he was a writer of some note, as well. In later years he bought a house at Burnham Norton, overlooking the fresh marshes. What a fantastic view he would have had – of the windmill, the saltmarshes and all the coastline, including Scolt Head, from Brancaster to the Holkham pines. No wonder he could be inspired, sitting there on his veranda. Imagine a big tide all over the marshes, a very light east wind, and all the birds coming in. Sheer magic!

A sad note was struck in 1959 when Mrs Metz and her sister, Miss Edwards, arrived for their final stay at the Hut. They were by themselves this time. Both were in their eighties and Miss Edwards had become deaf. Her health was failing and she obviously sensed this would be her last visit. Each day I delivered their stores to the Hut; but the day before their departure they had forgotten to order enough bread to last them. I told them I should return on the evening tide with some.

It was a calm sunny evening Phyllis and her parents decided to accompany me and as this September spring tide was one of the highest of the year, completely covering the saltmarsh, it allowed the boat to sail right up to the edge of the sand dune and the steps leading to the Hut. The two ladies had followed our progress and were standing on the veranda waiting for us.

Both were dressed in black, their calf-length dresses revealing calf-length buttoned boots. With lace shawls draped over their shoulders, and black bonnets tied loosely under their chins, they looked as though they had stepped straight out of the 1850s.

While I talked to them my family climbed Flagpole Hill – the highest sand dune in Norfolk. The wind was a light easterly, the sky a clear blue. Visibility under such conditions is fantastic – with the naked eye they would have seen all the coast, from Gibralter Point to King's Lynn, together with all the shipping from the Wash ports. At this time of year, on such easterly winds, many species of birds arrive, rest and feed, before continuing their journeys south. On this occasion a group of whimbrel was calling as it passed overhead.

'What a fantastic sight and sound,' I declared. 'This heralds the approach of autumn and the longer nights!'

Miss Edwards asked me to repeat what I had said. This I did, adding, 'They're still calling.'

I whistled close to her ear imitating the passing whimbrel. She cried out, 'I can hear them! I can hear them – something I never thought to do again!'

While waiting for their nephew to collect them in his car Mrs Metz thanked me for making their stay so memorable. Her sister had been so thrilled to hear again the call of a whimbrel – a sound which, wherever she happened to be, always reminded her of Scolt Head.

CHAPTER FOURTEEN

Black-headed Gulls
and Shelduck

In common with wardens at other terneries my father had discouraged black-headed gulls – known to be egg-eating birds – from nesting in the ternery. I have known six hundred complete common tern clutches to be taken by predatory gulls in some seasons, while each season a considerable number of eggs and chicks was taken. It was no easy task to prevent this from happening. However, although Father had had an idea that not all black-headed gulls were 'rogues', he couldn't see how to separate egg-eaters from the others. All that entered the ternery were therefore shot. Until 1952 I continued as he had done, destroying indiscriminately – twenty-two in my first year. By 1957 the total of black-headed gulls I had thus 'discouraged' at Scolt was 87.

Observation showed up a tendency for Sandwich terns to nest round an oystercatcher, if one were present in their chosen area. They would not, however, nest close to a common tern, because – unlike oystercatchers – they were too aggressive.

For a couple of seasons I watched the black-headed gulls closely. If after seven to ten days at the ternery no robbing had been observed, I knew the gulls present must be non-predatory. During the period before laying these birds remained at the nest site except when leaving the ternery to feed. On the other hand, black-headed gulls searching the ternery were certain to be predatory egg-eaters.

One experiment I carried out in this connection was to place strategically a number of bantam eggs (which are small and almost tern egg size) on the perimeter of the ternery on a convenient embryo dune. Any gull alighting and eating an egg was shot. This method was used for eight seasons until 1960 with satisfactory results.

So I at last solved the problem of distinguishing the egg-eating black-headed gulls from others. They proved to be birds which had no association with the ternery other than the robbing aspect. They were always individuals, opportunists out to snatch an egg or chick where possible. Their persistence – even though their number was small – meant that few eggs survived until the main lay commenced.

It proved simple to distinguish these from the benign birds. Gulls which flew down the beach to the ternery, either singly or in pairs, without calling and taking no notice of anything, were all right. But those which came down incessantly calling 'kak-ak, kak-ak' would be birds which had already robbed nesting birds. They would be waiting for a response from the birds they were now interested in robbing. They would hover nervously over a nest, repeating the kak-ak call expecting the sitting bird to go after them. Even when repeatedly driven away from a particular nest they would return to hover over it.

After pinpointing and destroying these suspected rogue birds the crops and gizzards were examined in order to discover if I was really on the right track. (It would be a brave warden who could state categorically that every bird killed was a rogue, without such proof.) Virtually all of them did contain either shells of tern eggs or day-old chicks. Some contained eggshell and chicks of ringed plover.

A large percentage of these rogue birds, when examined, proved to be immature males, who had possibly been 'taught the business' by their parents.

After three seasons without predation by black-headed gulls I considered those remaining to be 'safe' and allowed them to nest successfully. Nesting numbers increased – to twenty to thirty pairs by 1964/5 – and only an occasional rogue bird now had to be destroyed. Once the gulls established themselves the Sandwich terns followed. One beneficial result of this was to do with human disturbance – people who walked up from the wreck early on in the season, or allowed dogs to run wild while they themselves were miles away. The terns in general would be up long before we could get there. If even a single dog came through at this juncture, when there might be some thirty to forty Sandwich terns on newly laid eggs we would lose the birds. But when established on their nests gulls, being much less sensitive to disturbance, would come back quite quickly onto their eggs and this would encourage the terns to follow – which they did.

I had slowly discovered that black-headed gulls had a beneficial effect upon the terns' nesting success, and that the latter were in fact attracted by and orientated to nest around the gulls. My observations all pointed to this conclusion: the gulls nested first, followed by the terns. I understood that the

Sandwich terns got security from the gulls. If they saw the gulls nesting they knew it was also safe for them to do so.

An additonal idea was to use this black-headed gull colony as a 'barrier' for the Sandwich terns against ground predators such as stoats and weasels, which operate principally at night. Some years tern egg and chick losses were high to these. The new intake of gulls was 'manipulated' to nest at the eastern end of the ternery – the principal direction from which such predators would enter it.

Allowing the black-headed gulls to nest proved to be one of the best things I could have done for the tern species nesting on Scolt. Following a total loss in 1961 the Sandwich terns returned and nested there every year, slowly building up their numbers until the entire Norfolk population was nesting there.

Having been taught that when man gets away from nature's 'norm' side-effects can develop, I wasn't surprised when, in 1970, a behaviour pattern which had not been observed at Scolt Head before emerged. From the middle of the breeding season Sandwich terns were being intercepted and easily robbed of fish by black-headed gulls nesting at the ternery. The terns lacked the experience to avoid them.

Sandwich terns in Norfolk carry only one fish at a time in their bills, although those in Scottish colonies may carry up to five (like puffins). Gulls are scavengers; filling the crop, they regurgitate its contents onto the ground for the chicks to pick up. Initially they concentrated on robbing terns carrying large sandeels (8 to 12 cm in length). As each season passed, however, the robbing intensified. Fish as small as 5 cm became the target, resulting in the starvation of sixty per cent of Sandwich tern chicks. Common terns were not robbed, probably because the fish they brought to the ternery were too small.

During windy conditions chick mortality increased further, due to fish being more difficult to obtain. This was also evident when fifty to sixty black-headed gulls at one time patrolled the nesting area, waiting to rob the terns as they arrived. Subsequently common gulls joined in – no doubt stimulated by the black-headeds.

Few fish were getting through to the designated chicks and even when the parent terns did succeed in running the gauntlet a host of gulls would pile onto the chick, snatching the fish before it could be swallowed. If by chance the chick succeeded in swallowing the fish, the sheer pressure on it from the gulls forced it to regurgitate.

To put things in perspective, before the robbing took place Sandwich tern chick mortality was expected to be on average ten per cent during normal weather and up to fifty per cent in windy conditions prolonged over a four to five day period. The fledgling success in any given year depended on food availability. I felt that the high chick mortality rate was mainly my own doing. Had I not allowed the gulls to nest in the first instance this unwanted situation would never have arisen. However, I still felt that in the long run the terns must benefit by the presence of gulls. In the end the method I adopted and operated over the seasons to reduce the fish robbing proved not detrimental to the two species involved. Early gull nests were individually marked for positive identification at a later date. These were not to be removed, and thus left a nucleus not only to attract other gull pairs to nest, but also to stimulate the return of those pairs whose nests we did subsequently remove. Thus when the main gull hatch took place a high percentage of Sandwich tern clutches had already hatched.

With numbers of the latter species rapidly increasing when robbing did later become rife the outcome was little or no tern chick mortality. The gull colony at the ternery thus became manipulated at approximately three hundred breeding pairs.

One lasting effect that the fish-robbing had on the Sandwich terns was that after a few seasons they overcame the problem by leading the chicks – even if hardly dry – away from the nesting area to where robbing was less intense. Previously the chicks had remained at the nest site until well developed.

A species which was formerly 'manipulated' for a completely different purpose by man is the shelduck. This big dappled bird, which resembles more a goose than a true duck was once a rare nesting species along the North Norfolk coast, only increasing significantly in numbers after the introduction of bird protection laws. According to my father, less than twenty pairs were nesting when he had been a lad. Many hours would be spent watching and waiting for a pair to return to the nesting burrow.

A pair of shelduck flies round to make sure that the nesting area is free from danger. Then the duck (female) separates from the drake and quickly disappears down the nesting hole (usually an old rabbit hole). The drake takes no part in incubation. Holes would be watched and the eggs carefully collected for hatching by a broody domestic duck.

On hatching the duckling's wing tips – containing the primary feathers – would be nicked, making it impossible for them to develop. Even as adults these birds could not fly and were sold to adorn the ornamental lakes which were the vogue at that time. Each bird could fetch the sum of ten shillings – a week's wages for an agricultural worker.

A most important factor in the successful rearing of shelduck emerged: if the ducklings did not feed from the muddy creeks the majority died before reaching the age of six weeks. They apparently required essential properties found in the mud.

Professor W. H. Thorpe, an eminent zoologist, needed fifty shelduck eggs to hatch in an incubator in order to study their behaviour without adult influence. I collected them for him under licence and mentioned the difficulty in rearing shelduck, owing to the essential feeding in the creek.

'What utter rubbish,' he exclaimed. 'With our present-day scientific knowledge these old-fashioned ways and ideas don't even enter into things!'

I said that before the ducklings were released I should like to ring them, in order to follow their progress in the wild after being hand-reared, adding, 'How many do you expect to return?'

'Between thirty-five and forty,' he replied.

When they were fully feathered and could fly he brought them back to Brancaster Staithe. On opening the crate I ringed eight, and asked where were the others.

'They died,' he replied. 'Laboratory analysis found no scientific reason for their deaths – it's a mystery!'

Shelduck do differ from other species of surface-feeding ducks in that they pair for life and also undergo a total wing moult, like geese. They are unable to fly until new wing feathers have developed. Shelduck are maritime feeders. During the breeding season, as soon as the ducklings have hatched, the adults escort them to feed in the creeks and mudflats on the edge of the saltings.

During July an exodus of moulting birds, both breeding and non-breeding, takes place. Although some birds head for Bridgewater Bay or, in recent years, remain in the Wash, the overwhelming majority head for the German Bight, a vast area of sandbars and relatively shallow water, where the wing moult takes place in an ideal area away from the threat of any ground predators. Here there is sufficient food to support a population in excess of 60,000 until the moult is complete. This is in mid-September, when they return to their wintering areas. Each year at Scolt, throughout July, I recorded flights of shelduck numbering many hundreds heading east during the last two hours of daylight.

According to *The Handbook of British Birds*, when the adults leave to moult broods unite to form packs, with one pair of adults in attendance. The notion is that, by design, foster parents are left to tend the ducklings. I have certainly seen as many as sixty-one ducklings in one 'brood' – their ages ranging from day-old to six weeks – attended by one pair of adults.

My explanation of how these unnaturally large broods are formed and why a limited number of adults stay behind to look after them differs somewhat from the one commonly accepted since the days of the pioneer ornithologists. Over

Original Scolt Head Committee – Charles Chestney looking out of the window

Brancaster Staithe village green, Dial House and Harbour Road

The harbour viewed from Dial House showing concrete sea defences

Above: August 1944 in the army

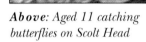

Above: Aged 11 catching butterflies on Scolt Head

Right: Sept 1945 after being wounded, convalescing at Western-super-Mare

Scolt Head Committee 1954 left to right: Dick Bagnell Oakley (Norfolk Naturalist Trust), Vera Powell (NN Trust), Nicholas De Basil Corbin (National Trust), John Cadbury (NN Trust), Bob Chestney (Warden), Dr William Thorpe (Scientific Zoology Camb), Mr Shearer (National Trust), Prof. Alfred Steers (Chairman Geography Camb

Wardens left to right: Charles Chestney – Scolt Head (National Trust), Ted Eales – Blakeney Point (National Trust), Billy Bishop – Cley Marsh (Norfolk Naturalist Trust)

Above: Bob with the ferry – Father standing by to assist. *Left:* With Father – a press photo 1946. *Below left:* At my observation hut and shelter Assistant Warden Ken Spencer talking to Eric Poachin, children's books writer. *Below:* As reserve warden standing by the notice board erected on beach point 1955.

Repairing the hut, showing pebble work in form of compass outside

Recapping at the end of a tour

Above: Shelduck – note broader band on the male. They pair for life

Little tern at nest ....

.... and feeding chick. Note the fish is longer than the chick

Right: Common terns at nest

Fish presentation during courtship of Sandwich terns

Oystercatcher on nest

Arctic tern in flight – lacking deeper black primaries and no black tip to bill, as in Common tern

Brent geese in foreground. Terns in background – winter and summer species overlapping

Ring plover returning to nest

Observing the tern colony

A mass of Sandwich terns on the breeding ground

John King and I (with Jip and Elsa) after the dawn flight on North Creek 'gush'

Gordon Howell, my invaluable assistant for 25 years, now living in Australia

Peace and tranquility in Brancaster Staithe harbour

Foam being deposited on the beach after a storm – brings death to nesting birds

Viewing the hut after 50 years showing compass design in Pebbles

Ted Ellis, the well known Norfolk naturalist

Self, Phyllis and daughter Sally after receiving the M.B.E. at Buckingham Palace

One of three people receiving an honour as a Norfolk Hero at the Hotel Nelson at the opening of their new Trafalgar restaurant

Chestney family toasting father's retirement. Left to right: Sally, Phyllis, Catherine, self and Sandra

the years I frequently observed what happened when two shelduck families met while swimming along a creek edge. The two drakes, without exception, fought. Although they were obviously challenging for supremacy, I am uncertain as to whether this was over the ducklings or the feeding area. (Drakes certainly are more aggressive when they have a brood of ducklings.)

These fights can be horrific, continuing for several minutes with feathers flying. By the end of a fight a champion has emerged. The defeated drake has been driven well out off the area of the first encounter, the ducklings have become widely scattered, and the duck of the defeated drake joins him. This pair then usually flies off and makes no attempt to return to its young. By repeated calling the winning pair gathers all the ducklings. There appears to be no recognition by voice (as there would be in terns, in a similar situation). The ducklings home in on the particular call of 'aaruk aaruk' from any shelduck pair.

A particular event helped satisfy me that this assumption was correct. Ducklings were brought to me after being trapped in local gardens while they were being walked from the Common (where they had been hatched) to the creek – a distance of some three-quarters of a mile. While the tide was in I searched the creeks by boat to find an adult pair with ducklings. Naturally the family scattered on my arrival.

Quickly releasing the captive ducklings I retreated to a safe distance where I could watch and hear what happened. Within minutes the original brood and the ones I had released had been called to the adults. There was no aggression by either adult towards the newly acquired family. This suggested that any pair of shelduck with a brood of its own will accept into that brood any duckling, irrespective of size or age. The number in any particular brood must, therefore, be controlled only by the physical ability of the drake to defend it.

CHAPTER FIFTEEN

Terns or Sea-Swallows

By 1961 the need for a competent permanent summer assistant had become paramount – I had wasted too much time on trying to train people who were not suited either to the job or local conditions. During a long talk with Professor Steers, I mentioned that I knew someone who I thought would be ideal.

The man I had in mind was Gordon Howell, whom I had caught as a fifteen-year-old egg-stealing with his mates. In the interim six years they had all spent time with me on the island, learning at least the basics of the 'trade'. After some thought the professor agreed to meet Gordon during his annual holiday visit to the Hut in August (he always spent his birthday there).

After making the introductions I made the excuse that I had a party to escort and left, knowing Gordon would be more at ease without my presence. On my return about an hour later I found them chatting away together. When Gordon left I stayed to hear the professor's verdict.

'You are quite right, Bobby,' he said. 'He is a rough diamond, but his knowledge and understanding of Scolt are first class. I should be pleased to own some of the many artifacts he tells me he has discovered at the Roman campsite, and his stamp collection contains at least three which are missing from mine – but he will not consider parting with them!'

I persuaded Gordon to apply for the post in 1962 and, fortunately, he was appointed. I pointed out to him that some people would try to take liberties, especially when I was absent from the ternery. However, humans were not very highly rated by Gordon – he especially resented them when they disturbed the terns in periods of unfavourable weather. He was a rough diamond and not the world's best-dressed gentleman – at least while on Scolt. He somewhat resembled Man Friday, though his pet bird was a crow, not a parrot. He didn't crave bright lights, actually enjoying the solitude of a rather lonesome, hermit-like existence at the ternery. Within a few years of his appointment virtually nothing would be able to move by day or night in this area without his knowledge. He would be my summer assistant for twenty-five years.

Relations between the Nature Conservancy and the local wildfowlers remained amicable until 1962, when the former announced summarily that wildfowling on Scolt Head would cease. Not even I had been consulted prior to the statement being issued.

I had explained the complex situation in which Scolt and to a lesser degree the whole area found itself to the regional officer on each of his visits. A satisfactory working arrangement had been fostered by my father between the local committee of the National Trust/Norfolk Naturalists' Trust and the local population, and I had hoped that under NC management relations would have continued in the same vein.

From 1951 until 1960 I had persuaded nearly all the fishermen to refrain from collecting driftwood while terns were nesting – in itself something I considered a fantastic achievement. The loss of their support and cooperation would result in the complete waste of at least ten years' hard work at the ternery; but apparently all my advice had gone unheeded. When officially told to implement a total ban on shooting I again emphasised the disastrous effect this would have.

In retrospect I realise that it was the result of a new intake of staff exercising bureaucratic authority. Anyway, the outcome of it was that wildfowling did cease for that season, as it was uncertain whether the Conservancy did in fact have the power to overrule a long established tradition. One can imagine the hostility directed against the NC and, to a certain extent, myself – everyone thought I had been aware of its intentions. The following shooting season the wildfowlers took the bull by the horns and ignored the ban. Wildfowling continued in subsequent years and the legal arguments dragged on and eventually arrived at stalemate.

In the very hard winter of 1963 all the creeks and saltmarshes became frozen. These had always been an ideal feeding ground for ducks and brent geese. The latter, until now a wholly maritime goose, had depended on a variety of marsh and foreshore plants for food. Now they were forced by the severe weather conditions to change their habits and they started to feed on the winter cereals close to the saltings. (Within ten years their feeding range would increase several miles inland; according to farmers they became 'pests'.)

The world population of eastern race, or dark-bellied brent, had at one time been estimated at 80,000. By 1954 this number had dropped to just 20,000. Not only had brent declined internationally but so had the surface feeding ducks. There had been a noticeable decline in numbers of mallard, teal and wigeon, not only in the Brancaster area but also nationally. Local wildfowlers were under the impression that the brent geese, feeding in the same area as the ducks, and fouling the ground with their droppings, while puddling up the marsh with their feet, were the cause of the decrease in duck numbers. On the other hand, ornithologists argued that shooting was responsible for the decline. Neither argument was absolutely true – modern farming, loss of habitat, wetland drainage, dressed corn, plus poor breeding seasons were all contributory factors.

At this stage nothing had been resolved – Conservancy and wildfowlers were still at loggerheads. The situation had become intolerable; I was 'piggy in the middle'. The NC image locally had sunk to a very low ebb. As the NC's solicitors themselves were uncertain of the legal position they refrained from taking any action. When this became known the floodgates were opened and there was more wildfowling on Scolt than there ever had been before! Shooting restrictions were few. Anyone could shoot anywhere on the Crown foreshore – the so-called 'marsh cowboys' (new wildfowlers) being principally responsible for causing the disturbance. Many travelled fifty miles or more with their guns and a hundred cartridges. They shot until the cartridges were expended – nothing that moved was safe!

The Wildfowl Trust, researching into the reason for the decline in brent numbers, found that birds were arriving at their nesting area in the high Arctic later than previously recorded. This resulted in retarded laying. Being hatched late the young were then not sufficiently advanced before the onset of winter weather to be reared successfully.

Brent take three years to reach breeding status. A certain reserve of fat is required before they can commence the six thousand mile journey to northern Siberia (the Yamal to Taymyr peninsulas). It was principally unwarranted shooting which kept them off the feeding grounds prior to migration – thus preventing them from adding the requisite fat reserves and delaying their departure.

Our third daughter, Sally, was born at Dial House on March 3, 1963. (On checking my records all our children appear to have been born after 'quiet' tern years!) On top of growing family commitments Phyllis still had the students to look after. In addition to the changing attitudes on their side, with which she had to cope, when she added up all the costs she discovered that she just wasn't making any money out of what was certainly hard work. She informed the Conservancy – who had set the tariff – that she would no longer be able to provide accommodation on this basis. From then on students stayed at the cottage next door, which was converted into self-catering accommodation.

For an all-too-brief period Dr Bruce Foreman became our regional officer for the Nature Conservancy. As well as being fully sympathetic towards Phyllis's point of view, he also fully endorsed what I was trying to do at Scolt Head.

Until now our only shelter on the island had been two sheets of corrugated iron on poles, with some canvas sheeting round them against the prevailing westerly wind. Some mornings I had woken up unable to move – literally having to roll about in the sand to get my circulation going again. One day I asked Bruce, 'Don't you think it's time we had a better shelter?'

He answered without hesitation, 'Yes, we must have a hut for you.'

Within a month one was acquired. Measuring six feet by eight, it cost £84, delivered on site! The date was May 28, 1964 and we managed to erect it two days before a terrific westerly wind got up. In those days there was no vegetation to the westward (as there is today); the blowing sand would sweep across, drifting and obliterating everything. Some days from 10am the wind would reach a force eight and gust to nine during the day. The whole area would be transformed by blowing sand. Nests and chicks could not survive such conditions. By seven in the evening it would die away.

On this particular day the wind gusted harder and harder; the hut started to lift up, actually leaving its supports. There was little we could do except stand right up in the doorway, with the door closed, in the southwest corner and hope that our combined weight would anchor it down onto the piers.

This worked and in the lulls between the fierce gusts we rushed outside and filled sandbags which we put on the floor – sitting there until the wind abated. When we got up we could see that the hut had moved six inches downwind! We had to get some timbers and jack it back again onto its supports. After this experience we decided to dig three by two inch baulks at each corner, bolted to the hut, and the hut served Gordon as summer accommodation for many years to come.

Knowing the long hours I was working, Bruce suggested that we have an 'official' nature trail to take the pressure off me. He asked if I'd like to write out something suitable for the visitors. Even with the nature trail I still met visitors, on landing, and took them round; but afterwards, instead of asking me, for example, 'What was that tern with the red beak called?' they could refer to the leaflet. Bruce agreed to this and the system proved successful.

From 1961 the quantity of plankton in the Wash slowly reduced; suitable round fish for terns became scarce. Data were supplied to me by a friend at the Ministry of Agriculture, Fisheries and Food (MAFF). Prior to this reduction in fish terns travelled an average distance of seven to ten miles before returning with fish for the young. This had taken them some twenty to thirty minutes. Now a distance of thirty miles from the ternery became the norm, thus extending the time between feeds to two-and-a-half to three hours.

A major contributory factor to the reduction of plankton and fish stocks in the Wash was, I believed, toxic chemicals washed from the land into rivers and ultimately into the sea. Concurrently there was a reduction – and in some cases disappearance – of mussels, cockles and even barnacles, due to lack of spawning. Flatfish such as dabs and butts, and roundfish such as sea trout also virtually disappeared at least in the local area.

The first indication that something was amiss with birds was the national decline of the grey ('English') partridge and birds of prey. Even the kestrel – hitherto our most common raptor – became something of a rarity. Dr Norman Moore of the Nature Conservancy was the first to point out that agricultural sprays were, by their large-scale use, harmful to wildlife. I became involved when he monitored seabird eggs from Scolt over a period of seven years. During the first three years of the study toxicity was recorded in tern eggs – some registered three separate toxic chemicals in one egg to a maximum eight parts per millilitre. It was largely Dr Moore's evidence that resulted in the phasing out of most toxic agrochemicals in favour of non-toxic substitutes, when the toxic residue found in tern eggs dramatically reduced (by 1975 it had become just measurable). His findings were published in full in his *Detailed Analysis of Toxicity in Sea Birds.*

Television natural history programmes had become instrumental in making the public aware of the disastrous effects toxic chemicals were having on their surroundings; but it was the suggestion that they could also be harmful to humans that really got the ball rolling.

Anthony Clay, a wildlife photographer with the Royal Society for the Protection of Birds, asked to film terns at Scolt Head to convey that it wasn't only land birds that were at risk from chemical pollution. He would also show that seabirds had the added hazards of an ever-increasing number of human visitors overrunning their nest sites (few people were yet aware that an enjoyable day at the seaside for them could turn out to be a disaster for ground-nesting birds) and was pleased to agree to this request. I had known Tony for many years. He had visited Scolt frequently, was familiar with the mammoth tasks we faced and was a keen ornithologist and a photographer of the highest standard.

During the winter prior to filming we spent many hours planning and discussing the most effective and realistic shots for the programme. I certainly didn't want the result to be load of 'slush'. Not everything in a ternery is perfect and I felt it should be made clear that not all eggs hatch and not all chicks survive. I felt that the many and varied reasons for this should be demonstrated.

At the start of the season Tony and his assistant would stand by ready to come to the island at a moment's notice. I should organise hides well in advance and advise him when each required sequence could be shot. We realised that the film couldn't be completed in one year. The first year we should concentrate on the birds at all stages of their breeding cycle. The second would involve filling in the 'gaps', shooting necessary retakes, plus natural hazards over which I had no control.

One of these was wind-blown sand which, especially on strong westerlies, could sweep across the nesting area, covering eggs and chicks to a depth of up to six inches. Another was foam which was created by onshore winds of force five or more pounding the waves onto the beach. Creeping forward like lava from a volcano at a height of two to four feet was equally deadly, continuing to advance until the wind abated.

On Tony's first day his assistant was unwell. He and I started for the ternery at eight thirty in the morning in the old fourteen-foot wooden dinghy with its outboard Seagull. The wind was a fairly strong northerly and it was forecast to freshen later in the day. As we rounded the corner by the Ninth the open sea was dead ahead. Although the wind seemed to have eased the waves were steep and close together though not rough enough for me to become concerned. I decided to continue and we passed through the choppiest part of the harbour safely. A further six hundred yards would see us safely at the ternery.

We reached almost the identical spot to where Alfie Chilvers had turned back on Coronation Day. The dinghy was making good headway against the wind and waves but through the spray I could see a hundred yards ahead that the tops of the waves were being whipped off by the wind, and that the swells were much larger – a sure sign that a sudden increase in wind strength was imminent. Even the terns could not fly against it and were being swept towards us. Above the noise of the wind and engine I shouted to Tony, 'I don't like the look of it ahead! If we're swamped grab an oar – it'll at least keep you afloat.'

At that time life-jackets were a luxury. Very few small boats carried them and when operating the ferry my solitary lifejacket had been found on the shoreline at Scolt! We watched the waves increasing in height as they came nearer. My only hope was to keep the bow of the dinghy straight into the wind and waves and ride it out, and to remember my father's advice from his naval experience – that a wooden boat wouldn't totally sink, so stay with it and grab anything, such as an oar, that floated, to increase your chance of survival.

I soon realised that what I was trying to do was impossible. The waves were too large and too close together for such a small boat to survive. I shouted to Tony to hang on and, as we hit the first of the big waves, the bow swung round with the wind. The next moment we were full of water to the gunwales. The weight of the outboard was dragging the stern down; so, with waves breaking over my head, I struggled to undo the clamps holding it to the stern. Eventually I succeeded and the boat returned to a more even keel.

Having to stand up, we acted as sails. I steered with an oar the best I could. As it tore downwind the dinghy would have submerged had we not repeatedly adjusted our weight distribution in it. With great relief we finally reached shallow water, on the tip of Beach Point the most southerly part of Scolt. Throwing the anchor out we waded through waist-deep water. Huge waves still rolled round us and when we eventually reached dry land my legs felt like jelly. We collapsed, totally exhausted.

After a rest we battled our way on foot against the headwind for a mile until we reached the safety and shelter of the observation hut at the ternery. Gordon had witnessed the whole episode and was waiting with a cup of tea. As we drank it, without looking at us he said, 'What a stupid thing to do! Who in their right mind would venture out in these conditions without a lifejacket between you – and you a coastguard.' (Both Gordon and I were members of the Coastguard and Rescue team.)

It was Gordon's only comment; but it made me feel how utterly foolish I had been to endanger both our lives like that. I should have known the risk involved. We were the only idiots afloat in the harbour that day and had we been washed away from the dinghy there would have been no chance of rescue.

The wind was still at gale force when we had finished our tea and were feeling refreshed; so we decided that as the foam would be at its height we should film it. On reaching the northern edge of the dunes we were met by an incredible sight. Foam reached from the huge waves pounding on the shore to the dunes where we stood – a distance of fifty yards. It was three or four feet deep and stretched as far as the eye could see on either side of us. Several hundred terns were hovering with great difficulty over their foam-covered nests. It was impossible for the birds to return to them. After filming the footage we required we hastily retreated – there was nothing we could do for the terns.

Through the afternoon the wind slowly abated and by six o'clock it had eased to a moderate breeze. We decided to check the ternery area which had earlier been covered in foam to see the results. What we saw and found was heartbreaking. There was utter devastation. A brownish, greyish sludge, dried by the wind, covered everything it had contacted. At least seven hundred pairs of common terns, plus oystercatchers, ringed plovers and thirty-five pairs of little terns had been nesting within the foam-covered area. Not one nest was now being incubated, nor had any chicks survived. We also picked up thirty-eight adult common terns covered in the dried sludge. They were either dead or in a very weak state. These were birds which must have remained at their nests to incubate, even when covered with foam.

The film *Terns or Sea Swallows* was duly completed, Phyllis and I being invited to its premiere at London's Royal Festival Hall. I was very pleased with its outcome. It truly did portray the many and varied hazards that terns are presented with. One sequence was of visitors arriving at the island. As they left the landing stage they wandered about, totally ignoring the notices telling them what to do and where to walk, and oblivious of the fact that they were treading on nests and destroying eggs.

Some people had been of the opinion that this sequence should not be included in the final compilation; but Tony and I had insisted that it be shown. When it appeared on the screen, with the eggs being trampled underfoot and destroyed, a spontaneous gasp went up from the audience. No doubt it was a shock to them; but it was true to life. I knew the point we had being trying to make had been appreciated.

Since that first showing the film has been seen by many thousands of schoolchildren and by many societies. Though it was not *Gone With The Wind*, *Terns or Sea Swallows* did become a 'classic' in the sphere of natural history films. Bearing in mind that when it was first shown the general public was not so nature-orientated or 'green-minded' as it is today, it really was 'things to come'!

CHAPTER SIXTEEN

Gordon Howell – Lifesaver

With Gordon now established as the permanent summer assistant on the island, some of the local boys were encouraged to come over to Scolt Head to join us. Among them were Stephen Loose, Philip Everitt and Jonathan Brown. They used to spend the day with me on Saturdays, Sundays or both – I took them down by boat and brought them back. Some others would also come, but only for a couple of weekends. They would have a look round, find it none too interesting and then I'd never see them again.

The 'regular' local lads were beneficial to Scolt. They were good ambassadors, going back and telling their parents and friends what was going on. Above all else they saw it themselves and made it clear to everyone that young terns were dying – even though it was hot and there was plenty of food – in the disturbed areas, whereas in the undisturbed area everything was all right. After twelve years I finally managed to get through to locals that what I was trying to do wasn't detrimental to their livelihood, or contrary to what they had done in the past.

Each year in July one old fisherman, Tom, landed at the ternery on his way home from fishing – claiming it as his 'right' to do so. Each time I walked out to meet him before he could reach the main ternery. There was never any trouble – he just remained where we met. The conversation was virtually the same each year.

'Hello, Tom. I don't want you to go any nearer the terns.'

'Well, why not?'

'You know the reason. But I will explain it to you again.' This I always did, adding, 'I have no legal right to stop you.'

'I can't see what good that is. Your father never worried about visitors walking in the ternery. Since it became a bird island there are less birds than when I was a boy – and we used to take the eggs!'

Instead of arguing with him I agreed, saying, 'I hope to achieve, in the next few years more birds than you have ever seen.'

'I don't believe it!'

To have presented statistics to Tom would have been pointless. I continued pressing home my 'case' as we stood there, knowing that he would return to his boat when the tide was sufficiently high for him to motor up to his moorings. (His brother had been landed on the beach earlier to walk home and light the copper fire, so that the water would be boiling when the whelks arrived.)

With the assistance of Gordon and Mike Softley (by now officially appointed an NC honorary warden) the ternery was kept virtually free from human disturbance. Not only was this beneficial to breeding birds but also to resting ones. The adjacent beach was undoubtedly one of the few coastal areas where seabirds could rest undisturbed while on migration. Each year numbers of birds quickly built up when one late July day we were expecting Tom: the time, tide and day were right. In the afternoon a light aircraft flew low over the ternery area, putting every bird to flight.

At a rough estimate there were 22,000 Sandwich terns (including nesting birds and fledged young), 3000 common terns plus young (the highest number I ever recorded on Scolt), 22,000 kittiwakes, 1000 gulls of other species and 1000 oystercatchers – a total estimated at near fifty thousand birds.

I told Gordon, 'If Tom lands today and does what he normally does, this amount of birds will work for us! You go low down the beach and get behind them. When I've been talking to him for ten minutes run up the beach, waving your shirt.'

As anticipated Tom landed. As he walked towards the ternery from the harbour channel I met him. Gordon went to play his part. When we met the usual conversation passed between us. Then he added, 'You should have had a good season, what with the fine weather. We have caught more mackerel this year by watching the terns diving.'

I only had time to say, 'I must admit this has been one of our best years,' when from behind the low ternery dunes poured thousands of birds (Gordon could not be seen, being behind the low dunes).

I don't suppose Tom knew what they all were; but even to me it was a most impressive sight. 'Fantastic' even! Tom looked without saying a word.

I said casually, 'That's some of the birds that have been nesting, and their young!'

'I don't think I've ever seen so many birds on Scolt Head.'

'Not even when you were a boy?'

'No, that I hain't,' Tom affirmed. 'You seem to know what you're doing.'

'I couldn't have done it without all the fishermen's cooperation.'

As I accompanied him towards his boat his parting words were, 'You ount see us again.'

That was perfectly true. Neither he nor any other fisherman gave me any anxiety concerning the ternery and the nesting birds from that day to my retirement – though in retrospect I am still not entirely clear whether it was purely that incident with the birds that changed Tom's mind. One of my young 'ambassadors for Scolt' was Tom's nephew!

Four years later, in 1968, the revised Bird Protection Act would give me authority to restrict the disturbance both to nesting and resting birds.

Being a coastal warden entailed involvement with events at sea – not, however, always from choice. Some, like the following account, were very sad.

On the morning of Sunday July 6, 1966, Martin Gethin, a local lawyer, and his friend Maurice Pegg decided to take a trip round Scolt Head in their speed-boat – something they had done many times before. Though Martin was an experienced water-skier and swimmer, Maurice was less so. Leaving the Hard at Brancaster Staithe they motored through the creek dividing Scolt from the mainland. When they reached the harbour mouth at Overy Staithe the weather had become unsettled and squally showers had developed. During these squalls the wind gusted to force four to five, then died away completely, so they decided not to venture out to sea during the squall but instead visit Overy Staithe for an hour.

When they returned the wind had died and the sea was calm; the only waves breaking anywhere were on the beach. The squall had passed so they decided to continue their trip round Scolt. However, as they reached Brancaster bar another squall developed. The wind quickly increased from calm to force five, making the waves at the bar steep with white tops. With only fifty yards to go to calm water a huge wave took them from behind, picking up the boat on its crest, speeding it forward totally out of control and twisting it to one side before capsizing it. Both men were thrown from the boat.

This particular Sunday I was on Scolt with Bruce Foreman and the Nature Conservancy's chairman, Lord Howick. For no apparent reason a group of Sandwich terns suddenly took flight staying in the air for about half a minute, before slowly returned and settling down. As we allowed a whole minute for birds to remain in the air before investigating the cause, I was convinced that all was well. Within two minutes, however, they were all in the air again. This time they did not return to the nest.

I shouted to Gordon, 'Has anyone got in without our knowledge?'

No way! he replied, nevertheless setting off to investigate.

After being lost to sight behind some small dunes, he reappeared two or three minutes later, a hundred yards to the north, disturbing virtually the entire ternery in the process. Knowing something must be seriously wrong for Gordon to do this, I told my companions to stay where they were and ran towards him. (It was one of the very few occasions when the terns took second place.)

I found Gordon on the shoreline, kneeling over someone obviously more dead than alive, who was coughing and choking. When we had removed most of the water from his lungs he managed to gasp out that his friend was still out in the water; but scanning the sea with my binoculars I could see nothing. The water was very choppy, due to another imminent squall, so I moved to a higher vantage point and searched again. Nothing was in sight.

Meanwhile Gordon had continued to apply artificial respiration. When I returned the half-drowned man was gabbling on and making no sense. His body was stone cold and purple all over. He was undoubtedly suffering from hypothermia. We dragged him to his feet, but he was incapable of standing so, half-carrying, half-dragging him we got him the four hundred yards to our observation hut.

Gordon and I dashed back to the beach and stood on a higher dune to scan the now much calmer sea. First I picked out the partly sunken boat, bow uppermost. It was stationary, causing me to believe that the anchor had fallen out and was holding it firm. Following downtide from the boat, about two hundred yards away I saw a person in the water drifting slowly westward. Taking off my jacket I waved it over my head. The man responded by waving his arms above his head; but on bringing them down he disappeared under the water. I watched him being carried slowly away from the shore.

While I was thus occupied the other man – who turned out to be Maurice Pegg – had been carried to the ferry and taken to Dial House by Bruce and Lord Howick.

They explained the situation to Phyllis who had been a reporting member of the coastguard service since 1959. (She was, incidentally, also the first lady coastguard.) As she later explained, when someone is brought to your house apparently dead you think, what do I do with him? It was obvious that Maurice was in urgent need of medical attention and since it was impossible to get in touch with the doctor by telephone, Phyllis jumped into the car and quickly drove to his house. Luckily he had just arrived home and hurried post haste back to Dial House.

Maurice was quickly undressed and put into a warm bath, which made his condition more stable, though he remained very weak. Later he was transferred to bed with masses of hot water bottles. Phyllis sat beside him, rubbing his hands for four hours to keep him warm and the doctor kept popping backwards and forwards to see him.

She described it as a 'horrendous day'; while she was trying to revive poor Maurice she also had to prepare an important lunch for Bruce and Lord Howick. At the time she was relatively inexperienced at this kind of entertainment; nevertheless, in between bringing Maurice back to life, she accomplished it. After resting for only two hours he wanted to get up and return to Scolt to look for Martin who, he believed, must have reached shore somewhere.

Twenty minutes after I had last seen the person in the water the helicopter arrived. I gave the exact position to the pilot when he landed on the beach; but after searching the immediate area for an hour and a half they gave up.

By six o'clock we had searched the shoreline down to the water's edge. The tide was near low by seven thirty; the speedboat was only thirty yards offshore, but the water was rough and it was impossible to swim out to it. We walked to the water's edge to check if by any chance he had reached the boat and was hanging on. The vast tidal area of the Wreck Sand, to the west of the ternery, was now dried out so we decided to search here also, returning along the low water mark. Although it was still impossible to reach the boat, we did identify it as *Pearly Mist* and it was only then that we then realised who its occupants had been. A coldness came over us as we looked at the boat; our feelings cannot be described.

On the evening flood tide a group of twenty people came to search for the missing man and confirmed that he was Martin Gethin. I told them what I had seen and that there was very little hope of finding him alive so after searching the shoreline until near dark we all returned home. It was now ten o'clock.

One outcome of the tragedy was that the King's Lynn Round Table, of which Martin had been a member, organised a memorial fund in his name and I was asked what could be bought with the money to help if a similar situation arose. I believed that Martin might have been saved had we been able to make immediate contact with the mainland and rescue services. The time between Maurice being found and the helicopter's arrival had been one-and-a-half hours (at that time it took twenty minutes from the 'alert' to arrive at the ternery). I suggested that radios should be purchased from the fund.

Three were bought: a base set, installed at Dial House to contact the coastguard and helicopter, plus two hand sets ('walkie talkies') with a range of approximately five miles. Gordon, Mike and I had to become coastguards (reporting members) to operate the sets legally.

This led to Phyllis's TV 'debut'. At the presentation by the Round Table of the radio sets its spokesman said that if they 'helped in saving one life they would more than pay for themselves'. Phyllis repeated this in her television interview. She felt that, since a great many people had given money to the Martin Gethin Memorial Fund they would appreciate knowing to what good use it had been put.

This was the first time I had had contact with the mainland from Scolt Head. The radios certainly proved their worth over ensuing years.

In 1977, Phyllis's vital role in the coastguard service was recognised by the award of the Queen's Silver Jubilee Medal. Local knowledge and expertise helped to save many visitors' lives over the years when people have been stranded on one of the many sandbars, lost on the saltings after dark with a rising tide, or carried out to sea in their dinghies, unable to sail against the strong ebbing tide. Even when the tide is out it is unwise to wander in the harbour. There are many hazards, including deep soft mud caused by springs that have ceased to be active – the hole having filled up with a slurry of mud and sand of varying depths.

With the arrival of summer visitors on Brancaster beach hardly a weekend went by without hordes crossing the main channel to visit the wreck – a distance of about three-quarters of a mile. Few were aware of the dangers involved if they were cut off by the incoming tide. Gordon and Mike made it their responsibility to warn visitors prior to the tide flooding by walking a distance of two-and-a-half to three miles along the north and south sides of the channel, at some risk to their own safety, to make sure that no one crossed – although some still crossed when the tide was coming in! I have no doubt that many visitors to Brancaster and the Wreck Sand owe their lives to these two brave men. Without their vigilance many more would have drowned – all in the pursuit of a casual look at a hunk of rusting old iron! Between 1966 and 1985 three more drownings did occur; but with the help of Gordon and Mike, plus the radios, I am positive that many more were saved. The radios paid for themselves many times over.

My role was less hazardous. Over the years I developed arthritis and because of this stayed at the ternery on a high dune from where, through my binoculars, I could cover the majority of the vast bleak expanse of sand. I could, by radio, point out any developments and keep them informed of the state of the tide. Over the years we experienced many hair-raising situations, including the unpleasant task of searching for and recovering the bodies of drowned people.

Although this final story represents something of a 'leap ahead' in terms of chronology, it seems fitting to round off this chapter with a story of a rescue performed by Gordon Howell single-handed. It should also be seen as a tribute to the heroism of both him and Mike Softley.

In 1980 the harbour channel divided, adding another hazard not only to visitors but to the rescuers themselves. With the tide flooding both channels simultaneously we decided that it was essential to have a dinghy standing by at the spot where the bulk of visitors crossed. On busy days Mike patrolled the extreme north side of the Wreck Sand which covered the open sea – and then returned on foot to the observation dune, while Gordon took the dinghy, left it at the main crossing and then walked to where the harbour channel emptied into the open sea. As he went he warned people, with a loud-hailer, of the incoming tide.

One particular Sunday the tide was predicted to flood the channels at five o'clock. Gordon and Mike started their usual patrol one-and-a-half hours prior to this. We estimated that about eight hundred people were to-ing and fro-ing on the Wreck Sand.

The tide was flooding up the channel at the harbour mouth as six adults were attempting to cross. Anticipating their intention, Gordon ran the quarter of a mile to warn them. As he arrived opposite them they were wading waist deep, and were already halfway across the channel. Through the megaphone he warned them of the incoming tide, and said the water would deepen quickly if they went on. They took no notice and continued. Suddenly, without any warning, the leader dropped into a hole and was swept off his feet, being carried down by the force of the tide. The others, at last realising the danger, struggled back to the beach and the one in the water, after a great effort, also reached the shore.

Due to this little episode Gordon decided to walk directly to the boat, to avoid any unnecessary delay. When almost there he heard screams for help coming from the channel. Although unable to see the situation, as the steep bank obscured his view, he raced towards the noise. A woman was standing up to her waist in water in the channel. Even more horrifying was the fact that she had four children clinging to her!

As Gordon started to wade towards them, two of the children let go their hold and were carried down with the current. Shouting to the woman to stay where she was, Gordon dashed ashore and ran along the channel edge ahead of the youngsters, in order to try and catch them as they floated past. Before they reached him one disappeared under the surface, while the other was thrashing about like a demon but luckily the water was clear so with one hand Gordon grabbed the submerged boy and with the other managed to reach the second child. Wading ashore he dumped them above the rising tide and returned to the screaming woman and the other two children – by this time in a state of panic. Getting hold of the two children he tucked one under each arm and, persuading the woman to hold on tightly to his radio strap, he again waded ashore.

Here he turned his attention to the first two he had rescued. One was OK, but the other, who had been underwater, was vomiting so Gordon picked him up and slung him over his shoulders in a fireman's lift. By the time they reached the boat most of the water had cleared from his lungs and insides. In just this short space of time Wreck Sand had virtually disappeared under the incoming tide!

The rescued became much calmer as he rowed them in the dinghy across to Brancaster. Even the child who had nearly drowned was now capable of sitting on a thwart. The woman told him that only one of the children was her own. After hearing Gordon's warning she had gathered the other three, who had apparently wandered from their parents, sunbathing in the sand dunes. Foolishly, she had allowed them to finish the sandcastle they were building before attempting to recross the channel. By then it had been too late. Amazingly it turned out that she was a non-swimmer! When they gained the safety of the beach she thanked Gordon for saving all their lives. They then walked up the sands and were quickly lost in the crowds.

I doubt that few, if any, people had witnessed the drama. Through my binoculars I had only seen part of the action, hearing the full story from Gordon himself later. He was so 'up tight' about the incident he was unable to drink the cup of tea that awaited him on his return. He said that there was no doubt that without the dinghy they would all have been drowned long before the rescue helicopter could arrive, as they were all non-swimmers.

In retrospect, I now regret that Gordon was never commended for a life-saving medal. He richly deserved one.

CHAPTER SEVENTEEN

Perphigus Trahernii Fosterii

B y 1966 the wildfowlers' attitude still showed no improvement, and some influential locals associated with Scolt asked the director general of the Nature Conservancy, Max Nicholson, to intervene in what was now an inflammatory situation. He chaired a meeting at Brancaster Staithe village hall. Many had expected a battle royal; but instead the meeting was carried through in an orderly fashion. Local viewpoints were put forward, along with details of the traditionary rights dating back over a century which had been exercised over the reserve, and the satisfactory arrangements that had existed prior to its takeover by the NC.

The chairman said that he understood the complex situation existing at Scolt, including the provisional registration of 'certain common rights' appertaining to the island. Rights were claimed for the whole of the tidal area and sand dunes, and certain areas above the high water mean tide level, within the parishes of Brancaster, Burnham Norton and parts of the foreshore owned by the Holkham estate. The NC agreed to await the Common Commissioners' judgement but in the meantime the wildfowling ban would be lifted forthwith.

The commissioners did not, in fact, sit until 1980. Scolt and its surrounding area was virtually the last case to be sorted out, taking longer than anticipated due to its complexity. The outcome of the meeting was that all rights claimed were granted.

Certain donkey dealing went on between the Conservancy and the common rights claimants in establishing these rights. After the meeting the wildfowlers expressed their goodwill and got together to re-form their club. In doing so, with the claimed rights and with support from the National Trust, Norfolk Naturalists' Trust and Nature Conservancy, they were able to control indiscriminate shooting by outsiders. They also agreed to set aside approximately 300 acres at the western end of the reserve where ducks and geese could feed and roost undisturbed.

After the experience with Tony Clay we had had some other bad trips in the old boat. By this time Bruce Foreman had left the Norwich office, where his replacement as regional officer was Dr Martin George. I suggested to him that it was high time we had a boat capable of getting us to Scolt safely, without having to suffer the anxiety of wondering whether or not we should get there and back.

He thought about it for some time. Then he said, 'There isn't much money Bob. You can have a new diesel engine, but you'll have to find a second-hand boat suitable to the engine.'

'There hasn't been a boat built since 1939,' I pointed out to him. 'There just aren't any good ones available.'

However he sent me a letter restating the position so I approached the Conservancy's maintenance officer, Ivor Owen. During the war he had been responsible for installing Merlin engines in high-speed torpedo-boats, motor gunboats and air-sea rescue craft but he was above all a practical down-to-earth person.

Ivor pointed out that it wouldn't be feasible to put a new diesel engine in an old boat, expertly presenting the case for a new one. While the matter was pending we had another visit from Martin George. This was in early May the wind was a strong easterly and the tide flooded about four to five o'clock. When the wind is against the tide it does pile the sea up, so I wore my waterproof Barbour coat. Martin had prepared himself less well. In fact he didn't have much on at all: short wellies, jacket, trousers; no mac.

When we left the ternery drain it was quite rough. I steered the old boat alongside Long Hills, in the lee where there was just enough water to keep going. In order to return to harbour, however, I had to go through the Hole. The tides were medium to big, and as soon as we hit the water in the Hole against the wind the short swells threw up and over the boat. Although I was quite happy in my mac, poor Martin got badly drenched and seemed quite relieved when we eventually got through the cutting and headed for home, in the lee of the Slough. When we landed the water was dripping out of him.

'They're the conditions I have to contend with,' I told him, as I threw the anchor out. 'You should come up there with me when it really blows. In my present boat it will give you some idea of how dangerous it can be.'

He didn't say much as he removed his soaked jacket; although I asked him in for a cup of tea but he preferred to drive off home.

Whether it was this unfortunate experience or Ivor's report which finally convinced him I'm not sure, but I did get approval for a new boat to the design I had had in mind all along.

That was the origin of the *Sea Swallow*, built by two local boatbuilders, Lester Southerland and Freddy Lingwood. Launched in 1966 she served me well up to my retirement, twenty years later.

By the time she arrived the season was all but over; the last of the Sandwich and little tern chicks were about to fly. The day in question was sunny and warm, the sea like a mill-pond.

Gordon said, 'Must be some mackerel out there. Look at those terns diving.'

'Why not go by sea on the last of the tide,' I suggested. 'Go up to House Hill first, moor the boat off the beach and check the noticeboard there. Then go on to check out the little terns at Breakthrough and finish up at Overy end, to check that noticeboard. Take the mackerel gear and on the way back have a trawl for mackerel.'

He was lucky in catching twelve mackerel. The local fishermen were out there at the time and saw him. When one of them met up with our deputy regional officer, John Morley, he said, 'See the Conservancy is in the fishing trade now!'

'What do you mean?'

'Saw Gordon and the new motorboat out there fishing.'

Two or three days later John asked me about the fishing incident. 'I know where you got that information from, John,' I said.

'Where?'

I told him. He said, 'You're quite right.'

'Let's look in my diary and see what happened on that day.'

He opened it and read out what I had entered for the day in question: '"Thursday – tried new boat out at sea. Under my instructions Gordon left ternery, went down channel and out to sea to renew noticeboard at House Hill, check little terns at Smugglers' Gap and renew noticeboards at Overy end. After job was completed, on his return Gordon caught twelve mackerel."'

When he had finished reading, John looked at me and said, 'I can see what you're up against, Bob.'

Over the years I had acquired a reputation of being always 'on site'. Little went on without my knowledge and when restrictions were lifted at the ternery after the breeding season, I became free to monitor the whole of the reserve at my 'leisure'. Occasionally Conservancy or National Trust staff visited the reserve unofficially and unknown to me. At such times, not requiring my attention and having previously been shown the safe way down the track when the tide was out they could walk the mile or so quite safely. Nine times out of ten when they were walking to the reserve across the saltmarshes, following the old cart track used by the old fishermen in years gone by, I could see them and watch their progress.

During lunchtime, on one of the committee's annual excursions to Scolt, the usual leg-pulling and one-upmanship (mainly from me) was taking place. A committee member, on only his second visit and therefore not geared up to my sense of humour, said, 'What you're telling us is that you know everything that happens on Scolt Head?'

I answered, 'Of course I do.'

'You tell us that, but can you prove it? I was here the other day and you were nowhere to be seen!'

'Now just let me think,' I mused. 'Oh, yes – it was last Thursday. You walked down the cart road with a friend. You both went to the Hut and tried the door. It was locked. From there you walked to the north beach, taking the path through the 'blowout' [an area where the wind had created a huge hole in the sand dunes]. Continuing, you reached the water's edge and 'tested' the water. You looked around. There was not a person in sight. Thereupon you both undressed and ran into the sea, and frolicked in the water for about ten minutes. You then left the sea, picked up your clothes, walked to the foot of the highest dunes, dumped your clothes and, while the young lady remained, you ran to the top of the high dune – presumably to check who was about. Returning to her you stretched out nude in the sun, then you – shall I go on?'

'No, Bob. You've made your point!'

The committee roared with laughter. I continued my lunch. The person concerned never asked me another question like that!

I have no reservations about spending long hours on Scolt Head. It certainly wasn't a waste of time; but my one regret is having missed the opportunity of being with my children and of watching them grow up. It may sound ridiculous when I say I could not find time to teach them sailing, swimming or hauling the Hole, or of passing on to them all the little skills I had acquired by the time I was twelve. They were left more to their own devices than I had been, and had to amuse themselves in their own fashion.

Sally was an *outdoor* type – much like me. When the builders were at Dial House there was, as is usual in these cases, a pile of sand 'ready-made' for children's adventures. Sally loved animals, especially my ferrets. She spent a considerable time making tunnels in the sand until, one Saturday morning, she decided that she ought to have something in her tunnels.

To the amusement of everyone at the sailing club she went and got my ferrets. She played with them for ages – they would disappear in one hole and reappear from another. Even now, years afterwards, her exploits with these animals remain a talking point with those who witnessed them. Bill Adams still says, 'Sally used to entertain us with the ferrets. But we were terrified they would bite her!'

When she was still very young I had to have my old bitch put down, and mentioned this casually to Billy Daniels, whose own labrador bitch was in pup. In due course we popped over with Sally. There were seven lovely puppies in the pen. A light-coloured one took a fancy to Sal. Of course the attraction was mutual!

'Daddy, can I have a puppy? Can I have a puppy?'

I didn't particularly want a light one - it would show up too much when I was duck-shooting. Nevertheless I agreed we could have it.

'Can I have it as my puppy?' Sally asked.

Billy looked at her and said, 'I dunno. Have you got any money?'

'Oh yes. I've brought my money,' Sally answered. 'Daddy said we might buy a puppy so I brought it with me.'

Billy said, 'Ooh, dunno if you've got enough.'

'Yes I have,' she insisted.

'You show me what you've got then,' he said.

She gave him an old penny.

Examining it closely, Billy said, 'Just what a puppy's worth!'

We bought the puppy and brought her home. She was called Elsa, because she looked just like the lion cub in *Born Free*, a film Sally loved.

We didn't realise it, but that penny was very special to Billy and Aggie Daniels. He loved grey mullet and when I caught one I usually took it down for him. However on this particular occasion, years later, Phyllis went with the mullet and found Aggie cleaning her silver, brass and copper. She tipped up a copper jug and out dropped a penny.

'I bet you dunno what that is?'

Phyllis said, 'No.'

'Can you remember Sally buying a puppy from Billy? Well, we kept that penny because it was the cheapest dog he ever sold in his life!'

Phyllis's Mum came to live with us at Dial House in 1967 after Will, her husband, died. She had had a heart attack, and we felt that if we sent her home she too would have died. As it was she stayed with us until the end of her long life, a further twenty-two years.

I've heard many old tales and jokes about mothers-in-law; but I certainly couldn't make up any about mine. She was just a fantastic person. Gran (everyone, not just the family, called her Gran) always seemed to be working. We just couldn't stop her!

One Monday, as usual, she was doing the washing. At the time location shooting was going on in the harbour for the Oliver Reed/Suzie Kendall science fiction film *Where No Birds Fly*.

A knock came on the door. Gran went to the door and said, 'I don't know anything about Scolt Head!'

'Can you stop hanging your washing out?' an agitated voice asked. 'Every time you hang it out and we take a shot we get an extra two or three pairs of knickers in it. We can't get our continuity right.'

'I don't care about your continuity,' Gran answered. 'I gotta get my washing dry!'

One evening I was returning home in my motorboat on the first of the flood tide when I spied, on a sandbar in the middle of the harbour, the lone figure of a man walking towards the main channel. There seemed no sense of urgency in his stride; he was walking as though unaware that, with a rising spring tide, he was cut off from both Scolt Head and the mainland. As I got closer I could see he was not even suitably dressed for the beach. He was wearing a grey suit, trousers rolled up to his knees, shoes in his hand.

I had no choice but to pick him up – I realised that he was totally oblivious to the danger he had been in. The island he had been walking on was already fast disappearing. Had I not come along I dread to think what the result would have been.

Not knowing him from Adam, once he was safely aboard I said, 'You must be an idiot, wandering in the harbour – especially on these high spring, fast-running tides. Obviously you know nothing about tides!'

His reply was, 'I was told by Alfie the ferryman that it would be safe to cross the channel to Scolt Head up to six o'clock.'

'It's past seven thirty,' I pointed out. 'Don't you know that tide and time wait for no man?'

He made no comment but asked me to drop him off on Scolt Head.

'Why?'

Then he told me who he was and that he was staying in the Hut with a research student. That was my introduction to Dr John Treherne, Fellow and later President of Downing College, Cambridge. The very year in question (1968) he was Vice-president of the Royal Entomological Society and was awarded the

Scientific Medal of the Zoological Society. In later years he would become known to a wider public as a fiction writer.

I ferried him across the main channel to Scolt Head. When we landed I looked back for the island from which I had picked him up. It had vanished – a fact I pointed out to him. Then I gave him more advice on the local tidal situation; but he didn't really listen. Before departing he pulled out his wallet.

'How much do I owe you?'

I paused before replying, 'How much do you value your life?'

To judge from his facial expression John Treherne hadn't received my statement too kindly; but I had always believed in shock tactics to get a message through. That way it usually sunk in. Eventually, even in John's case, the ploy worked. Looking at me he said, 'You must think I'm an idiot!'

'Quite right,' I retorted.

Pushing the boat into deeper water I continued home, still having given no indication of my own identity. Meeting him in my official capacity the following day, I introduced myself. Naturally we discussed the previous day's episode and quickly became good friends. As a scientist he was easy to talk to; equally as important he was also a good listener. We talked and discussed Scolt's many facets.

On one of his visits to the ternery we watched and talked terns. He was the kind of person who never talked down to me and also had a keen sense of humour. I would give him practical demonstrations, in order to emphasise my points in a discussion.

He would say, 'You are a great practical man' (which I had told him, jokingly, many times) 'and I am a great scientist' (not a joke - it was perfectly true). 'Who knows what we can achieve?'

Although this was said lightly, it turned out to be no idle remark.

There can be no doubt that a host of mysteries still remains locked in nature's treasure chest, waiting to be solved. To discover a species new to the scientific world is not only rewarding but also very exciting. I like to think I had a hand in doing just that.

If my discovery had been a bird, 'twitchers' by the thousand would have trampled Scolt Head flat in their frenzied hysteria in order to tick it off on their 'lists'. However it wasn't a bird, nor even a plant, which might have brought botanists at least by the hundreds. It was, in fact, a lowly aphid – how uninteresting! And on a saltmarsh, too!

This must have occurred some ten years before my first encounter with John Treherne. I had been on this particular saltmarsh numerous times at this stage of the tide; but on the August evening in question the tide was higher than I had expected and had covered the marsh to a depth of five to six inches. The party that was departing from the Hut had to wait for the water to recede before they could walk to the departure point at Hut Creek.

It was a warm evening and there wasn't a ripple on the surface of the water. Sitting on the stern deck of my motorboat I watched the dead particles of marsh plants floating past on the ebbing tide. Some came into contact with the boat and collected in the eddy created by the stern. As I watched these trapped particles going round and round I noticed that some, of pin-head size and the colour of wax, were clustered together. I wondered if it was wax, as I had not seen this substance in the water before. Cupping my hand I reached down and scooped some up, putting the particles on the warm deck. The water soon ran off and the deck dried. I squeezed the particles with my fingers – they were too small for me to be sure what they were but they felt waxy. My beekeeping experience told me they had been made by a minute insect – but what sort or why I did not know.

Each year from then on, around mid-August when the tides flooded the marsh, I saw the same waxy substance in the water on the same sequence of high tides. As it was an annual event I wasn't too excited. It seemed to be of no great significance; but, although I thought no more about it, I did store the event in my mind.

It was while John Treherne and I were discussing and exchanging information that I asked him if he could tell me what the waxy substance might be. However, after I had given him all the details, he admitted he didn't know, suggesting I collect a sample to send to him.

The following year during his stay at the Hut we again discussed the waxy substance. I had sent him the sample he had asked for and he was able to confirm that it was definitely wax – a bubble made by an aphid species with which he was unfamiliar. A search through scientific journals had been to no avail and there was a possibility it was a new species of aphid. John was a specialist in these small plant-lice and these particular ones must be minute – it would take many to cover a pin-head, 'excluding the wax bubble'.

William Foster, then one of John Treherne's students, was given the task of researching its origins. At the end of three years three things emerged: the wax bubble was made by the female aphid; when filled with air it sustained the animal while it dispersed to saltmarshes, borne on the tide which covers the saltings in August and September, and that the remainder of the year, to combat the flooding of their homes it resorted to a mini-hibernation coinciding with the spring tides. Finally, it was a new species to the scientific world.

John suggested that it should have a name with Chestney connections; but this I rejected, saying, 'I'm a tern man, not an aphid man. The honour should go to those involved in separating it from known aphids.' (In retrospect what a chump I was!)

John gave the honour to William Foster, who named it Pemphigus trehernii fosterii in 1975.

CHAPTER EIGHTEEN

More About the Tern Colony

One theory I developed was met by considerable scepticism. When I first stated that terns identified their mates and chicks through voice recognition it was difficult to convince zoologists that this was possible. I had, however, carried out small simple experiments with adults and chicks that had convinced me.

After catching a pair of terns I marked them and released one, placing the other in a covered box. Only its own mate showed any interest in the box and the calls coming from it, returning to it repeatedly. Likewise, when chicks were placed in a similar box, only their parents were interested in their calls. By increasing the number of pairs caught over the years I became convinced that I was working along the right lines.

With time and practice I was able to separate male from female by their voices, and even to recognise some individual birds the same way the following year. Fortunately I found an ally in Professor Thorpe, a leading authority on bird behaviour (I have already written about him concerning shelducks) and a member of the Scolt Head Committee. I had known him many years and he was always interested in my research into birds. He told me that Bryan Nelson (at that time a PhD student), who was studying gannets on Bass Rock, had suggested the same thing. The professor, using a more scientific approach than me, at the end of three seasons' study established that my original theory of voice recognition was correct.

From knowing the variations in calls between the sexes I was able to establish that there was a surplus of males. It seemed likely that there was a reason for this. Perhaps the incubating female is more susceptible to predation – especially to ground predators – while on the nest, principally in the first half of the incubation period. The advantage to her of this 'pool' of unattached males is that should she lose her mate another male will be waiting, ready to fill the gap. Within three weeks the female has not only found another mate but can actually have laid a second clutch of eggs, providing there is sufficient food and time remaining that season.

Controlling ground predators became less difficult after a path was cleared through the dunes and kept free of all vegetation. Any rat, stoat or weasel crossing this area would obviously leave footmarks. It was checked each morning, before any moisture had been dried out by the sun or wind. Any animal which had dared to enter the ternery and remain there would be dealt with accordingly!

If a stoat, weasel or rat hunted the ternery in daylight, terns (especially common), skylarks and meadow pipits warned of the intruder. They hovered over it in considerable numbers, calling and following it as it hunted. I have even seen common terns hover over a long-tailed fieldmouse, especially immediately after rain at the end of a dry spell when it had been tempted out in daylight by the smell of moisture. These birds will hover over any strange new object, only dispersing after establishing that it is harmless, or if there is a lack of movement.

On one occasion, after several days of northerly winds and waves almost reaching the dunes, the terns were to be seen continually hovering in the same spot. I investigated several times in the space an hour, but saw neither movement nor anything alarming. I finally decided to stay forty yards away from the place of attraction, to watch and wait. Within seconds of my sitting down the terns returned and hovered over the same spot as before. I still could see no movement or danger; so, pinpointing the exact spot, I went to investigate. Lying on the sand, sealed in a polythene bag, I found a koala. With its black plastic feet and life-like eyes this furry cuddly toy looked alive even to me – how much more so to a tern! No doubt it had been washed onto the beach – but from where? I gave it to Sally, to whom it became a great treasure. (It is still in the family today, being the proudest possession of her daughter!)

A hedgehog was a surprise cause of commotion in the ternery. At the time this was a rare species; so after being caught it was taken to the observation hut and placed in a fish box. When I returned home I put it my side-bag but during the walk back a considerable number of fleas decided to desert their host and crawl onto me. On reaching Dial House I placed the bag near the back door and hurried to change my shorts and pullover; after which, placing the hedgehog in a polythene bag in the boot of the car, I took it to the edge of the common, where I released it. Over the next three or four days I had to de-flea the cat and the two spaniels, as they were forever scratching! This was the only hedgehog recorded on Scolt, at least in the sixty-one years that Chestneys were wardens. How did it get there!

An unusual non-predatory species was the natterjack toad. At least six were seen at the ternery between 1970 and 1980. Some people thought they had been deliberately taken to the island but I finally became convinced that it was possible for them to have arrived entirely by their own efforts.

One morning the dew-covered sand revealed the tracks of a toad walking through the cleared pathway to the west. Easily followed, it was found sixty yards inside the ternery and turned out to be a female natterjack – distinguished from a common toad by the yellow stripe on the head and tail end of its back. Its back had a scaly appearance, as though singed or burnt.

There had been a dune fire at the west end of Holkham pines – seven miles from where the toad was found. It was well known that natterjacks bred in the pools there, and it seems likely that there is a movement of toads to the west – the direction taken by the six toads monitored on Scolt. I don't think that the fire stimulated the movement of this individual – it was coincidental.

To return to predators, I must admit that there has to be a limit to the amount of persistent predation tolerated, when this leads to moves by nesting birds to new territory or a new ternery. Persistent short-eared owl predation of common terns over four seasons resulted in two separate reactions. Firstly, pairs deserted Scolt ternery and moved to Titchwell beach, approximately a mile away; predation of incubating adults also occurred. The remaining birds nesting at Scolt overcame the nightly attacks with a manouevre I have yet to find recorded.

At dusk there was an exodus of birds from the breeding area to the north shore, a hundred yards away, where they remained until dawn. Then, with one accord, and calling, they all returned to their eggs or chicks. At first I couldn't believe that birds could successfully combat this form of predation, let alone so quickly or so naturally. I had to prove it to myself. During five consecutive days I counted the number of occupied nests containing eggs or chicks. I also checked the same area for five consecutive nights. The maximum number of nests occupied was 175 during the day, but only six during the hours of darkness.

It is never really dark at this time of year, even without moonlight; there is sufficient light to see birds flying forty feet above their nesting territory. Those on the north shore could not only be heard when taking to wing but also be seen. Thus my suspicions were confirmed. With one's 'finger on the pulse' little could go on without any knowledge!

Another puzzle emerged. Chicks from newly-hatched up to five days old were being taken nightly, while older chicks were not – even when these were the more plentiful. However, they would be taken when all the smaller ones had gone. The answer proved simple. When the younger chicks were deserted by their parents at night they became chilled, and their squeaking calls attracted the owls, who homed in on them. Older chicks retained their body heat and remained silent. This proved to be their salvation.

Chipping eggs suffered the same fate as small chicks. Chicks inside the eggs called loudly enough to be heard thirty yards from the nest on a still night. I am certain that this was how these eggs were located (at no time did the owls take eggs that weren't chipping).

Ringing many pairs of common terns provided me with interesting information. The longest surviving pair nested for nine consecutive years at the same nest site – a partnership which was ended when the female was beheaded by a short-eared owl while she was incubating at night. Although each clutch laid by the pair during this period had hatched, not one chick had successfully fledged due to weather or stoat and owl predation. One season we thought they had succeeded. The chick flew in the morning, only to be taken later in the day by a redfooted falcon stooping on it. This broke the chick's wing. Though it survived a further six days, it eventually died due to infection.

When the short-eared owls nested for the first time, after an absence of eleven years (back in my father's time) I was not over-excited, but it did give me an opportunity of monitoring which species they were taking for food in any given season. My father had seen the nesting owls – assisted by the autumn influx of their species decimate the mammal population for seven years before they turned to the young of small birds such as skylarks and meadow pipits. This was a sure indication that insufficient food was being found at night and why tern chicks and adults had become their nightly prey. Interested to see if the same food pattern would be followed, I found that for the first two seasons the main food source was indeed mammals.

Due to myxomatosis small rabbits were far fewer than in earlier years but the mammal population in general was high, due not only to a lengthy absence of breeding owls but also to a decline in their numbers on migration. Halfway through the third season, when many tern nests had hatched, chicks started to disappear at night. This was no surprise since the previous week the male owl had been seen hunting during the day – an indication that food was short at night. Within a week tern chicks disappeared at night as soon as they hatched, and by the end of the season some 300 common tern chicks had died this way.

During the fourth and subsequent seasons both Sandwich and common tern chicks diappeared as from hatching. As the seasons progressed adult birds were also taken – two actually on the wing, carried to and eaten on the ternery boundary during late evening. The majority, however, were carried to the owls' nest site, two miles to the east.

In connection with this predation, I witnessed an extraordinary incident during a night-time observation from a hide. Through the slit opening I saw, by the light of the nearly-full moon, a dark shape slowly moving around the incubating birds which made no attempt to take to flight. It was, in fact, a short-eared owl, stalking from bird to bird. The tern nearest to the owl got off its nest, giving a repeated guttural call; but it did not alert the rest of the colony. This particular nest contained only an egg. The owl moved on to the next nest, and again the tern got off, calling gutturally; but this time the owl seemed to ponder. Then, taking a chick in its talons, it departed.

This ritual went on until dawn. Knowing the state of the colony prior to the owl's visits, I deduced that 22 chicks (none older than three days) had disappeared in five hours. Some had gone two at a time, one in each talon! The owl had made no attempt, however, to take or eat any eggs.

Had I not experienced this happening I would have been convinced that an owl at a breeding tern colony – even at night – would have caused a commotion. However this procedure reoccurred for not less than five summers – until that particular male owl ceased to return to Scolt.

The ninth year turned out to be the last for the nesting short-eared owls at Scolt. We checked the nest area as usual at the end of the breeding season for indications of food taken. Dispersed over a wide area we found 184 relatively fresh pellets (there were undoubtedly others we didn't find). Upon examination these were found to contain common and little tern legs, common, little and Sandwich tern skeletons, the ring from our previously-mentioned longest breeding tern and the remains of a newly-hatched short-eared owl chick (the latter was thought to have been eaten by the older and bigger owlet).

During the period the owls nested the estimated numbers taken at night (excluding the first three seasons) were: common tern chicks 2400, adults 140; Sandwich tern chicks 800, adults 50; little tern chicks 190, adults 25. Though these figures look horrific, things weren't as drastic as they seem. Even with maximum predation control common terns on Scolt fledged on average only one chick to every three pairs.

My theory was that five chicks could be taken from the same three pairs, or, pro rata, 145 chicks from 100 pairs that nested before the owl effect would reduce the total number that naturally survive. Scolt Sandwich terns could rear 90 chicks from 100 pairs and this fledging success allowed them to double their colony every five to six years, ample numbers to allow considerable predation of this nature. Little terns enjoy a similar success rate to common.

Why were the short-eared owls allowed to nest for so long? My answer must be that, although terns were what the majority of visitors came to see, they were only a part of Scolt Head nature reserve and its many facets. Less than a hundred pairs of these owls nested in the southern half of the British Isles, whereas a few years previously that number had nested in Norfolk alone. Such was the effect of pesticides on wildlife – especially birds of prey. On the other hand between four and five thousand common terns were nesting in Norfolk. It seemed to me a case where a common species could subsidise a minority one, even though the former was already showing signs of a slight decrease in breeding numbers. The owls did not take any mass of breeding adult terns, when they were re-laying.

By preventing the owls from nesting I should not have discovered how the common terns combated, adjusted and finally overcame a form of predation entirely new to them. (I doubt if any of the original birds were still alive from when the owls had previously nested.) Observing carefully, manipulating and managing a reserve for the benefit of all species that are threatened or are finding successful breeding difficult without the help of man is what I consider conservation is all about.

I have mentioned in a previous chapter that one year short-eared owls were known to have killed five stoats, without eating them. This was the only time I recorded such behaviour – confirmed when I disturbed the owl (a young bird of the year) from the fourth and fifth victims. When these were examined their bodies were found, like the others before them, to have been punctured four times as though by a needle. The heart and lungs had been penetrated and internal bleeding had occurred. In evidence was the pungent skunk-like smell ejected by the stoat from a gland when danger threatens. Was this why they had not been eaten, I wondered?

The magic and fascination of walking through the main tern colony and seeing hundreds of nests, with the birds screaming overhead, was undoubtedly destroyed for visitors by my restrictions. Certainly, disapproval of my methods was registered by many of those who had wandered at will through the colony in my father's time. Once they had been generous benefactors, helping to maintain the financial viability of Scolt Head; now they stayed away. I refused eminent photographers, zoologists and ornithologists the unlimited access they had been used to. My image wasn't good; but that was the least of my concerns. I do not consider myself a sentimentalist but without visitor control the main feature which got to me was that soon after hatching common tern chicks in the disturbed area acquired a pitiful weak little cry. Within four days they would be dead, still in the nest. I called the cry their 'death knell', and found that it applied not only to terns but to oystercatchers, ringed plovers and redshank too.

The way I presented my explanation for these 'unnatural' occurrences to sceptics was to ask them, 'Would you expect your children to be strong and healthy if they weren't getting their food at the right times, thus becoming too weak to be able to accept the food when it did arrive?'

I remembered my days in hospital during the war. The doctor had said that my pneumonia had been brought on by shock and weakness; it had had nothing to do with temperature. Could not a weak chick (due to an extended incubation) be unable to accept food and ultimately die of pneumonia? When parent birds were put to flight, instinct prompted newly hatched chicks in the undisturbed areas to scurry away from the nest. They were not capable of accepting that very important first fish. This resulted in a much higher number surviving during the initial four days.

One person was interested in what I was trying to do in my early days: Dr Jennings, of the Pathology Department at Cambridge. After visiting Scolt and being interested by my ideas, he suggested analysing complete nests of chicks which died within four days of hatching in the disturbed areas. His findings proved my theories: the stomach gut was empty and the cause of death was pneumonia, which, it was suggested, was brought on by starvation.

Sandwich terns were found to be particularly susceptible to continuous human disturbance, either deserting the site prior to nesting or the nest after eggs were laid, before five days of incubating. Fragmentation of the colony and in some years total desertion of the ternery for that season occurred.

During disturbances, when a nest contained a chick and an egg yet to hatch, parents took the chick a considerable distance away from the nesting area, to a creche, where it remained until fledged, away from human impact. The second egg was left unattended, the chick ultimately dying in its shell.

I discovered that when human disturbance, including wardening, was kept to a minimum, none of these things happened. Pairs of eggs successfully hatched; chicks remained in the nest for two weeks and stayed in the actual nesting area until fully fledged, instead of forming creches. Prior to disturbance control Sandwich tern chicks were very 'mobile' before they had fledged up to 600 yards from the actual nest site – an area virtually void of human disturbance. Although the system of visitor control may have seemed 'regimented', statistics prove that since its adoption in 1951 tern – in particular Sandwich tern – numbers increased considerably. By 1961 the main nesting area (some fifty acres, out of a total of 1800 acres of reserve) remained undisturbed for the whole season. Until this time there was little change in breeding numbers. Fledging success averaged thirty per hundred pairs for Sandwich terns – quite good, as the average figure for common and little terns was between ten and fifteen per hundred pairs. By 1961, however, I had become more familiar with tern behaviour and had tried various simple experiments to reduce disturbance to nesting birds.

Firstly I worked out a counting system to an accuracy of within two per cent, which eliminated the daily counts and disturbance from when nesting started.

Three physical counts during the season became sufficient, unless adverse weather had reduced the food supply and retarded the final laying group. The first physical count was made twenty-four days after the first bird incubated. This covered nests containing two eggs – the second egg is usually being laid two clear days after the first.

Physical counting was carried out every subsequent twenty-four days. By the second count all the first clutches (apart from addled eggs) had hatched. On the third count the second batch had hatched. Any nests after this count were 're-lays', birds which have retarded their nesting due to insufficient food prior to nesting.

Information I gleaned during my first ten years of wardening was considered revolutionary; it was only eventually accepted – and then half-heartedly – because my methods proved successful (then it was hinted that I was 'cooking the books'!)

From 1935 until 1961 Sandwich tern breeding numbers remained stable in Norfolk, at 1200 to 1400 pairs. Numbers fluctuated each season between Scolt and Blakeney Point. Fledging success at each ternery was estimated at thirty to forty per cent. With a change in management at Scolt from 1961, the Norfolk breeding population increased year by year. By 1975 it had increased to 4850 pairs and principally favoured Scolt Head, undoubtedly because the fledging success during the previous fifteen years there had risen from 35–40 to 85–90 per cent on average. One season 130 chicks were estimated to have fledged from every 100 pairs that nested. It was said that the increase in nesting pairs was at the expense of European terneries; but on checking terneries and numbers I found that this was obviously not so.

One thing of which I did soon become aware was that anything I said about terns that had not previously been written in a book was treated as suspect. Much of the time my arguments appeared to fall on deaf ears and I felt that I was 'flogging a dead horse'. I became frustrated; so in the winter of 1967–8 I decided to write an article quoting results of the terns' breeding success prior to and after human control. In its original form it is doubtful if anyone could have understood it and I was grateful to John Morley who, after some persuasion on my part, made the final draft for me. (Incidentally, had John been a zoologist he probably wouldn't have entertained the idea but fortunately he is a geographer!)

The article was sent to the Norfolk Naturalists' Trust for publication in their *Transactions* and, for his comments, to Dr Coulson at Durham University. The latter was responsible for research into tern behaviour on the Farne Islands. When he returned it he had virtually filled the fly-leaf with remarks such as: 'How did you arrive at such sweeping statements?', 'How many birds were involved and for how many years had you studied them?', 'There is insufficient evidence to support your claims,' etc. He also wrote a personal letter to John Morley saying: 'Regrettably Chestney lacks scientific experience and expertise. He has no concrete scientific evidence to support his claims, but should be encouraged to continue his research under guidance.'

I realised that most of the criticism was true and thought the article would die a natural death; Bob Chestney had been brought to heel!

However the Lord moves in mysterious ways (some call it luck). Whatever it was, it came my way in the shape of Euan Dunn, a student of Dr Coulson, who was researching Sandwich terns on Coquet Island and the Farnes. He wanted to visit Norfolk to study the fishing success of young terns and to see how quickly they achieved the success of adults. Since Scolt was a stopover area for terns fledged farther north, he could extend the season of his observations. I invited him to stay with us.

From the time he arrived until his departure we talked terns (I should say that Euan occasionally got a word in here and there!) On his return to Durham I believe he saw terns in a different light. When he arrived he was shy and retiring; but living with the Chestneys (including three young girls who enjoyed his company) brought him out of his shell. They all enjoyed playing the guitar and spent many happy evenings strumming away.

Euan's first visit to Scolt ternery was on August 14, 1969. All the nests had hatched; fledged and unfledged young were on the outer ternery shingle beach. Some birds with fledged young had already dispersed, leaving 3000 adult sandwich terns from the 3500 pairs which had nested.

Colour rings were placed on the legs of chicks, each colony having its own colour coding, thus establishing the place of origin of these birds. After checking the adults for rings through the telescope I said to him, 'In four days' time the bulk of these adults will have gone, leaving about three hundred here. Since very few Sandwich terns have nested at Blakeney this year, I suggest you concentrate your observations here. We can go there later on.'

On the second and third days we checked the adults carefully. Euan said, 'I can't see any departing by tomorrow.'

'We shall have to wait and see,' I answered.

As soon as we arrived on the fourth day I noticed that the volume of noise was greatly reduced. Although I knew from this that the bulk of birds had indeed left, Euan had not noticed it. We walked to the observation hut, after dumping our kit a hundred yards from where the terns congregated on the ridge. I said, 'Notice anything different from yesterday?'

'I can't see anything different.'

'You just listen.'

After listening a few seconds I could tell from the expression on his face that he had registered my meaning. Looking at me he said, 'How did you know that most of the adults would be gone by today?'

I didn't tell him, though he asked again several times throughout the day. I have found that the easiest way to make a point is by a practical demonstration. It never fails to impress. We counted 318 adults on the ridge – none of them ringed.

While we continued watching the terns busily feeding their young, an adult flew past, calling and carrying two fish. I said, 'Ah, listen to that call, that's one of your birds. I'll guarantee that's either from Coquet or the Farnes.'

Euan said very seriously, 'There's no scientific evidence that Sandwich terns from different colonies have different calls.'

'Just listen to it,' I reiterated. 'Can't you hear that Scottish 'och-aye', instead of our Norfolk 'aye-uck.'

We watched it fly round the group of terns on the ground and eventually land, still with two fish in its beak. I said, 'I bet it's got one of your rings on its leg. Check it out with the telescope.'

I didn't bother to look, as I did not even expect the bird to be ringed – I was just 'winding him up'! However, Euan looked at it through the telescope for a few seconds, then exclaimed, 'It's not possible! It's not possible!' Straightening up fom the 'scope he said, in a voice which betrayed sheer amazement, 'It is one of mine. It's got one of my rings on its leg!'

Without batting an eyelid I said, 'I told you so.' (The Lord had once again been on my side!)

'How could you tell it was one of mine?'

'It's taken me eighteen years to find out all I know about terns and their behaviour. I'm not going to tell you in five minutes. But before you go back to Durham I'll let you into the secret. I bet you'll kick yourself when I tell you!'

During the rest of the day he asked me several times to reveal my secret; but each time I refused, laughing it off by telling him that one day he too would be a 'great tern man' – like me!

On returning home I noticed that he was quiet, and thought this was due to the obnoxious way I had behaved to him. In an attempt to improve the situation I suggested a 'wee dram' before dinner. When we all sat down even the girls remarked how quiet and serious he was. 'Is he all right?' they asked, and, 'Come on, Euan, eat your dinner.'

The meal was roast pheasant (the last two frozen birds) saved and cooked especially for him, as he couldn't recall having ever eaten pheasant.

'I can't eat a thing,' he complained, 'until Bob explains how he can tell a Sandwich tern from Coquet.'

I could see that he was serious about not eating his meal. 'OK,' I agreed. 'I told you that you'd kick yourself when you knew the answer. Well, nesting Sandwich terns on Scolt and – as far as I know in Norfolk generally, have never been recorded as carrying more than one fish at a time in their beaks, whereas on Coquet, the Farnes and Sands of Forvie they have been observed carrying up to five at a time, like puffins. The chances of the bird having nested in Norfolk were, therefore, slim. It must have come from a ternery in Northumberland or Scotland.

As you know, the early nesting pairs disperse from the breeding area prior to flying south. Scolt birds with young have been sighted in northern terneries around August the eleventh. A southerly movement of northern birds is also recorded at Scolt about the same time of year. As for the voice at each colony being different, that's eyewash, though it is possible to tell male from female by their calls. As to how I knew the bulk of terns would be gone in four days – I think I'll keep that up my sleeve and leave you guessing!'

During the period Euan stayed with us we exchanged many snippets on tern behaviour. He read the article which Dr Coulson had vetted, and I voiced my opinion of the comments on it. He suggested that I visit the doctor at Durham and said that he would arrange a meeting at which I could discuss my Scolt findings with him.

The meeting with Dr Coulson was arranged for the end of April 1969. As we intended making a short holiday of the trip by going on from Durham to

Scotland, Phyllis accompanied me. The day of the meeting I was nervous and apprehensive about his attitude, after the comments he had made about my article. Nevertheless I tried to keep an open mind. Euan had told me earlier about him and the work he and his students had done over a twenty-five year period. Had I been too bold in coming to see him? Surely his research had covered mine – had I come all this way just to be made a fool of? I asked Euan to introduce me and stay to give me moral support.

I did not feel at ease in Dr Coulson's presence. Looking over his reading glasses he said, 'So you are the person who is going to revolutionise tern colony management.'

'Certainly not,' I replied lightly, thinking, if this is going to be his attitude, get stuck in Bob! 'Information I have gathered does, however, suggest that a shake-up is urgently needed before terns become museum specimens! Although the main theme of my article was the effect of continuous disturbance on nesting Sandwich terns, I also stated that the status of terns in general was declining, giving my reasons for this. You said that the article was 'sweeping'. But the end result was sufficient evidence in itself.

'After reading your paper on the reasons for so many chicks dying in the egg just before hatching, I totally disagree with your conclusions. If you followed the Scolt system you would arrive at results like mine, and the fact of dead in shell just prior to hatching would be eliminated.'

At this point Euan left. However I was past the stage of needing moral support! Dr Coulson was adamant that his scientific data proved that chick mortality just prior to hatching was due purely to the hard texture of the shell. He showed me a pile of statistics which, though doubtless to a scientist impressive, meant nothing to me. I could not understand the equations he talked about.

Discussion became rather heated, until I remembered what my father had always emphasised: 'Lose your cool, lose the argument'! So I calmed myself down and again tried to press home my own point.

In my father's time, and until I became warden, the high number of chicks which died just prior to hatching was expected and accepted as the 'norm'. We were convinced that continuous disturbance was a key factor, but didn't know how or why. I was determined to find out.

'My article explains my observations over a period of eighteen years,' I told him. 'My experiments during that time were far from scientific – I relied on clues.'

My first clue was that the number of Sandwich tern chicks which died in the shell was related to the number of clutches of two eggs in any given year. The second egg to be laid was always the one that was deserted. In single clutch nests it was rare to find a chick dead in the shell, even with the same amount of disturbance. I therefore assumed that these eggs were deserted because the parents were orientated more to the chick already hatched, and less to the remaining egg.

Prior to restricting visitors to the colony, during the morning on a showery day I had observed that nests containing both a chick and an egg would be occupied. The nest cup would be dry; but by the evening, after the many visitors through the day, only the egg remained and the nest cup would be wet. The mobile chick would already be with the parents, twenty yards from the colony – something not typical of this tern species. To make doubly sure that the eggs had been deserted I stood five of them on end in the sandy nest cups, points down. If the birds returned to incubate, any eggs would be returned to the normal incubation position.

The following morning at seven o'clock I checked the nests. All five eggs remained as I had positioned them the previous evening. Picking up the nearest of them I found it to be cool – air temperature (65 degrees Fahrenheit) instead of the 80 to 85 degrees of an egg when the incubating bird has been away from the nest for three or four minutes. I felt to see if it was chipped and found that it was. Putting it to my ear I carefully listened for several seconds for any sound, but without succcess.

Hearing no sound I presumed that the chick was dead, and took the top of the egg off with my knife. I wanted to discover at what stage the chick had died, so emptied the contents of the egg into my left hand. The amount of yolk remaining unused is an indication of this.

As it lay there I saw the chick move several times and was surprised that it was still alive, knowing that the parents must have deserted it for a minimum of twelve hours, including overnight, when the air temperature is at its lowest.

I then had a 'brainwave' – why not place the other four Sandwich tern eggs in four separate nests, which each contained one chipping egg? I knew by the dry nest cups and by the warmth of the eggs that at these particular nests the birds were incubating. To ensure that I should recognise these nests again I added walnut-sized stones of a particular colour.

Within forty-eight hours each egg had hatched, including the original ones in the nests – though the foster chicks were less active and more 'tired' than those originating from the four nests.

While in the nest the foster chicks' legs were painted with white paint; those of the original chicks I left black (the paint remained positive for five days). The following day the four nests were empty. I saw the birds leave their chicks as I arrived, but searched and found the marked chicks. They had walked away from the nests, encouraged no doubt by their parents, towards a group of young which had hatched earlier, fifty yards away from the area where they had hatched. This was undoubtedly to get away from the continual disturbance by visitors looking at them.

On the third day they were on a shingle ridge, well away from daily human disturbance, with an earlier dispersed group of young. Apart from the paint on their legs I couldn't tell the foster chicks from the others. By their development each seemed strong and equally well-fed. After that day I discontinued my search for them, as I had confirmed the point that I had hoped to make. I continued with these experiments for a number of years, arriving at the same results and drawing the same conclusions each time.

This was sufficient evidence to warrant closing the main breeding area to visitors. The result of isolating the main ternery from human disturbance was the elimination of chick deaths in shell prior to hatching and the formation of a creche after ringing, which took place when the first hatched chicks were twenty-four days old. Finally, after I ceased ringing, the chicks remained near the nest, eliminating the formation of a creche.

'That is my case,' I told Dr Coulson, 'with the results I have obtained at Scolt. This success has not been equalled, as far as I am aware, at any other ternery in Norfolk and I am determined that it will continue while I am warden.'

He sat pondering for a few seconds before replying. I thought, wait for it, Bob, he's going to disagree again. All he said, however, was, 'More research is needed. It has been very interesting but I have another appointment now.' (Which told me it was time to go!). I thanked him for sparing so much of his precious time – I had been talking to him for over an hour.

We stayed at Durham another two days. The day we should have gone to the Farnes it was too rough to make the crossing. However I didn't mind as Euan and I had plenty more to discuss.

Phyllis and I continued to Aberdeen by train. It was a six-hour journey and we arrived in the rain so not knowing the city or our whereabouts, we thought our best plan would be to take a taxi to the Caledonian Hotel, where we should be staying. To our dismay, however, the taxis were all on strike so we had to ask directions and walk.

On arriving at last we decided to shower and rest before dinner. Reception rang; Phyllis answered it.

'There's a gentleman here to see you.'

Our caller was Nigel Langham, who had been the MAFF coordinator involved in the colour-ringing programme with me. We went down, had drinks together and a long talk before he left.

Next day we met Alastair Smith, an old friend of Bruce Foreman. A police inspector in Aberdeen, he was also voluntarily wardening Sandwich terns at the Sands of Forvie. It had been Bruce's idea to bring us together, to discuss – what else? – terns. Alastair picked us up after breakfast. What a contrast in weather from the day of arrival; the sun was shining and it was a beautiful day. What a contrast in personalities too from Dr Coulson! Alastair was patient, a good listener and was interested in my findings.

He took us out to the Sands of Forvie, which was yet another contrast for us. After Scolt the area of mobile sand was vast (location shooting for *Lawrence of Arabia* had been done here). At first he was dubious about my Scolt Sandwich tern results. Here, the birds had just arrived and were starting to establish nest sites. Their nesting habitat was quite unlike that at Scolt or Blakeney, and was quite a surprise to me, being on top of dunes some thirty to forty feet high (like Scolt's Long Hills) in sandy areas among the long marram grass, there being none of the couch grass here that Norfolk Sandwich terns favour.

Alastair had a little old hut at the bottom of the dunes. He said, 'I'd better get my hide up. You stay here.'

He got inside the four-foot square canvas-covered frame and picked it up by the handles. Then, to my utter amazement, he walked right up to the establishing Sandwich terns in it and plonked it down. Naturally the terns departed. Alastair got out and walked back to us. I said, 'Is that what you normally do?'

'Oh, yes. But there's no guarantee where they'll nest. I like to get it on site, but sometimes I have to move it three or four times before they finally settle down!'

'I'm not surprised – that's diabolical! The hide should either be erected before the terns arrived in an area where you think the terns will nest, or slowly walked up, stage by stage, when they are settled. If you choose the latter course of action there's no reason why the group should not establish. Otherwise you'll disperse them all every time,' I warned, 'as in previous seasons.'

After returning to Aberdeen and visiting the University we went to Fraserburgh. This was something entirely different from anything we had seen before – steep cliffs, with guillemots and puffins flying below us. It was a glorious day. That evening we had dinner with Alastair and his family and, after two more days in Aberdeen, returned home to Norfolk.

Alastair agreed to give my recommendations a try. Throughout the winter we exchanged information and the following season he and his family visited Scolt. He was pleased with his past season. Fledgling success had noticeably improved and he hoped that this would continue.

Indeed, within two or three seasons he had achieved a fledgling success comparable to Scolt. Looking back he said, 'I can understand now why you looked at me in horror when I walked that hide up!'

I felt that my trip to Aberdeen, with regard to the Sandwich terns, had been most satisfactory.

Incidentally, a few years after my visit to Dr Coulson I was told by one of his students that he was working on the effect of human disturbance on Sandwich tern chicks that died prior to hatching. He was about to publish his findings.

CHAPTER NINETEEN

Birdwatching in Holland

In 1967 I was invited by Anglia TV to go to Holland, as assistant cameraman to Ted Eales, to film for their Survival series of natural history programmes. They wanted shots of birds coming into the northeastern polders, an area of some 177,000 acres which a few years previously – prior to a massive drainage scheme – had been the open sea of the Zuider Zee.

We set off on January 3, in possession of a letter from Prince Bernhard (husband and consort of Queen Juliana) which guaranteed us the freedom of virtually the whole country. It was a freezing cold winter. Although we were travelling in a Dormobile camper we intended staying at hotels for bed and breakfast.

Unfortunately, prior to my leaving, Sandra had contracted mumps. (As a child I had somehow escaped all the childish complaints.) We departed from Harwich on the *Queen Wilhelmina*. It was a hell of a trip; we literally had to hang on to stop ourselves being rolled out of the bunks, it was so rough. We arrived at The Hook about 7 am, following seven hours of this. After clearing customs we drove along the road in the dark towards Amsterdam, where we had to present ourselves to the Minister of Agriculture. Ted was driving, I was navigator. Suddenly we realised that a huge illuminated Coca-Cola truck was heading straight for us, on the same side of the road as ourselves!

'He'll turn to the left in a minute, Ted,' I declared confidently.

Soon, however, we came bumper to bumper with it. Its driver was sitting in his stationary vehicle, grinning like a monkey! I had a sudden thought. 'Ted, shouldn't we be on the other side of the road?!'

In Amsterdam we thought we were getting on well – on the correct side of the road – until we suddenly heard a bell ringing.

'Pull over, Ted, there's a fire engine coming up behind.'

Ted pulled over but the ringing still continued. I beckoned the vehicle on, wondering why it didn't pass us. Only when I leaned right out could I see it was a tram. We were on the tramlines!

We found the Minister of Agriculture to be most pleasant and helpful. The following day he arranged for us to be taken out on a fishery protection vessel, to look for birds in the Goes area of south Holland. Although the water was five or six feet below the banks, from the wheelhouse we were just above the level of the ground. There was a lot of wildfowl about, including all the usual duck and goose species. Suddenly I spied four other geese, with yellowish legs and bills. I asked the minister if we could stop and take some film, explaining that I believed them to be bean geese.

'No, no,' he said. 'They're not recorded in this area.' However after a while we finally convinced him and from then on we were the experts! We saw literally thousands of ducks and had an incredible day, which included lunch on board.

Next day we travelled north, stopping at Over Flakkee, to view the picturesque town and its huge cheese market. Ted wanted to buy some china from the famous Dutch porcelain town of Delph.

I should say at this stage that we were not dressed in our best clothes. The weather was very cold, and there was snow on the ground. Night temperatures were usually below −4 or −5°, sometimes plunging to −16°. Consequently we were well wrapped up – Ted in his black woolly balaclava, khaki-coloured airborne jumping jacket and thigh-boots, myself in short wellies and dufflecoat. We didn't normally shave until night – so we must have looked like a pair of real desperados!

About 11.30 in the morning we went to the International Bank for Ted to draw some money. When we walked in lots of people were there; but the doors were shut fast after us.

'Blast, Ted,' I said. 'We only just got here in time!'

An armed security guard stood by the door, letting people out as they concluded their business and left. Ted drew out the money he required and back we went to the door. After our departure it was left open and the only conclusion that we could come to was that they had thought us to be a hold-up gang!

We continued north to Amersfoort, where we stayed overnight in an hotel. Next morning when I got up and looked out of the window just after daybreak, a rough-legged buzzard was sitting in a tree not more than twenty-five yards away from me – quite a sight! Our journey continued via Zwolle to Emmeloord, on the Noord Oost Polder, then southwards again to Lelystad on Oost Flevoland, where they were still reclaiming some land. It had been drained and a seawall built; so, leaving the Dormobile on the seawall, we went through the reedbed to shoot film.

It really was a birdwatcher's paradise. In addition to the thousands of ducks, geese and swans present there were also harriers, short-eared owls and large flocks of bearded tits. (It was after the draining of these areas of the Netherlands that this latter species erupted to eastern England and started breeding there again, after a long absence.)

A white Volkswagen car came screaming along the seawall and, to our surprise, stopped by our Dormobile. We had earlier ignored a notice on a gate forbidding entry, but were nevertheless surprised when two policeman got out the Volkswagen and came over and asked what we were doing there.

I explained, but they didn't understand. So I suggested to Ted that he show them Prince Bernhard's letter. Ted put his hand in his pocket, and the policemen immediately went for their guns! Eventually, however, we calmed them down and Ted was allowed to put his hand slowly into his pocket and take out the envelope containing the letter and hand it to them. They read it and discussed it. Then they put it back in the envelope and returned it. Stepping back a pace, they saluted, then off they went. We never did have any more problems with the authorities after that.

We were fortunate enough to meet someone who had a shoot in this area. How it came about was that we wanted to go onto some farmland where there were literally thousands of geese flighting in from the sea just after daylight to feed on the grassland but had no idea of how to get there.

Knowing that the land was owned by the government, which then leased both farmland and shoots to tenants, I made enquiries and found that the tenant of this particular shoot, of some 1000 hectares, was a Mr Kukan. We met and I explained the situation to him. He couldn't believe that we were both conservationists and shooting men, but nevertheless invited us to his home.

We didn't realise that he was actually a Dutch millionaire (he was the Netherlands' biggest importer of agricultural machinery) until we visited the little house where he had been born alongside his huge bungalow – it was like a matchbox alongside a two gallon can! He still didn't believe our claim so, after a few drinks, and when we had warmed up a bit, I gave him a convincing demonstration with one of his guns. Next day he took us out with him but instead of shooting the geese we filmed them, from a hide that was actually a tilting platform some twelve feet long (it tilted some six inches when the geese flew by, so that you were out of their view). We got some lovely film that day.

We stayed at the Vohhoye Hotel at Emmeloord for four days, visiting the north-east polder and the Ijsselmeer, and going even farther north, right up to Groningen. There was only one 'fly in the ointment': on awakening one morning I had to tell Ted, 'I've got the mumps!' (Of course, I didn't report it – I had to keep going.)

At this time the Dutch were starting to build a power station and the new town of Drontden. However there were still sand dunes, though it seemed strange to see them miles out in the reedbeds which had been planted in the not inconsiderable stretches of remaining open water.

We could see there had been terns nesting on the dunes I asked a Dutchman close by what species of terns had been nesting there. Fortunately I had done my homework: as his knowledge of the English or scientific names was non-existent I had to use the Dutch ones I had learnt. Apparently grote stern (Sandwich tern) and visdiefje (common tern) had nested there for over twenty years, but never dwergstern (little tern). Now their tenure was at an end, the site was to be bulldozed and made into a dock.

In our short time there we got to know the country reasonably well. Eventually, however, it was time to motor back down through Amsterdam and Rotterdam to The Hook, and to undergo yet another rough sea crossing. Then came the road journey back from Harwich to Cley, where Phyllis met me.

I arrived home on my birthday, January 19. Phyllis and Gran had got everything ready for a celebratory party for me – but I was too ill with mumps to enjoy it! I went straight to bed and was ill for a whole six weeks. When the film was eventually shown on TV, however, it was exciting to see the footage Ted and I had taken.

One of my subsequent filming ventures, however, had a less fortunate outcome. In 1974, a very good friend, John Coast – who had been a regular visitor to Scolt since my father's time – said he was prepared to finance my taking shots there with a 16mm cine camera. He knew my feelings about and knowledge of terns and said he thought that similar shots to those I had already taken with my Super 8 Cine would be suitable for a television programme.

John knew a producer of TV natural history programmes at Bristol who was always on the lookout for new material. He had been a prisoner of war in the Far East, along with hundreds of others serving in the Royal Norfolk and was subsequently an adviser on a documentary film *Return to the River Kwai* which gave an account of their ordeal. He also financed and directed a film portraying Javanese national dancing and culture.

After filming was completed, an edited clip was sent to the BBC producer at Bristol. His comment to John was that its quality and content were 'acceptable', but that as I wasn't a union member, the material couldn't be used. However he was prepared to send a natural history film unit to Scolt to film similar sequences and sufficient material to illustrate my point of view. I rejected this suggestion. A full production team was out of the question, as I considered the disturbance too great. I had filmed over two seasons at the terns' leisure, when it was convenient to them.

CHAPTER TWENTY

Famous Visitors –
Rare Birds

In 1969 there was no money to pay Gordon. When I argued with the office I was told, 'Well, there's very little happening on Scolt Head – it runs itself! Therefore, as we've got to cut back, we shall cut back on Scolt Head. A summer assistant really isn't warranted!'

It was demoralising – it took the wind out of our sails; but I had to work out a plan to keep Gordon with me for the season at least. Apart from anything else I felt some moral obligation to him; upon becoming the 'permanent' assistant warden he had given up his farm job. I told him, 'I can't afford to pay you (his take-home pay was £38 per week – which was peanuts, considering everything he did as assistant warden) but to help out financially you ferry people to and from the Hut, in your own boat, and make a charge, £10 a round trip.'

Undeterred by the lack of money from the NCC Gordon continued to soldier on, as always starting just before the terns arrived, in mid-April, and continuing, staying in the little observation hut right up until the last chick flew in August. It was a shame that it was not realised what a dedicated man he really was; being a bit rough and ready, not being able to express himself too clearly, worked against him.

By the time the NCC got its act together we had made our own arrangements. Prior to this period we had been at everybody's beck and call, carrying stores to the Hut daily for the visitors. I pointed out that, with modern dried milk and preserved foodstuffs, there was no need for this. I felt that it was up to them to look after themselves, with the proviso that if they did want anything extra they could come down to the ternery and let me know what they wanted. I could bring whatever was required back to the ternery the following day and it would be up to them to come down and collect it.

During that summer of '69 we received the first of a series of visits from a family whom we came to treat as rather 'special' – not because of their status, but for the wonderful people they were.

Gran loved Dial House and spent most of her time in the kitchen, at the sink. On this particular occasion she was peeling the potatoes. Phyllis was writing. Needless to say, I was on Scolt Head. Gran went to answer a knock on the door, wiping her wet hands on her apron as she opened it.

A smart well-spoken lady whom Gran had never seen before stood there. 'I'm making enquiries about going to Scolt Head,' she said.

'Phyllis, there's somebody wanta go to Scolt Head,' Gran called out. 'When do you wanta go?' she asked. 'Oh? Thursday. Hang you on.'

'Can't find the tidetable,' Phyllis said loudly. 'They'll have to ring back.'

The lady went off. Twenty minutes later the phone rang and a voice said, 'The Duchess of Kent wants to go to Scolt Head.'

'Oh yes,' Phyllis replied. 'Well, if she'd like to get in touch with us.'

'She got in touch with you twenty minutes ago,' the voice said. 'You hadn't got a tidetable to hand!'

This was in August and the birds were finished nesting. We arranged for Gordon to take the party over to the island in his boat.

'Bill,' the Duchess said (she called me that, for some reason, though she called Gordon by his name). 'Bill, if it rains, where can we shelter?'

I replied that if it was all right with Gordon they could shelter in the observation hut. Since he was sleeping there at the time (it was his 'home' for the summer months) I said she must ask his permission too. This she did.

Gordon looked at her and drawled, 'Yeah, I reckon that 'ud be all right!'

Many eminent people visited Scolt over the years. Aubrey (now Lord) Buxton frequently brought friends over; but on one particular occasion he asked if it would be possible for his party to be the only people at the ternery. Though I was not told the reason for this request, I had my suspicions. I suggested that the party be ferried to the ternery on the last of the tide, and then walked back. It was the only way I could guarantee freedom from other visitors and the proposal was agreed to. I told Gordon about the visit and who I thought one of the party would be, adding that – as it was two weeks away – to keep the knowledge to himself, because they wanted no publicity.

His comment was typically, 'Oh ah, yes.' He appeared neither interested nor excited.

It wasn't often I commented on Gordon's clothes; but on the day in question

I said to him, 'As this is a special occasion, at least for Scolt, will you tidy yourself up a bit?' His hair, not having been combed or washed recently, was knotted, his beard had been trimmed about a fortnight previously but was still four inches long and his shorts and fisherman's smock were covered in mud. As very little was left of the upper parts of his sand shoes they were held on his feet by string.

On meeting the party I explained the policy at the ternery and the importance of Gordon's role. I emphasised that none of the achievements would have been possible without his dedication. Gordon himself was waiting for us at the observation hut. I felt quite proud of him. He looked so smart! His hair and beard were combed and he was wearing clean denim shorts (albeit with a broken zip!) and an almost new pair of shoes. These he had found washed up on the beach. They had but two drawbacks – one was blue and the other white, and both had been designed for use on the left foot!

I introduced to him to our 'star' guest – the Duke of Edinburgh.

'How ya goin' on?' said Gordon.

The Duke obviously found difficulty in answering this remark and looked at Gordon in a rather strange way. I felt that the impression he was forming of my assistant did not quite tally with the one he had gained from my earlier remarks. He nodded and said, 'Hello.'

To minimise disturbance we walked round the edge of the main group of nesting common terns. The Duke asked to walk directly through, but I explained why this was not advisable. As we approached the Sandwich tern colony the birds took to flight. 5000 of them were in the air – a most impressive sight. Almost 2000 chicks stampeded away from us.

I pointed out that the chicks now out on the open beach were vulnerable to predation by gulls and risked drowning or being swept out to sea when the ridge flooded, as it often did when the tide was forced up by a north wind, adding that unruly dogs could kill considerable numbers before their masters could stop them.

Withdrawing again to the ternery perimeter, we continued to where a group of common terns was hatching. (Their nests are more widely scattered as, unlike the Sandwich tern, some individual birds can be very aggressive.) As we neared the first nest the incubating bird took to the air, circled and dived straight at the Duke. It deposited a 'message' on his head and jacket.

Why him, he asked. I jokingly answered, 'Terns are not selective. That's what they do to me – they class us all as ruddy nuisances!'

Whether it was the smell of the excreta or my remark I wasn't sure, but he was certainly not amused! When we returned to the observation hut, Gordon's offer of tea was declined and, after resting for ten minutes, I walked the visitors back across the mud and sand to the mainland. On our arrival at the Hard, where the cars were parked, there was not a person in sight. Only the terns had been aware of the royal visit!

I wasn't too popular with members of the press corps; they had asked me to keep them informed of VIPs visiting the island. I also received a reprimand from the regional officer for not informing the office of the Duke's intended visit. I was told curtly that it wasn't the warden's duty to entertain distinguished visitors. My reply was that, over the years, Aubrey Buxton had brought many distinguished people, including the present director general of the NCC, to Scolt Head. I added that it had obviously been a day away from the Duke's many official duties and that I had particularly been asked for no publicity – a request that I had carried out to the full. I heard no more about the incident.

It has been said that when Bob starts talking about terns and Scolt Head it is a hard job to get away from him! I make no apology for this; I am only too pleased to pass on the knowledge I have gleaned over the years. Observing tern behaviour from arrival to departure I became at first aware, and finally totally convinced, that they inherently pick up atmospheric waves or changes. This 'built-in barometer' mechanism is so sensitive that they receive these waves three or four days in advance of the actual change in the weather.

It is a scientific fact that the hours of daylight control birds' migration to the breeding areas, their nesting and departure. It seems likely that terns have an inborn 'radar' system, worked on a polar flux or field, governing their direction of flight on migration. Taking this hypothesis a stage further, could a similar system operate to locate their nests (ie eggs) in total darkness, I wondered?

When deliberately disturbed at night an incubating bird on its return alighted ten to fifteen centimetres downwind of the nest and walked directly to the eggs. (The nest area had previously been ringed with a margin of sand, to pinpoint the exact landing spot.)

Birds cannot automatically leave when nesting is complete; changing from the breeding state to that of migration takes twelve to fourteen days. Their imminent departure is indicated by their behaviour during that day. I have frequently observed terns after nesting congregating on the shoreline, preparing to migrate. They usually leave at sunset and I have noticed that if a group on the point of departure in the evening stays until the following morning, a change of weather is on the way. Low atmospheric pressure appears to control their final departure, and I have known groups to stay for an extra four days, due to unfavourable weather, rather than actually go with little or no improvement in conditions. However, by midday on their last day weather conditions would have improved.

It was many seasons before I realised that terns reacted to atmospheric changes – not only to what was happening on the day in question but also to changes up to four days away.

These observations had led me to tease poor Euan Dunn, concerning how I knew when each particular group of terns would depart.

Many people have listened to me predicting the weather – even four days in advance! – by tern behaviour. To some it was a 'good laugh' though their laughter faded when my forecasts frequently turned out spot on! It was, however, taken to the extreme by two dear old ladies who met me on Scolt Head.

Having heard my reputation, they asked me, 'If you took a holiday at Brancaster, which month would you choose?'

It had been dull or wet for all but two days of their fortnight's stay, so I knew the enquiry was no 'legpull'. What could I say? With tongue in cheek I declared, 'Next year take your holiday during the first two weeks of August – you can't go wrong!'

Thanking me they went off happily. The following year I met them again on Scolt Head, at the end of their two weeks' stay. After the usual 'hellos' the topic turned to the weather. They said, 'We have had two fantastic weeks. The sun has shone every day, just as you said it would. We shall tell all our friends about you, and how you can predict weather conditions in advance.' In actual fact it had been the hottest and driest summer for years!

My reputation encouraged gardening neighbours to follow my lead when hoeing, when they could expect dry weather for a couple of days, or setting out their plants (especially brassicas) when they hoped for rain within twenty-four hours.

For many years a friend, David Jarwood, had spent his holidays in the village, fishing and sailing. Due to adverse weather most years the actual number of days he could take his boat to sea had been few.

Eventually one year he asked what the weather prospects were for the following two weeks. (He had heard of my predictions for years but had never taken them seriously.) The previous three weeks had been mainly fine, sunny and warm, with light to moderate west-south-west winds.

I said, 'According to the terns' behaviour this fine spell will last until Tuesday. So get as much fishing in as you can over the next four days, and then look out!'

The next three days I saw him going out in his boat. Then, on the Tuesday morning, he called in at the ternery on his way. The time was nine fifteen, the weather fine and sunny. The air temperature was 74 degrees Fahrenheit, and there was hardly a ripple on the water.

'What's happened to your weather prediction, Bob?'

I must admit that I thought I – or should I say the terns – had made a mistake; but as we talked the entire common tern colony took to the air for the second time in an hour. This was the fourth day they had been 'dreading'. When the majority of birds had returned to the nest I said, 'You have witnessed it for yourself. The four days are up. That's a sure indication that a change to bad weather is imminent.' (Though looking at the clear sky I wasn't too convinced of the truth of my own statement!)

David said, 'I'll have a little bet with you, Bob, that there will be no change in the next twenty-four hours.'

'OK, let's make it a pound. But I'll also bet that by six o'clock on the flood tide you'll be only too glad to reach the shelter of the harbour channel, and that you'll be wearing your oilskins, thigh waders and sou'wester!'

We shook hands on this and he left for his day at sea, wearing only shorts and a shirt. At midday the thermometer registered 81 degrees Fahrenheit, the wind was light south-west and the cloud cover nil.

Again, looking at the sky where the blue reached right to the horizon, I decided that the terns had let me down for certain. My interpretation of their behaviour was 'rubbish'. What an utter fool I should feel when David returned!

About three o'clock I was talking to six visitors who had walked to the island from the mainland. Suddenly I felt a cool breeze and realised the wind had veered to the east. To the north a black cloud, low on the horizon, was moving towards us. As it came nearer the wind freshened and veered north. A noticeable drop in temperature followed, causing me to put on my shirt and pullover. I suggested to the six visitors that if they didn't want wet shirts they had better make their way back without delay; so off they set. The menacing black cloud continued landward, completely blocking out the sun. By five o'clock the wind had reached fresh to strong northlwest. Upon checking the temperature I found it had dropped to 59 degrees, and as I made my way to the observation hut I felt the first spots of rain. This soon increased and visibility deteriorated, until it was impossible to see the ternery, let alone David's progress up the harbour channel.

About six o'clock I heard footsteps on the wooden approach to the hut. The door was locked to stop it from being blown open and when I unlocked it, there stood David. It was only with a great effort that we closed the door and relocked it. Cursing, he removed his sou'wester and oilskins. While he dried himself I made a pot of tea.

'You and your bloody terns! I thought my bet was a dead cert. Before I left this morning I rang RAF Marham met office for their latest weather report. They assured me that there was no change on the way in the foreseeable future. When I get back I shall ring and ask what went wrong with their forecast!'

The following day the weather had improved somewhat; but not enough for David to go fishing. On my return home in the evening he gave me a call from the sailing club. Over a pint he told me that the RAF said that a small depression had developed very quickly and that this had made it impossible to forecast what was going to happen.

'I told them,' he concluded, 'that in future they should contact you. With the help of the terns on Scolt Head you would be more reliable than all their sophisticated equipment.'

Incidentally, he parted with his pound – and I have won many more pints since!

Stan Woodell, head of botany at Oxford University, and an adviser to the Nature Conservancy, was researching into the high saltmarsh plants – sea lavender and thrift – at Scolt. He had some fifteen to twenty fixed points to which he returned each year to take photographs by which to record changes in distribution of these species. During twenty-five years of his visits I had got to know both him and his wife Becky, a very keen ornithologist, well. One day he said, 'I consider that what you've found out about Sandwich terns is very interesting. If you write it all up, I know someone who might publish it. I'll edit it for you,' he added, obviously sensing my hesitation.

With Stan's help, extracts from my article were subsequently published in *Biological Conservation*, in the *International Journal* – a journal of ideas and information. At the time the Israeli government was starting out on a conservation programme which included nesting terns. Having read my article they contacted me in late 1969 for more information on the subject of tern management. Their common tern colonies reared on average ten per cent of young figures identical to those achieved on Scolt before visitors had been controlled.

I supplied the information they requested and the following summer the 'Bob Chestney' of Israel visited the British Isles to look at terneries including Scolt. Unfortunately his English wasn't good, and my Hebrew even worse, but we managed to understand each other by drawing symbols and images in the sand. After three days on Scolt he understood what I was trying to put over. I also wrote down the information that I had given him with the comment, 'Don't expect to achieve it all in a few seasons.'

He had tern colonies on many small islands comprised of slabs of rock and sand with little or no vegetation. Near a main beach they were frequently visited by boats, whose human occupants, having no thought for the birds, stayed for most of the day. The chicks naturally scurried away from the nests and shelter of the rocks on the humans' arrival, exposing themselves to the intense heat. Thinking our two otherwise dissimilar areas, many miles apart, might have something in common, I emphasised the importance of monitoring his island, both with and without human disturbance, and after the heat of the day.

Next autumn the officer in charge of the Israel Conservation Department, a man who spoke excellent English, visited Scolt and their past season's results, based on the information I had supplied, had been even better than I had anticipated. On the islands with the minimum of disturbance forty per cent of pairs had successfully reared one chick. On the island with no visitor control the figure had remained unchanged – ten per cent of pairs had reared one young. It was clear from the results that the banning of visitors from the islands was the answer.

Many zoologists from overseas, when visiting Britain, made a special effort to come to Scolt Head. They came from the USA, Canada, Thailand, India, Israel, South Africa, France, Italy, Belgium, the Netherlands, Germany, Switzerland, Sweden, Denmark and Pakistan. Those interested in terns all took away with them the 'Scolt Head Method' and I felt so pleased that I had, in a small way, been able to help terns virtually in 'another world'!

Scolt was also the site for pioneering studies and experiments and studies over the years. The International Synthetic Rubber Company from Southport, Lancashire, ran a pilot scheme on the island to stabilise mobile sand. I have already described the devastating effects that blown sand could have on nesting terns and it was the ternery area at the western end of the island which was chosen for these experiments. A solution of rubber, oil and water was to be sprayed on the mobile sand. A chemist and a botanist were sent from Southport to set up the programme.

The first year was taken up with perfecting the consistency of the solution, to get it to go through a commercial spray. The experts plotted out the area that was sprayed; I monitored the effects of the solution. Bamboo canes, placed in each plot, were painted in two-inch strips, in a variety of colours. The depth of sand which had either eroded or accreted could therefore be easily studied. The study continued for three years, at the end of which I was asked for an opinion on it by interested parties from Australia, Israel and the USA – eager to find out if the scheme could be adapted for use in the vast desert regions of their respective countries. It was certainly successful at Scolt.

Another experiment of the same period which I particularly remember was

173

that carried out under the direction of Dr Kitson and Professor Steers. Radioactive pebbles were placed out to sea (roughly in bucketfuls at a time) to study longshore drift. Piles of these were deposited a quarter of a mile, half a mile and three-quarters of a mile out to sea, to confirm what their distribution was. The pebbles were similar in size to those known to occur naturally in the areas they were placed. They had been drilled out, small radioactive particles inserted, and sealed with aerolite, at Harwell. They could then be picked up by geiger counter for some thirty weeks afterwards.

My job was to go out in the boat and assist. The recording gear was in the boat, and we would trawl around until we found them. The distance they had been dispersed by the tidal movement could then be assessed.

Although terns, and in particular Sandwich terns, employed a very large amount of my time and effort, nevertheless they were not the only birds which concerned me. I have already written about some of my childhood experiences with other birds at Scolt Head and even today, without referring to my notes, I can vividly recollect where, when and on which part of the island I saw my first great bustard, little stint and eleven tern species – all of which I was able to identify virtually straightaway. Apart from the 'regular' tern species, I've been lucky enough to see Caspian, gull-billed, bridled, sooty and white-winged black terns at Scolt Head.

Mention of the sooty tern brings to mind Dick Bagnall-Oakley, one-time geography master and head of the ornithological team at Gresham's School, Holt, and president of the Norfolk Ornithologists' Association. Every year he brought his pupils over to Scolt Head. They were very keen, and always asked me, 'What have you got, Bob?'

This particular year I was able to answer, not without a certain pride, 'We have a sooty tern here at the moment.'

'Oh, yes,' Bagnall-Oakley replied casually. 'There have been a lot this year.'

I knew what was in his mind – many country people still call the comparatively common black tern (a marsh-nesting species which bred in England prior to the drainage of the Fens) a 'sooty' tern. The actual sooty tern, which is much larger, is a rare visitor to this country from the tropical Atlantic.

'Aren't you getting your Chlidonias niger mixed up with your Sterna fuscata?' I asked.

This brought a different reaction: 'SOOTY TERN! Where is it?'

This bird had been present for some time and had a call which I had learned to imitate. Each night at about six o'clock I would hear it and call it up. This evening proved to be no exception. I called it up, and in it flew. Bagnall-Oakley was able to take a photograph of it flying round us. (This later appeared in the

Norfolk Bird Report.) The bird stayed on the North Norfolk coast for a fortnight in all.

The most species I ever saw in one day on Scolt was eighty-four, on May 18, 1948. By 1983 298 species had been identified there – not a bad total for such a comparatively small area. It must be said, however, that I never did go looking for birds ('twitching'). Being on Scolt for the hours I was I didn't need to.

My first rarity was a great reed warbler. I've also seen Bonelli's warbler, gyrfalcon and black wheatear – the latter by accident! There had been a considerable amount of wood washed ashore by the big April tides. I went over on a big tide in early evening, so it wasn't too far to carry the wood. I brought it over the hills to the Cockle Bight, on the south side of the island, where I noticed a bird on the beach. I remember the date – it was April 29. A number of common wheatears were present, along with this other bird. It had a typical wheatear stance, and flipped along, showing a white rump. Otherwise it appeared wholly black like a small blackbird. At the time I couldn't figure out what it was; but later on I was able to look it up in the field guide.

Other Scolt sightings included snowfinch, little egret, white-tailed eagle and osprey.

There was also an American mockingbird – which 'experts' said couldn't possibly have flown the Atlantic. (Did they make the same complaint about the red-breasted nuthatch, which turned up unexpectedly at Holkham in October 1989? No – because thousands of people saw it!) Less likely 'rarities' included harlequin ducks and budgies.

If I saw a really rare bird, with my luck I sometimes saw two! That was even worse – who would believe you? This happened when I found what would have been the first (two) county record(s) for red-throated pipit. In those days there weren't so many people birdwatching; but now scarcely a section of the British Isles has managed to escape the attention of birdwatchers. Nowadays this species, while still creating a stir among twitchers, is seen comparatively frequently in Norfolk.

One bird (again two!) which, to my knowledge has never again been recorded in Norfolk (and which was unacceptable to those who 'know about' these things) was the brown flycatcher. Becky Woodell was with me when we came across this unusual little bird at the Hut. We both managed to get within a few yards of it.

Not everything that turned up was a rarity, however. One day, two eminent ornithologists were walking up the Hut steps with me when I picked up a bird from the side of the steps. Taking out my rule I recorded its wing and other measurements. None of us knew what this smallish, brownish passerine was; but suddenly we had a bright idea after examination, when released it might call, thus enabling us to identify it. So we took it out onto the marsh and released it. It flew away and, as we had hoped, called: 'piou!' It was a skylark!

The same two men were down at the ternery with me when we spied a bird standing on tiptoe in the couch grass.

'What is it?' we all asked, almost simultaneously. The size, we all agreed, was that of a redshank. It was definitely a wader; but we could not determine the species. Eventually we flushed it and it flew onto the beach, landing beside a ringed plover. Suddenly it had shrunk in size! It wasn't as big as the ringed plover, let alone anything like a redshank in height. It was a dunlin in winter plumage!

These two instances taught me a great lesson – unless you're positive about a bird in your own mind, forget it! During the long hours I was looking at birds on Scolt Head I could have conjured up anything I liked, had I wanted to.

As we have seen, my father encouraged me from an early age to become involved with the island and its birds. In the summer holidays I was allowed to assist with the catching of tern chicks. One of the first 'recoveries' was a chick which had been ringed two summers previously. Caught and eaten by an inhabitant of Senegal, in West Africa, the ring had been taken to a mission where the finder was paid one (old) penny. I remember saying, 'Is that all?!' However, it was pointed out to me that annual earnings there were then around £16. From then on I had become much more interested in the ways of birds, rather than in merely shooting them with an airgun!

I also recall my first bird recovery after I became a qualified 'ringer'. It was a common tern, ringed as a chick in July and found in September on Skegness beach. It had only travelled nineteen miles, not a spectacular recovery, but an interesting one all the same.

To become a qualified ringer involves very stringent training under supervision, with various species (both adult and young). The trainee has to pass as competent before a licence is granted. Much valuable and interesting data has been recorded from birds recovered (which is usually after their death). For instance I ringed a male blackbird in December. In June it was caught at the nest in Poland. A starling I found dead on Scolt had been ringed three years previously three hundred miles east of Moscow.

It might seem horrific to be catching birds at the nest but I can truthfuly say that, of all the pairs I caught – not only of common tern but also ringed plover, oystercatcher, black-headed gull and even the wily redshank – not one deserted the nest. After being released, without exception, each bird flew to the nearest water, to wash, preen and readjust its feathers. Then it flew back to the nest. If the mate had returned to find the nest unoccupied it took over incubation; but relinquished that status when the 'on-duty' bird arrived.

I must make it absolutely clear that passerines (small land birds such as meadow pipits, reed buntings, skylarks and linnets) won't tolerate being caught at the nest while incubating.

The longest a common tern (only this tern species was caught while nesting) was away from its nest after being released was seven minutes. Of the waders, a redshank held the longest record: seventeen minutes.

The oldest breeding bird on Scolt Head was an oystercatcher female. When I first saw her nesting I noticed a ring on her left leg. I knew for sure this wasn't a Scolt bird, as I always ringed on the right leg during the incubation period. I caught both male and female and, for future identification, colour-ringed them, as well as obtaining data from the ringed female.

They nested in the same spot for seven consecutive years. One morning when I arrived at the ternery I found that the eggs had been deserted. Both birds were in the 'off-duty' area – a position in the nesting territory normally adopted by the bird not incubating at the time. This by itself suggested that all was not well.

The following morning the birds were in the same position. I saw them frequently throughout the day and noticed that the male spent most of his time with his head under a wing. He looked a very sick bird. On my way home I walked towards them. The female flew off but the male was too weak to stand. He was extremely thin and, on examination, I discovered that the lower bill had been broken at the tip. At least half an inch was missing, thus preventing him from feeding. He had probably sustained his injury in an encounter with a stoat when he was incubating the eggs. By the next morning he was dead and there was no sign of the female. However, twenty-two days later she had returned to the same nest site, accompanied by a new unringed male. During incubation, when he had become more 'tame', I caught and colour-ringed him.

This particular partnership continued for eleven seasons; and then, halfway through the season the nest was deserted for five days, both birds remaining in the off-duty area. The following morning the male was dead. There being no visible signs of injury, I conducted an elementary post mortem which revealed that the gizzard was badly infected due to the presence of a single number five shotgun pellet. Our female oysteratcher was 'bereaved' a second time; but within a month she had found a third male. They returned to the nest site, and successfully fledged one chick on August 29 – a very late date.

They continued nesting until 1987, when the female was thirty-seven years old. In 1988 they were again present; but I cannot confirm whether or not eggs were laid. On checking my records I established that she had laid at least forty-two clutches of three eggs (clutch size never varied). This made a total of 126 eggs. Over the years the eggs became reduced in size, from 58 mm in length to

50 mm, and in width from 42 mm to 33 mm. Finally, therefore, she was producing an almost round egg. The bold overall markings of little-fingernail size had become reduced to the odd spot.

During the last five years, although the eggs hatched, the young were in a very weak condition, surviving only for about seventy-two hours and dying near the nest.

On a place like Scolt Head, bird experiences are bound to be many and varied. How many people, for example, have seen a young cuckoo, not quite feathered, in a meadow pipit's nest – the foster parents having to work incessantly to satisfy the ever-hungry chick which even at this stage was as big as them? (I think a newly-hatched cuckoo the ugliest chick I know – reminiscent of some prehistoric creature.)

Another experience I shall never forget occurred the evening the local Women's Institute visited the ternery. The weather was fine and sunny, but an east wind made it rather cool. On their arrival I gave my usual introduction to Scolt and its nesting birds; then I continued with the conducted tour. After I had shown them a representative selection of nesting seabirds, we made a sortie through the dune vegetation and bushes where small passerines were nesting.

Prior to the party's arrival I had checked out each nest, to discover the stage of incubation, as passerines disturbed prior to being well into their fourteen-day incubation are likely to desert. However I gave the visitors the impression that the nests were all new to me, and told them how sensitive land birds were to disturbance. The most incredible thing happened when we went to look at a linnet's nest, concealed in a seablite bush. I expected the incubating bird to have departed; but as I parted the branches, exposing the nest, there was the male bird sitting tightly.

'I shall have to put him off, so that you can see the eggs,' I said, slowly lowering my hand towards the nest. The bird, however, did not bat an eyelid!

When I placed my fingers under its breast, to my astonishment it jumped onto my finger and stayed there while I showed the ladies the four eggs and one chick – the latter only a few minutes old. Then I slowly lowered my hand and, turning my fingers downwards, returned the bird to the nest, to continue brooding. My last task was to let the branches back to their natural concealing position.

I said, without any conviction, that this was what could be done if one understood birds. Someone said, 'You must love your birds.'

I replied that it was far more important to understand their behaviour. (What should I have said to a lady who compared me with St Francis of Assisi?!)

In fact I think that the reason for this bird's strange behaviour was quite simply that the air temperature at the time was well below normal, due to the east wind.

There must therefore have been a difference in temperature between air and nest of 40 degrees Fahrenheit (21°C). Under these conditions there is a strong impulse to keep the chicks warm, which overrides the natural fear of man.

I have experienced other situations where birds appear to have shed this fear. One morning in early October, just after daylight, while walking across the high saltmarshes on Scolt I saw flying towards me at great speed (only about three feet from the ground) seven small birds. A larger bird was in hot pursuit. As they drew closer I saw that the smaller birds were redshank and that they were being chased by a male peregrine.

I stopped, telling the dog to sit. It appeared that the peregrine was trying to get beneath the redshank; but they were refusing to rise. The line they were taking was straight for me. Any moment I expected them to veer away; but when they were within a few yards their close formation exploded, and all seven dived into the vegetation around me. Whether the peregrine had seen me earlier I don't know; but within ten yards of me it shot into the air, its wings making a sound like calico being torn.

When at a 'safe' distance it circled twice overhead before flying off. The dog and I remained in the same positions for at least three minutes before I gave the order to 'put them out!' She hunted the area where I am sure we both knew the redshank had dropped; but not one was flushed. So we left them hiding.

A similar episode (what I call man/bird relationship) also occurred on Scolt. I was walking along the north shore at midday when a turtle dove shot over the dunes, not a hundred yards in front of me. It was pursued by a male peregrine.

The dove turned sharply to the left and headed straight for me. After the redshank experience I, of course, stopped again, telling the dog to sit. The pair continued on the same course until, within fifteen yards of me, the dove crashed onto the beach. The peregrine, in close pursuit, shot skywards, though without the 'calico-rending' sound I had heard before. The dove picked itself up, unhurt but panting and gulping for air as it inflated and deflated its lungs.

The dog and I did not move for at least two minutes, by which time the dove had regained a normal breathing rhythm (no doubt its 'second wind'). It turned its head and, though no doubt only in my own vivid imagination, I swear by its facial expression it was saying, 'That was a close one!'

Fluttering its wings and adjusting its feathers it took to flight, returning the way it had come.

I experienced other similar occurrences, in which I felt that birds were less concerned with man than with the situation that confronted them. This suggested to me that they had the ability to use us as an additional source for survival outside their inherited instincts – man being the safer of two evils!

CHAPTER TWENTY-ONE

My MBE

On November 20, 1974 the postman delivered a long brown official-looking envelope to Dial House. Phyllis picked it up and read 'On Her Majesty's Service' at the top. Bringing it in to me she declared, 'There's a letter from the Inland Revenue. What have they written to us about? We don't owe them any money.'

We had a look together and discovered that it wasn't from the tax office but from the Prime Minister. Phyllis said, 'What the devil does Harold Wilson want to write to us for?'

We opened it, and she gasped. 'You've been nominated for the MBE!'

I read the letter. It informed me 'in strictest confidence' that the Prime Minister: 'had in mind, on the occasion of the forthcoming list of New Year Honours' to submit my name to 'HM the Queen with the recommendation that her Majesty be graciously pleased to approve that you be appointed a Member of the Order of the British Empire (MBE).'

My immediate reaction was that I couldn't see how a simple country boy like Bob Chestney could have such an honour bestowed upon him. What would all my friends think? What would they say?!

'I don' want that!' I told Phyllis.

Phyllis said, 'Oh, come on, Bob, it'd be nice.'

'No. What have I done to get that? We aren't going to the Palace!'

She made me sit and talk about it for a while. In the end she said, 'Well, wait until the children come home tonight. We'll see how they feel about it.'

On first reading the letter I had completely failed to grasp the significance of the award, not only to myself but to my family; and I had not fully comprehended the fact that it would be as a tribute to my contribution to conservation. It was the highest award I could have obtained for my services within the United

Kingdom. (The OBE – Order of the British Empire – is for services rendered also outside the UK.)

When the girls came home Phyllis said, 'Guess what? Daddy has been nominated for the MBE.'

'What's that.'

'It's a medal we assume for all his work for conservation, and it means we can go to Buckingham Palace to the Queen, to collect it with him.'

'Ooh, yes, Dad – let's do that!'

'Oh, I dunno,' I replied guardedly, but eventually, still with some reluctance, I agreed. So I filled in the form that had been enclosed with the letter and sent it back.

On January 1 1975 the newspaper deliveryman was met with great excitement! The paper was scanned eagerly and, sure enough, there was my name in the Honours List.

Later I received a letter, inviting me to an investiture at Buckingham Palace on February 11.

Of course, everything started to 'happen'! What does one wear to go Buckingham Palace? We weren't really earning a great deal of money. Phyllis said, 'Well, I don't know what I can wear!'

As our local policeman, Les Brackpool, had to go to Norwich he offered to take Phyllis with him.

It was a dreadful morning. On arriving at Norwich Phyllis made her way to Garlands store, where she was greeted by a female assistant.

'Can I help you? You wanted something special?'

Phyllis said 'Yes.'

'The bride's mother?'

'No. I'm going to Buckingham Palace!'

'You need our Cresta range.'

When Phyllis saw the prices she thought, I can't afford this – Bob will blow his top! Nevertheless, she took an immediate fancy to a dress and coat outfit which looked both smart and warm. Although it fitted beautifully the price made her gasp – £55. However, she decided to buy the outfit, saying to the assistant, 'My husband will go berserk when I get home!'

Having got the coat, Phyllis remembered that she now had to get a hat, which entailed a further walk all over Norwich, from shop to shop. In the end she chose an emerald green 'bowler' style hat.

When she arrived back no-one was at home. She had a headache and felt sick. She lit the fire and, though not normally a whisky drinker, made herself a 'hot toddy'.

The children arrived and asked if she had bought something.

'Yes,' she answered flatly.

She had hung her new outfit up behind her. The girls saw it and exclaimed, 'Ooh, that's nice!'. 'Lovely!'

'I don't know what your father's going to say.'

'He won't worry,' Sandra reassured her.

Phyllis didn't hear me come home; but the girls did. They came to meet me before I went into the sitting room. 'Don't say anything, Daddy, but Mummy's ever so upset. She's bought this dress and coat and it cost her fifty-five pounds. She's worried what you're going to say. She's feeling quite ill.'

They went back into the sitting room; after a while I followed them. I didn't let on what the girls had told me. I said to Phyllis, 'Did you get anything?'

'Yes.'

'Where is it?'

'There, hanging up behind me.' She didn't look up at me.

'Oh, that's good,' I said. 'What'd it cost – sixty-eight pounds?' Phyllis breathed an audible sigh of relief. 'Oh no, only fifty-five!'

For my part there was only one thing I could wear – a morning suit. So we had to make a hurried trip to George Goddard's shop, in King's Lynn, for me to be fitted.

The trip to London was a highlight for the Chestney family. It was the very first time we had all been away together. (It would also prove to be the last.)

Some friends, Sheila and Duncan Marshall Andrew, who lived in London but had a holiday cottage at Brancaster Staithe, had kindly arranged all our accommodation and transport. (Their firm had had the painting contract for the Throne Room at the Palace.) They sent a car to pick us up at Liverpool Street station. We were driven in style on a tour of London, before being dropped at our lodging in Ebury Street. In the evening Duncan and Sheila took us out to dinner. That sort of kindness is something you never forget.

Next day was the great day. Previously we had driven round in a taxi, so that we knew all five of us could go. Today, however, a policeman was standing outside as we left Ebury Street – so five were not allowed to share a single taxi. Phyllis, Sally and myself got into one cab, Catherine and Sandra followed on behind in another. Off we travelled to Buckingham Palace.

On arrival, sheer excitement and nervousness began to take grip. When Phyllis got out of the taxi her hat came off and went rolling down the street. I felt highly embarrassed, all dressed up in my morning suit. (What a contrast to my usual Scolt Head dress of shorts and shirt, or thigh boots and oilskin coat!)

Unfortunately, the invitation had made provision for only one child to accompany Phyllis and I into the Palace. Between them, Catherine and Sandra had agreed that, as the youngest, Sally (then aged twelve) should have this honour. Their only proviso had been that they should be included in the visit to London. They now remained outside the Palace gates while we three went in.

It was like stepping into another world; but, strange as it may seem, my shyness and embarrassment started to evaporate. I soon felt at ease, even among the breathtaking splendour I now discovered about me.

Sally thought the Household Guards in their bearskins were stuffed, since they stood absolutely motionless to attention. 'Are they real Mummy?' she asked Phyllis.

'Yes. I'll wink at one.'

She did – but he didn't even bat an eyelid in response!

We were ushered the length of a long mirrored corridor into the Throne Room, where I left Phyllis and Sally. I was taken into an anteroom, where all the recipients were briefed and had to wait until called for. It was a very relaxing atmosphere, with the band playing light music on the balcony.

Eventually I heard my name called: 'Mister R. F. Chestney!' With my heart knocking like a drum I approached the Queen. She was standing on a dais about a foot high, and I was surprised at how tiny she was. She looked rather tired (who wouldn't be, after shaking hands with six hundred people, one after the other?). After a brief chat and congratulations, the medal was pinned to my lapel.

After bowing, I turned to my right, and the ordeal was all but over. I rejoined Phyllis and Sally and we left together. When we came out we were all highly elated. We had our pictures taken and were met by another great friend, Timothy Potts, who took us for a celebratory lunch at the Spaghetti House, in Knightsbridge.

The meal was wonderful; but unfortunately Sally got drunk on the wine. So we had to walk her up and down Knightsbridge until she was sober again before we could get a taxi and take her back to Ebury Street.

When we got home to Brancaster Staithe, to my considerable disappointment, not one of my old friends said, 'Well done, Bob we're proud of you!' However, in spite of all my childish white lies, thieving and scheming, I am sure my old schoolteacher, Miss Kaye, was proud of me. Just prior to her retirement, a few years previously, I had met her on her final school trip to Scolt Head. (During all the years my father and I were wardens at Scolt there had been an annual school visit by Deepdale School.) On that occasion I had asked her if she was satisfied with her life and with teaching such poor scholars as myself.

Her reply had been: 'Without your missing school and going to Scolt with your father, and learning the business from him, I doubt that you would have achieved what you have.'

On congratulating me after I had received my MBE she said jokingly, 'I must admit you were not one of my star pupils!'

It was a very proud and memorable moment, and I was so glad that my family had persuaded me to accept.

Chapter Twenty-Two

Phyllis and I move from Dial House

I first met Pat Murray at Brancaster Sailing Club one Sunday in August 1975. I had just arrived home from Scolt Head and he and his wife Kay, who lived in Switzerland, had come over to stay with Bill Adams for a month's holiday. Despite visiting the area regularly over a period of years, neither Pat nor Kay had been to Scolt Head – a situation we rectified next day.

A consequence of their visit was an invitation to visit Switzerland, as the guest of the Swiss Ornithological Society, whose members were keen on the idea of me going to talk to them. As it would cost a considerable amount of money to get me over there, would it be possible for me, instead of just talking to one group of people, to speak to groups in Berne, Basel and Zurich their letter of invitation requested?

I replied in the affirmative, adding that there was one proviso: I didn't go anywhere without my 'secretary'. This was agreed to, and the dates confirmed for the following April.

As Phyllis refused to fly, we travelled by train and boat – a long and very tiring journey. We finally arrived in Zurich at 8.30 the following morning. Somewhat to my surprise I discovered that I had to follow Margaret Thatcher. She had been lecturing here recently, and I was their next 'star turn' (quite an honour!)

The slide and lecture show seemed to go off well and we travelled on to Berne. Here we were met by Dr Mandac, an officer of the Swiss Ornithological Society, and shown the new wildlife park of the Berne Museum. We were taken along the river and shown the bears in their pits. Our hosts insisted we have steak while we were there. So we ate steak – in every shape and form! It was really too much – but we felt that we had to keep on eating it.

We had a wonderful time! Despite being asked to go back to Switzerland we haven't yet found time to do so; but we really did enjoy ourselves there.

Although 1976 brought with it several happy occasions, it also caused us further problems at home – and not just short-term ones, either. For the second time in a quarter of a century, Dial House was flooded. Although we were better prepared than we had been in '53 – all the important things had been placed above the old flood-line – the result was still misery.

We had believed that such a disaster just couldn't happen twice; but it did! Once again we cleaned up and tidied up as best we could after the event but the flooded area remained damp. Replacement carpets turned mouldy, metal objects, such as our cutlery, rusted, and mildew covered everything, including our clothes in the wardrobe.

Two years later, in 1978, the NCC asked me to take promotion to senior warden. When I asked how this would affect me and my work at Scolt Head I was told that my salary would increase by £300 per annum, and that I should be required to liaise between reserves.

Since this would leave me only a limited amount of time for Scolt, I told them I should have to think it over and discuss it with Phyllis. Of course I already knew what my answer would be!

When I turned down the promotion I was told I lacked initiative and drive. Insofar as the NCC was concerned this was doubtless right, but how naive it was to think that I could desert Scolt Head and its terns! As their self-appointed spokesman, and knowing what I did, turning down this promotion was the only decision I could have made.

That same year, when discussing with the regional officer the important part played by warden's wives in general, and Phyllis in particular, I remarked how well she coped with the hundreds of visitors who came into her kitchen every year. I said that most of them were provided with a cup of tea.

He scoffed at my remark, saying, 'You do run on, Bobby!'

I carried the conversation no further!

(During the final year at Dial House Phyllis kept a note of visitors entertained in her kitchen: from January 1 to November 5 1468 people drank 856 cups of tea – a figure that was by no means exceptional.)

Returning home one November evening I found her in tears. Another large section of plaster (enough to fill a wheelbarrow) had fallen. I rang the building officer the next day to ask when repairs were to be started, explaining in no uncertain terms the conditions we were living in (perhaps 'enduring' would have been more appropriate!). Once again I received the answer, 'due to financial climate nothing could be done in the foreseeable future'.

This statement was the last straw! Although Phyllis had never been too 'house-proud' she had always liked a tidy home. She was adamant that she was leaving. 'If you're not coming with me,' she told me, 'I'm going by myself!'

On November 5, 1979 Phyllis and I moved to 26 The Close, at Brancaster Staithe. It was a sad day when we left Dial House, ending an association between it and the Chestney family which had lasted for fifty years. Once again the property changed hands and John Morley, supported by Professor Steers, urged the National Trust to buy the property.

The Trust had purchased part of the Manor of Brancaster from a group of philanthropists, who had previously bought it from the family of the lady of the manor, Mrs Rose Southerland, following her death. The actual area extended from Brancaster Beach Road to Overy Bank – double the size of Scolt Head. Thus it made good sense for the Trust to acquire Dial House too. Subsequently the National Trust warden, Richard Lowe moved there, the cottages and outhouses were converted into hostel accommodation and the old barn into an information centre.

Richard after ten years moved to South Creake. Dial House now stands empty.

Whatever the loss, in terms of sentiment, the move from Dial House was certainly the best thing we could have done from a financial aspect. It had cost a fortune to live there. My army pension had been spent for years just running the old place. Now we were 'quids in'.

1979 was a memorable year in other ways, too. Firstly, because of the party we held on Scolt Head for Professor Steers's eightieth birthday – later described in the *St Catharine's Society Magazine*:

Early on the morning of August 8 the family came over to the island, before the many guests from the Nature Conservancy, National Trust and other organizations were due to arrive. But the amusing prelude to the celebrations that Alfred enjoyed so much was the ceremonial procession leading to the arrival of sea trout on a dish, ready cooked and garnished by Mrs Chesney (sic) at the hut steps for delivery to Alfred. It was a glorious August day with a mottled sky, typical of Norfolk at its best.

The sea trout, which I caught off Scolt and provided, was a twelve pounder. The girls from the Norwich office made their own contribution in the form of donations of salad and so on. The committee, all of whom came over for the party, presented him with a picture. His wife Harriet, his son and daughter and their families all came, together with many others who had been associated with Scolt over the years. In all some forty or more people were present. The professor was amazed that we had been able to transport all the food, plus wine and sherry, over to the island without his knowledge. He said it was a wonderful party and thought the same thing should happen every year. We suggested that this might be possible – if he paid for it in future; but he wasn't so keen on the idea then!

Mrs Steers was taken aback by it all and it really was a wonderful day – beautiful weather and a lovely setting. Absolutely perfect!

Less than three weeks later a tragic event occurred which was to have far-reaching consequences for all those holding high office or taking a high public profile in Britain. On August 27, in County Sligo in the Republic of Ireland, a bomb exploded on the boat of Admiral of the Fleet, Earl Mountbatten of Burma. It killed him, his fourteen year-old grandson Nicholas Knatchbull and a fifteen-year-old boatman. Three other people in the boat were all seriously injured. A seventh person, 82 year-old Dorothy, Lady Brabourne, died of her injuries the following day. The Provisional IRA (Irish Republican Army) claimed responsibility for the explosion.

Earl Mountbatten was a great-grandson of Queen Victoria and an uncle of the Duke of Edinburgh, and had been Supreme Allied Commander South-east Asia in World War II, and subsequently the last Viceroy of India and Chief of the Defence Staff.

Only three or four days before his funeral the Duke and Duchess of Kent came to Scolt. Every year for a decade I had taken them over. I would show them the stop-holes, which concealed the baby rabbits, skate eggs, Sandwich tern eggs, a seal or the eider out at sea whatever there was to interest them. Then I'd take their elder son, George, Earl of St Andrews, on a little tour of the island by himself.

This was always after the season was over, and we always had a fantastic day. At this time of year I took my fortnight's 'holiday'. Though most of it was spent on Scolt it was as a 'private individual' – I was *incognito*. No-one who saw him could ever have guessed who my young friend was either.

The whole family arrived – the Duke and Duchess, the young Earl, and Lady Helen and Lord Nicholas Windsor (then a baby). I took them down in the *Sea Swallow*. Very few people realised who they were.

'How long would you like to stay?' I asked.

'How long do you think?'

'Well, that's now about quarter past three. I'll carry the hamper up for you. When you've had a walk round and had your tea I'll ferry you back at your leisure.'

The Duchess, for some reason, had never quite got the hang of my name! She still called me Bill, even after ten years of coming to Scolt Head.

She said, 'But Bill, you're coming with us.'

I had mistakenly thought that they wouldn't want me prattling on after the recent tragic events. 'I didn't think you'd want me there,' I said. 'I thought you'd want to be on your own.'

'No, no. We'd very much like to have you with us. You're so interesting to listen to.'

Luckily we had a lovely calm sunny end-of-August day. They shook hands with me when they got out of the boat, saying that it had been a great pleasure.

I gave them my condolences once again, and said how futile I thought Lord Mountbatten's death had been – that it would solve absolutely nothing. It was the last time I saw them. The security risk, I am sure, had become too great for them to come Scolt Head anymore. However, their visits are yet another pleasant memory for Phyllis and me to look back on.

CHAPTER TWENTY-THREE

The Guardians

Sometime in 1980 I received an unusual and somewhat disturbing letter from a woman. It read: 'Do you consider that what you are telling children is beneficial?'

It went on to say that the writer had heard of a school party which had visited Scolt Head. 'I consider that Scolt Head is not the place to teach young children natural history,' the letter said. Its writer considered that it was a total waste of time to try and teach children of that age anything about conservation.

Anyone knowing me knows that I could not leave it at that! So I made some enquiries. Apparently, the writer had stayed in the Hut and had read the children's comments in the visitors' book. She had written to the regional officer to complain. The letter had upset me and I was determined to get to the heart of the matter. I soon discovered what had happened. The day in question had been a nasty one, towards the end of May. At 10.30, on the last of the tide, the boatmen had brought over thirty-four children, aged from about seven to eleven. I had left my dinghy in the Hole for Gordon to ferry them safely across it before they continued their walk back to the mainland, at 2.30.

They had only been on the island minutes when it started to rain quite heavily and the wind freshened. Knowing that the boatman had gone back, I realised that I had somehow to cope with them for four hours under these conditions.

Some cried; as they were wet and cold I set out along the beach with them, to have a quick look to see what we could find, before going up to the Hut to have lunch. There I lit all three burners on the stove, boiled a kettle and made tea for those children who wanted a cup. Within half an hour they began to get warm, and the crying stopped. So I sat chatting to them, telling them about 'when I was a little boy of your age' and so on. I managed to capture their interest, and explained to them why Scolt Head was such an important place.

When it was time, we walked back to the Hole, from where Gordon would ferry them back to the harbour. It had ceased raining, the children were much happier than they had been, and I thought that they had had a good time under the circumstances.

During my research I discovered that the letter writer was a schoolteacher. Another woman had been coming to the island with her own children for many years. At the end of their time, when the children and the others in the party had gone on and I was left alone with her, I thought I'd broach the subject on my mind.

'Can I ask you a question?' I asked. 'I want your answer straight from the shoulder. Do you think that what I tell the children is beneficial to them?'

'Oh yes,' she answered. 'The children love it! What I said to them was, "We can go to such-and-such, or to Scolt Head, to look at the birds and have a day on the beach". They've always chosen Scolt. They're always thrilled when you produce rabbits out of holes and show them chicks. They love everything about their day on Scolt. Why do you ask that, Bob?'

I went to the observation hut, thirty yards away, and found the letter in question. When I showed it to her she read it carefully, then exclaimed, 'What a stupid woman!' On seeing the writer's address and her name she added, 'Ah, but I know her! She's a right pain. She complains about everything. Take no notice of her – she would argue with herself. Oh, and incidentally, she's a great friend of your regional officer!'

I had been downhearted, thinking that perhaps the writer's attitude was typical; so my morale was boosted by this lady's comments.

Over the years I have received many compliments, and have had other kind remarks passed on to me. While Sandra was at work one day, in her office in King's Lynn, a black-headed gull hovered outside the window. She casually remarked, 'Oh look – a Larus ridibundus!'

Her boss, David Little, was in the office at the time and asked if she were a keen ornithologist. Sandra, despite knowing only about four birds by their latin names, including the black-headed gull, said, 'Oh yes, my father is the warden of Scolt Head.'

David said that it was a place he and his family would love to visit, so Sandra promised that, when the terns had finished nesting, I would put aside a day to spend with them on the island.

On the day of their visit, it was a neap tide (usually slow in flooding) and we had to wait for the motorboat to float. When it did so we headed down the channel, until we reached the point where it divides to Norton Creek. Here I switched off the engine and we drifted with the slow flooding tide for approximately half a mile.

On either side of the channel the mud was still exposed and wading birds were feeding. Being familiar with boats, however, they took little notice of us we drifted past and allowed us first class views of them. Migrating waders were passing through, too. I called down a golden plover, spotted redshank, greenshank and whimbrel to within twenty yards of the boat. They only stayed a few seconds; but it was sufficient time for a positive identification. All were 'new' species for my guests.

After landing on Scolt we walked to the Hut, to take in the view it commands. It had just gone high tide when we returned the boat. We motored back through the channel to the ternery, to spend as long as possible sea-watching. All the 'usual' birds were to be seen, including auks, fulmars, little gulls, eider and three of the four skua species – arctic, great and long-tailed – virtually all at the same time. Once again these were all new birds for them. I had never met a family so interested in birds.

The following Monday, and for several days afterwards, Sandra heard all about the day on Scolt from David. She suggested that they come again; so a date was arranged for three weeks hence. Unfortunately, however, the rest of the family couldn't come, so David arrived alone. The day was perfect and I think he gained the impression that it was the 'normal' thing to see so many species. We boated down at 9.30 and, as the tide was out until 5.30, decided to walk back before it flooded. After leaving the western end of the island we crossed the channel towards the Ninth, but hadn't gone a hundred yards when in front of us we saw a smallish wader.

It was one I was unfamiliar with. We approached to within twenty yards, but it made no attempt to fly away. It appeared very tired, and was feeding as though its life depended on it. The only bird it called to mind was a Baird's sandpiper – a very rare visitor to this country from North America. On landing I asked David if he would like to come into the house for a cup of tea, while at the same time I could look the bird up and confirm whether it was indeed a Baird's (this was in fact the case).

David looked at the many bird pictures adorning the walls of the lounge. As he was about to leave he spotted the photograph of Phyllis, Sally and myself, taken at Buckingham Palace.

'Did you really go there and meet the Queen?' he asked.

I described the day I received my MBE, said goodbye and he left. At work on the Monday, Sandra asked if he had had a good day.

'It was fantastic!' He said he'd been excited at seeing the Baird's sandpiper, adding that he didn't realise I had received the MBE.

Sandra gave him her description of this great day in our lives and told him why we thought I had received the honour. When she had finished, David said, 'But your father is so ordinary!' 'That's right – that's my Dad!' Sandra replied.

That evening she repeated the conversation to me. After thinking about it, and knowing David, we all considered it to be a compliment.

An event occurred in November 1983 which caused me personally considerable sorrow. My father's old friend and my mentor, Billy Daniels the gamekeeper, died at the age of 91. Being so 'involved' at Scolt Head at the time, I didn't hear of Billy's death and wasn't told of it by anyone until after the funeral had taken place.

One extra duty came my way during the three years prior to my retirement. Charles Johnson, the NCC warden at Holkham, retired. As he was not replaced at this time, I was asked to put in at least three days a week there, to keep an eye on things – no great hardship in the wintertime because there wasn't much to do there at that time of year.

For the first seven years I had been warden at Scolt Head, as I have said, I hadn't even had a rudimentary shelter. I was there in all weathers, often seven days a week, fourteen hours a day. Frequently I got soaked to the skin and had to dry out again in the wind. I sometimes slept down there, particularly if I knew there were egg thieves, stoats or rats about.

One day in 1975 I got terribly wet in a terrific thunderstorm. I have never been so cold in my life – I could not get warm! When I got home I had a hot bath but that day proved to have a lasting effect on me. It was when I first felt the arthritis which was to make life so difficult for me in later years. It was the principal reason why Gordon and Mike would go out onto the Wreck Sand on busy days, while I remained on lookout at Point Two – I had to adjust to what I could do.

The arthritis got progressively worse. By 1980 I found it very difficult to walk to and from the island; three years later it was too bad even to walk down to the beach. My arrangement with Gordon became that I worked the tides – I'd go down by boat on the last of the tide, say at 8 am, then boat back at five or six o'clock in the evening. If Gordon was taking anyone to the Hut in the evening I would stay until he returned to the ternery – sometimes eight, nine or even ten at night. They were still long hours – but I didn't have to walk.

In 1985 I was approached by Nick Duval, who was producing a series of half-hour programmes called *The Guardians* for Anglia TV. He wanted to include a portrayal of my thirty-six years as warden of Scolt Head and explained what he had in mind. Having been embarrassed by the way my job had been represented previously by radio, TV and the press, I didn't want a similar thing to happen, especially when I was on the point of retiring. I wasn't impressed with the proposed content, as it didn't seem to present a correct picture of my role. As with filming the terns, I viewed the whole project and presentation with suspicion, feeling that it would be of no benefit to Scolt in the future. So I told Nick, 'Sorry, I'm not interested.'

I told him the reasons for my refusal, but he wouldn't take 'no' for an answer! In the end he said, 'You tell me how you would present it.'

'Firstly,' I replied, 'there is too much of Bob Chestney. Why not portray more local situations? Most of them have connections with Scolt Head, or have Scolt at heart.'

There was the thriving local shellfishing industry, dating back to before World War I. Whelk fishing was now a dying trade, with only one vessel operating from the Staithe whereas twenty years previously there had been six. Gone was the sight and smell of the thick black smoke belching from the steam coal fires, boiling the coppers to await the return of the whelk boats with the day's catch. The smoke had always been a sure indication that the tide was flooding up the lower harbour channel. After a hard and sometimes rough trip at sea one of the boat's crew was landed on the shore to walk the last mile home to the whelk house, to light the fire and prepare the copper.

Nick listened patiently while I sketched these things in words.

'I should also like to show how, if we just stop for a change and let the world go by, that there is a host of interesting things at our feet,' I said. 'How many of us ever stand and watch and listen? So many things pass unnoticed. Regrettably, Brancaster Staithe, like so many small coastal villages, has joined the rat race. The long established village community and spirit, and the pleasure of hearing happy children laughing on their way to and from school will soon be lost forever. I should like to arrange for the local school to be the last one that I show nesting terns. It's closing in July, so why not record this historic event? It will be the last opportunity to portray local children in their own local school. They will be so excited at the prospect of appearing on television. I am sure that the headmistress, Miss Brenda Elsey, will agree to their taking part. Even though the breeding season will be virtually over, I can conjure up enough in the way of eggs and nests to make it interesting for them.'

Nick heard me out to the bitter end, while I covered some more aspects of life locally. Then to my surprise he agreed to my suggestions. Filming began early in 1985 seven filming days allotted through the season for completing the programme (the director was Graham Creelman – now head of Anglia's Survival team). On the first day the crew arrived with all their equipment. I had completely forgotten that they were coming and, in any case, it was impossible to cross to Scolt – there was insufficient tide. The weather was cold, with drizzle and an east wind so I suggested that they spend the day filming the fishermen sorting their mussels on the Malt House Hard. The area is exclusively for the fishermen's use and the sheds are for keeping their gear. The red-brick whelk sheds are of historical interest and together with the picturesque Malt House Yard in which they stand have proved a delight to artists over the years.

After completing the filming of the musselmen the crew turned its attention to the freshwater springs, which still pump out hundreds of gallons of water per hour, and are an important source of drinking water for birds, especially during hard winters. Another feature to find was cockles in the sand. (You look for two pinhead holes – one where the water is syphoned, taking in food particles, the other where the water is ejected, after passing through the stomach.)

Nick was satisfied with the day's results. I didn't tell him that most of it had been done on the spur of the moment; the rest of the filming days would be less haphazard.

On the last day the school was visited and the children filmed in the classroom during morning lessons.

At half past one they all arrived at the Staithe Hard for their visit to Scolt. High tide was at three o'clock, thus giving them ample time before returning to school for the final prayers and a last goodbye to Brancaster Deepdale School and Miss Elsey. I could hear them singing long before the two ferry boats arrived at the ternery. Gordon and Mervyn Nudds (who is both the harbourmaster and Alfie's successor as ferryman) ferried them to and from the island without charge.

The film was duly completed and shown on TV. I bet every house in Brancaster Staithe has a copy of the video and that those children delight in watching it again.

I have watched the *The Guardians* umpteen times. All my guests – if they haven't already seen it – get a viewing (or more than one!) The message is simply but factually put across, and I have not as yet been embarrassed by either the programme or its contents. Incidentally, I learned recently that it still being given an 'airing', being an item of in-flight entertainment on Virgin Airlines.

If given the opportunity to do it again I should make very few changes. I was told that there was enough material for an hour – half an hour hadn't proved nearly long enough to put across all the aspects of my work and what it was all in aid of. I must say that Nick Duval understood my feelings and what I wanted to portray with each situation and sequence. I felt that he was experiencing the same nostalgia as I was (he too has a deep interest in the world of conservation).

It was his genuine understanding, keenness and interest that fired me with enthusiasm and helped me to forget the presence of the director, Graham, the cameras focused on me and the bright artificial lights. The Anglia TV crew was the best filming crew ever to visit Scolt Head and a pleasure to work with. I was thrilled for Nick and Graham when I heard that the programme had won an award.

Retirement was now only months away. Every year the Norwich office staff of the NCC held a Christmas party. I received a note from the office suggesting that, as a secretary, Wendy, would be retiring on the same day as myself, the retirement party and a presentation to us could be amalgamated with the office party – to be held at Barnham Broome, near Wymondham, on December 3.

Phyllis and I were quite agreeable. It served a dual purpose, as this was also our wedding anniversary! A good crowd came to the party, including people from the NCC's Peterborough headquarters. We spread out round the restaurant at separate tables. Ours had ten people, including Sue Day (who had been a secretary at Norwich – a terrific lady, who had always kept me up to date with what was going on), Mike Schofield (then deputy director, NCC England), Wendy and ourselves.

When the band came in we were all having a really good time and thought, this is great – we're going to have a dance as well; but what about the presentation? When will Martin George make his speech?

However, nobody made a speech the tables were cleared, the music started and we all went dancing. Then, about 11.30, Joan Moore, the executive officer, came to our table to tell us, 'Oh, by the way, we're not doing the presentation tonight, we're not ready for it. You'll have to come to the Norwich office.'

What a fiasco! We had got dressed up in our best for nothing!

For some time donations towards our leaving presents had been requested – a good sum of money being collected. People kept asking Phyllis, 'What does Bob want?' Between us Phyllis and I agreed that we should have a little TV set, and I said I should also like a pair of Zeiss binoculars. Wendy was to be presented with a picture by a well-known Norfolk artist, Jason Partner. After this had been purchased, however, there was insufficient money left in the fund even for my television and we had to meet the shortfall ourselves. The set was purchased and put into a presentation box – by Phyllis (I was supposed to be 'in the dark')! I enquired whether Phyllis, who was coming with me, would be receiving a presentation. The answer being negative, I asked the chief warden, Martin

Musgrave, to get her a bouquet of flowers, adding that I would pay for them. I didn't want Phyllis to retire with me and receive absolutely nothing. (In the event, 'Muzzy' got the flowers and paid for them himself.)

After the fiasco at Barnham Broome, I was more than a little gratified to discover that the regional officer had nominated me for a 'Norfolk Hero' award, in connection with my contribution to nature conservation. Phyllis and I were invited to the Hotel Nelson at Norwich for the opening of its new Trafalagar Room.

To mark the occasion three local people, including myself, received certificates, plus cheques for £100. We were also treated to a veritable feast, which included caviare and champagne, by our hosts.

A month after my retirement, Phyllis and I went to the Norwich office for the long-postponed official presentation.

After finishing with Wendy's presentation, Martin George turned to Phyllis saying, 'Now Phyllis. She has assisted Bob during his work for the Nature Conservancy and the National Trust, and she will be remembered for cleaning and scrubbing the Hut out.'

What a 'testimony' to my wife's hard work and sacrifices for the past thirty-six years! Needless to say, I was not by now feeling in the best of humours...

Before making the presentation to me, he turned to John Morley and asked, 'How long has Bobby been working on Scolt?'

'Thirty-six years,' John answered.

'Oh, yes. Now Bobby will be remembered for being so good to the children.'

I just could not let him get away with these remarks! So, as he presented me with the gift-wrapped television, I looked at it, then at him and said, 'Whatever can this be? I know – I bet it's a bust of Martin George, to put on my mantelshelf!'

That is how I remember my retirement presentation. I went out like a lead balloon!

CHAPTER TWENTY-FOUR

Life Moves On

Naturally, I was slightly anxious, both about Scolt's future and how I should react with someone else as warden of what some people called 'Chestney's Island'. It had been my life – as both boy and man. Up until now I had been the driver; what would it be like to be driven? Having given this a great deal of thought I had made up my mind to keep a low profile once my successor was established at Scolt particularly after recalling an incident in my own first year as warden.

On the committee's annual visit to Scolt we had been walking along the north beach, chatting as we went. One committee member said to me, 'He was a remarkable man, your father. You will never be as good as him!' What a 'boost' to my morale, and what 'encouragement' to a young chap just starting out on his life's work! (Incidentally, some twelve years later, while walking in the same place, I reminded this person of his comments. He said, 'I can't recall saying that, but if I did I must admit I have been proved wrong!')

I didn't want this attitude to be taken towards the new warden. He would undoubtedly have his own ideas on how to run Scolt and he wouldn't want me saying, 'I didn't do it that way!'

I didn't know until a fortnight before I retired who was going to take over from me, and I had actually retired before he took over on March 2.

The NCC asked me to stay on for an additional two weeks – two weeks, I ask you! – to familiarise him with the reserve, tides and local involvement!

My successor was a tall lean Scotsman, Colin Campbell, previously warden of the Wildfowl Trust reserve at Caerlaverock, in Dumfries. When he visited the reserve for the first time, prior to my retirement, I tried to convey to him all the aspects of the job, in the limited time available. In the main I tried to put over the complex and unique situations which existed at Scolt, in particular the relationship between the local inhabitants, the warden and the NCC, and the situation appertaining to certain common rights exercised over the island. I sincerely hoped that by putting Colin 'in the picture' the change of wardenship might pass unnoticed.

By my last day I had formed the impression that Colin found Scolt a most complex situation. We had got to know each other fairly well and I told him that if he had any problems he shouldn't hesitate to call on me. I should be only too pleased to help out in any way. Colin thanked me for what I had done and said he would bear my offer of help in mind. Then he added a sentence which, for once in my life, rendered me speechless.

'I have been told to get totally away from the Chestney regime,' Colin said.

My heart dropped to the pit of my stomach; I was dumbfounded.

However I did persuade the NCC to employ Gordon in an advisory capacity at Scolt during Colin's first season, with appropriate pay. He stayed on for another summer season as an assistant, but decided, for reasons of his own, that it would be his last. Despite pressure from me to reconsider, he was adamant that he was quitting. I understood what a wrench it must have been for him to come to this decision.

It was a disappointment to me that Gordon didn't qualify to become my successor, though no great surprise. The prevailing theory nowadays seems to be that the new 'breed' of warden requires a university degree – not necessarily accompanied by any practical knowledge or experience. So the powers that be allowed Gordon to escape and the expertise that we both acquired over the years has been lost to Scolt.

Although admittedly a rough diamond Gordon had dedication to the job, plus a vast store of knowledge and expertise gained over the years, not only appertaining to the reserve but the entire North Norfolk coast. He was not only a good ornithologist and botanist but also an archaeologist, his collection of artifacts found at the Roman camp of Branodunum, prior to its being built on, being of considerable historical value. Some of his 'finds' caused great excitement among the experts on this period of history, while his depth of knowledge on the subject even surprised noted academics.

Gordon and his wife Nancy emigrated to Australia in 1987; but before quitting his beloved Norfolk he gave the greater part of his collection to the Norwich Museum.

I still visit the island and enjoy talking terns with Colin's summer assistants, who appear to enjoy listening to me. So it hasn't been so much of a wrench as I had anticipated. Perhaps Colin's statement helped me in getting Scolt quickly out of my system.

During the early wardening years pressure of work at Scolt had forced me to give up sports such as golf and tennis, which I had enjoyed playing. In the few years just prior to my retirement I had found time to play golf again, at the Royal West Norfolk, and I was also able to continue this pursuit for a few years afterwards. For the past two years, however, my arthritis has forced me to 'retire' from the sport once more.

A big help to me in retirement has been spending ten weeks in Spain in the winter, from where I have been able to view from afar both Scolt Head and my involvement there. On returning home I could see my retirement in an entirely different light.

The following year both Scolt Head and I personally lost a great friend and champion. Professor Steers died on March 10, 1987, aged 87.

John Treherne continued visiting me. Apart from being a zoologist and biologist he had also, since my first meeting with him back in 1968, become a best-selling author. I called him, jokingly, 'the poor man's Jeffrey Archer'. His books included *The Galapagos Affair, Strange History of Bonnie and Clyde,* and *The Trap.* The film rights to *The Galapagos Affair* have already been sold, while another work of John's, *Dangerous Precincts,* has been filmed for the BBC.

He suggested that I write a book – *On Reflection.* He would edit it, assisting me in any way he could, and use his influence to get it published. Sadly, however, he died after a second heart attack within twelve months, on September 24, 1989. His last wish had been that his ashes should be scattered on Scolt Head. John had taught me a great deal. Like so many who knew him, I shall never forget him.

Another great personal loss to us during the October of the same year was that of Gran – Phyllis's Mum – who had lived with us for twenty-two years. After a lifetime of hard work, she finally passed away at the age of 88.

Early in 1991 Phyllis and I travelled to Australia, for a five-month stay with Gordon and Nancy, at Bennison in Victoria. This was a great opportunity not only to travel round this vast and interesting country and see many bird species entirely new to me, but also to chat over old times. In fact, some sections of this book were conceived and drafted while I was there.

An added pleasure was the renewing of a friendship with Dick Roy, who had emigrated in 1976, after being the National Trust warden for the Manor of Brancaster for a number of years. He and his wife now live close to Gordon and Nancy, at Foster. Gordon, Dick and myself were photographed, and a piece published about us in the local newspaper.

While we were reminiscing, Mrs Roy recounted a tale concerning the birth of the great Norfolk hero, Admiral Lord Nelson of Burnham Thorpe, where she herself had been born: 'We all know about Horatio Nelson and the Battle of Trafalgar,' she said. 'How his body was preserved in a barrel of brandy. But few people know where he started life. You know his father was rector at Burnham Thorpe, and in those days everyone went to church. There was little else to do – it didn't mean they were any more religious!

'On the Sunday Nelson was born his parents went to church as usual, being driven there by pony and trap. They were to be collected at 12 noon, after the service. But young Horatio couldn't wait' and his mother started to walk home – a distance of about half a mile assisted by some of the local women. When walking became impossible for her, a wooden wheelbarrow was found to transport her. But before she got home the baby was born in the wheelbarrow!

'I know that's right,' she concluded, 'because my grandmother told me.'

So even his arrival caused a commotion, apparently. And his life progressed from a wooden wheelbarrow, through wooden ships to a wooden barrel at the end of his days!

CHAPTER TWENTY-FIVE

Ever Present Memories

In October 1986 a vixen arrived on Scolt Head, being joined by a dog fox in December. From this partnership four cubs were produced the following March. Although these were successfully destroyed, the adults eluded capture. Thus began a vulpine takeover of the island, which has continued until the present day.

As I have tried to show, stoat, weasel and fox control is, regrettably, a necessity. It is simple to know what ground predators are present and in which area they may be found – especially on Scolt – by their paw marks in the sand. My target was always to achieve efficient control by April at the ternery, and the results with nesting birds always proved the worth of these efforts. 1985, my final season, was an average one. Numbers of terns present and their breeding success was: common tern – 200 pairs nested, 70 chicks fledged; Sandwich tern – 2500 pairs nested, 2400 chicks fledged; little tern – 82 pairs nested, 51 pairs having one or more chicks; arctic tern – 1 pair nested, 2 chicks fledged; black-headed gull – 300 pairs allowed to nest ('controlled') with a reasonable fledging success.

Each year following my retirement the number of nesting and breeding terns and gulls decreased. The official report for 1989 stated: common tern - 159 pairs attempted to nest, 10 chicks fledged; Sandwich tern 1052 pairs actually laid eggs, but no chicks fledged; little tern – 63 pairs raised 12 young.

Continuous nightly predation by foxes of both eggs and chicks, over successive seasons, resulted not only in total loss but also an exceptionally early dispersal of Sandwich terns from the ternery. It is not known how many adult incubating birds were taken at night. By 1990, and in ensuing years, the actual tern nesting area on Scolt was virtually devoid of birds. There is no doubt that those formerly nesting there have established a new breeding area elsewhere, where they will remain so long as they breed successfully. Other groundnesting species at Scolt Head, including oystercatchers, redshank and ringed plover, have been equally unsuccessful. Most of the nesting shelduck were dug out and killed for food while incubating in their nesting burrows, and have now become a rare nesting species on the reserve. The havoc caused by this continuous fox predation is now apparent, and will take many breeding seasons to recover from, even after the situation is finally resolved.

Efforts made to eliminate foxes from the reserve in general and the ternery in particular include the erection of an electric fence east of the ternery, to cut it off from the rest of the island. However, this has proved ineffective – they pass round the ends of it at low tide!

Although the original foxes did 'disappear', after at least four years, others subsequently arrived to take their place. During my life I have had many disappointments; but to watch the most thriving tern colony in Europe virtually disappear in just four seasons, after sixty-one years of Chestney effort, has not been merely disappointing – it has been heartbreaking!

During my association with Scolt from 1946 to 1986 I spoke to over 300,000 people, lecturing both in this country and abroad, and talking to people away from the island. I believe that I not only entertained visitors but also passed on knowledge of its many facets. I saw Blakeney Point and Scolt Head as 'twin' reserves, with their sand dunes and lateral formations. The same skills are needed, both for wardening and operating a boat. Knowledge of the tides, currents and channels is essential, as is the ability to observe the weather signs when a change is imminent and expertise in the use of a gun.

From 1951 I was the first to control visitors walking through the main area of nesting birds. As we have seen, although some sceptics opposed this restriction, stating that it was unnecessary, I convinced them that the system was working – results spoke for themselves. No one 'lost out' – neither the locals, ornithologists nor photographers. My efforts were rewarded in 1961, when a prescribed route was finally laid out through the ternery at Blakeney Point, to restrict access of visitors to the main nesting area.

There were other achievements too. The western end of Scolt, even today – and hopefully for years to come – is a non-wildfowling area. This is under the agreement between the Brancaster Common Right Holders Gun Club and the NCC, referred to in an earlier chapter. Wildfowling is also restricted on the whole of Scolt to club members and those belonging to the Overy Common Right Holders Gun Club.

There is no doubt that this ban was instrumental in the establishment in 1979 of a flock of wintering pink-footed geese, feeding locally and roosting on Scolt

Head in the area closed to wildfowling. Commencing at just 100 birds, by 1985 this flock had built to a peak of 20,000 – twenty per cent of the UK wintering population at that time. Scolt thus became a major roost and haven for these geese in Norfolk.

I believe I was also instrumental in persuading local farmers that, as the geese had become regular winter visitors to Norfolk, and had acquired a safe roost, their food supply should be secured by leaving the tops of sugarbeet on the fields until late January or February, instead of ploughing them in as had formerly been done. This additional food source would also relieve the pressure on geese grazing upon cereal crops, since they could feed on the beet tops with the minimum of disturbance from shooting and birdscarers. In the event, these theories proved correct.

There is, however, some food for thought here: increasing numbers of sheep are at present being grazed on sugarbeet tops in the same feeding area as the pinkfeet. As yet the acreage being grazed by these government-subsidised sheep isn't detrimental to the geese; but it could be if flocks were to be increased further.

I was sometimes accused of being 'over-zealous' in the way I protected my terns; but what I couldn't have known when I started was that from the early 'sixties to the mid-seventies numbers of terns nationally and internationally would decrease, despite the stringent controls practised at Norfolk terneries.

I believe that had it not been for the zealous protection of these birds, using the Bob Chestney management methods, this decline would have been far more severe. Not all my predictions came to pass; but among those which did was that tern numbers – especially common terns – must surely decrease nationally. It was obvious to me that there were insufficient young replacement birds to cover the normal annual losses of adults. This was seen as one of my 'sweeping statements', and I was asked what scientific data I had based it on. I could only reply that it was on my observations over (at that time) an eighteen year period, along with information sent to me by tern associates from all over Europe, after their visits to Scolt.

At the time approximately 36,000 common tern pairs nested in the British Isles; by the time I retired this had dropped to 11,000 breeding pairs. The decrease was not entirely due to human disturbance at the terneries. A contributory factor was toxic chemicals polluting the sea.

I suggested that the extended laying date and the decline in fish stocks available to the terns were the result of toxic chemicals washed from farmland into the dykes and four main rivers that empty into The Wash. The shortage of suitably-sized fish taxed the terns in their quest for food, especially in unfavourable weather conditions. It wasn't unusual, in adverse weather conditions during the period 1960 to 1980, for the ternery to be virtually devoid of adult birds for four to five hours during the day. Their quest for food increased their searching distance by an extra twenty miles.

Between 1951 and the appointment of a permanent summer assistant in 1962, the number of hours I spent on the reserve increased until I was there virtually all the hours of daylight. Each season started with the arrival of the Sandwich terns in mid-April and finished when the last chick was fledged, about August 20. During this period one thousand hours would have been spent at the ternery alone; but it was still important to cover the remainder of the island, observing and recording events and installing visitors in the Hut, and delivering stores to them there. At no time was I bored, lonely or discouraged through spending many hours per day – even in the winter – on my own.

Since retiring I look back on my first ten years as warden, and wonder at the results I achieved. Perhaps the 'slap-happy' way I behaved sometimes was not to my advantage; but I didn't want to become known as a know-all or a bighead. (Others will have judged whether or not this was the case.) 'When Chestney retires we will bring in an academic to run Scolt as it should be done!' An NC officer told a friend, no doubt sincerely, and with the good of Scolt in mind. It suggested to me, however, that the speaker was totally out of touch with what was involved and how it was possible to maintain the results we achieved. The disastrous results since my retirement prove my point.

Scolt Head was unique. Very few such areas had retained their natural features, their birds and plants. There was no need for things to have happened in this way. I pointed out many times before retiring that Scolt is no ordinary nature reserve – wardening it requires special expertise,in order to maintain its Grade A status.

Another important factor was that the fish size became less varied. Fish between three and six centimetres long became scarce; the average fish size of six to nine centimetres was unsuitable for day old common tern chicks, but nevertheless suitable for Sandwich tern chicks of the same age, the latter being twice the size of the former.

Well documented was the effect on the Dutch Sandwich tern colonies when, in the early 1960s, a release of toxic chlorinated hydrocarbon insecticides into the Rhine poisoned the fish. These were eaten by the terns and other fish-eating birds, and also fed to the young. Between 25,000 and 40,000 pairs of Sandwich tern had nested regularly in Holland up until that period. By 1961-2 this figure had dropped to 12,000 pairs, and in 1964 2500 pairs. The following year only 650 pairs bred in Holland; but after the factory responsible reduced the effluent of the DDT-related compounds the tern population became stable.

Due to all the publicity and growing knowledge of their effect on both wildlife and on human beings, toxic agrochemicals were subsequently gradually phased out.

Scolt Head played a major role in the Chestneys' way of life. The many hours spent on the island, both by my father and myself especially during the period April to September each year – were considered necessary by us for the smooth running of the reserve, for the benefit of both terns and human visitors. With a nature reserve such as Scolt you cannot just shut the gate and go home, forgetting about it 'until tomorrow'!

I also suggested that it would be most unwise if Gordon Howell – for twenty-five years my assistant, and with all this knowledge at his fingertips – was not given the opportunity to succeed me. Perhaps – as with me – the book-work may have been less instructive, but the job would have been expertly carried out!

Without local knowledge academic qualifications are not sufficient to manage a reserve with such complexity. Thus the Chestney-Howell expertise gained over so many years has not been replaced. The long established and thriving tern colony ceased to exist in the space of four breeding seasons. This easily avoidable situation was the cause for grave concern.

Thank goodness 1993, five seasons on and with successful ground predator control, sees the return with success of the breeding tern colony. To celebrate their return one lesser crested tern appeared – a rarity to Scolt. During my wardening I recorded no less than eight rarer species – black, gull billed, sooty, caspian, whiskered, bridled, white winged black, and roseate. What a delight it would have been for the twitchers of this world to have ticked all these!

Index

Bold numbers indicate line illustrations within text